A Grassroots History of World War II

Eight Men in Granite

Robert C. Francisco - Henry E. Wise

George Reisinger - Robert R. Billard

Elmer L. Leech - William K. Belles

George M. Buzek - Donald A. Gibble

Richard J. Staats

HERITAGE BOOKS
2008

HERITAGE BOOKS
AN IMPRINT OF HERITAGE BOOKS, INC.

Books, CDs, and more—Worldwide

For our listing of thousands of titles see our website
at
www.HeritageBooks.com

Published 2008 by
HERITAGE BOOKS, INC.
Publishing Division
100 Railroad Ave. #104
Westminster, Maryland 21157

Copyright © 2008 Richard J. Staats

All rights reserved. No part of this book may be reproduced or transmitted in any form or by any means, electronic or mechanical, including photocopying, recording or by any information storage and retrieval system without written permission from the author, except for the inclusion of brief quotations in a review.

International Standard Book Numbers
Paperbound: 978-0-7884-4756-3
Clothbound: 978-0-7884-7525-2

TABLE OF CONTENTS

Introduction v

Chapter One - "Your Toughest Son" 1

Chapter Two - "Your Loving Son, Robert" 103

Chapter Three - Henry Bernard Wise, Class of '36 187

Chapter Four - P.F.C. William H. Bettes 228

Chapter Five - P.F.C. George M. Buzek 254

Chapter Six - Pvt. Donald Dibble, A Peaceful Man 279

Chapter Seven - George Reisinger, Jr., Seaman First Class USN . 290

Chapter Eight - Private Elmer L. Leech, Aviation Engineer 300

Epilog - 311

INTRODUCTION

It was a mighty fine gesture. Unlike the tilting, weather-worn, white limestone tablets for the Civil War soldiers, this 6' x 1' x 2' gray granite memorial would forever enshrine the names of the eight local World War II servicemen. The township trustees had formed a monument committee and voted for an appropriation for a memorial. Private funds were also donated toward the project. By May 17, 1948 the monument order was contracted to an Akron monument firm for $904.50 plus $27.14 tax. Delivery was promised for some time in July.

On Armistice Day in November, the solemn memorial dedication ceremony transpired in front of the town hall. (The eight servicemen being honored had perhaps gathered here as children for the Memorial Day and Armistice Day occasions.) Service organization delegates, tearful relatives and friends of the departed, and the youthful faces of the small high school band gazed at the veiled granite. Myriads of thoughts passed through their minds as the light November breeze stirred the American flags. (The red, white, and blue was a sacred symbol in these times - the blessed thirteen stripes and 48 stars.) The former high school principal delivered the keynote address, a more difficult task because he had personally known some of the servicemen. At last, the order was given to remove the shroud from the memorial. Ex-servicemen snapped to attention, some saluted.

Sixty years later, only a handful of relatives and friends of the eight men remained. Other than them, no one could remember what the men looked like. Even many of the eight men's nieces and nephews knew very little about their uncles. For the older generation, such tragedies were to be suffered with a stiff upper lip, true grit, and no whining. Besides, the memories were just too painful to dwell on, much less to pass them on to others.

The eight men were kids at one time, who loved to play ball in the pastures, fished the local creeks and ponds, and hunted the farmers' woods and fields for squirrels and pheasants. They had kids' dreams, some modest and others grandiose. They had family members who loved them and helped to celebrate their birthdays. They thoroughly enjoyed the 4th of July, the family gathering and feast at Thanksgiving, and Christmas. They had friends who enjoyed their company. They attended the local elementary school, and as teenagers they attended the small high school, where "everyone knew everyone." Some relished their high school days, whereas others dropped out of school to pursue other paths. They experienced the disillusionment of World War I - it seemed as if all the American casualties had gone for naught. They survived the Great Depression, and still were imbued with patriotism. By 1940, times were changing. Some folks complained of the political socialistic programs of the '30's; but most folks did not seek a handout or look at government assistance as a divine right - they just wanted the opportunity to make it on their own.

To be honest, most of the eight men - especially those with wives or sweethearts - would have preferred to stay at home than to yield their freedom to military life and then be shipped to a perilous situation in a foreign land. (The attack on Pearl Harbor changed all of that.) All expected to come home; none expected to be killed; at worst, a few thought that they might be severely wounded and dreaded the thought of being a burden upon those at home. Nevertheless, they and 16,112,558 other Americans did their duty with 291,557 of them losing their lives in battle. Whether or not they realized the concept at the time, they had relinquished their individual freedom so that millions of other people could be free.

Then there were those who the eight men left behind - permanent victims in their own way. An integral part of their lives and dreams of things to be were dashed forever.

The sentiments of the monument-makers were fine, noble, and enduring; but it is the purpose of this work to go beyond a name chiseled in cold stone. The first task was to add a face to the names. The relatives of the eight men gladly donated service pictures and any existing childhood photographs. They handled these treasured pictures with reverence. Second, each name surely had a unique personality, and an effort was made to determine what the serviceman was like - warts and all. The third step was to research the service record of each serviceman. In what unit did he serve; what did his outfit do; where did they go; and how did they meet their demise? (Until this research, some of the relatives did not know what happened to their World War II serviceman.) An effort was also made to present a sense of the times in which the eight men lived. The America of 2008 is far different from that of 1915-1945; and for better or worse, Americans of today are far different than the Americans of that era.

The author sincerely thanks the following people and organizations for their time, information, and support.

Lenora (Hillard) Foster, sister of Bob Hillard
Robert Foster - brother-in-law of Bob Hillard
Linda Foster - niece of Bob Hillard
June (Anderson) Buttermore - sister of Lucille Anderson, Bob Hillard's fiancee.
Quentin Unger, 2nd Lt. in the 3rd Chemical Mortar Battalion
Chris Unger, Quentin's son and e-mail correspondent
Dorothy (Francisco) Sanford - sister of Bob Francisco.
Howard Mangold - nephew of Bob Francisco.
Francis Knapp - nephew of Barney Wise
James C. Haahr - author of *The Command Is Forward*
Fred Neal - nephew of Vernon Neal
Mary Jane (Robertson) Brockett - sister of two WWII servicemen and wife of Scott Brockett
Sophie (Tymcio) Cogan - WWII WAC
Marie (Bettes) Kropp - sister of Bill Bettes
Betsy Bettes - sister of Bill Bettes.
Ann (Buzek) Jones - sister of George Buzek
Gary Buzek - nephew of George Buzek
Sam Buzek - cousin of George Buzek
Marguerite Kleckner - contributed yearbook information for George Buzek
Gary Dibble - nephew of Donald Dibble
Betty Tanaska - niece of George Reisinger
Sally Hickenbotham - daughter of Bill Leech, niece of Elmer Leech.
Sam Feciuch - friend of Bill Leech
Department of the Army, U.S. Human Resources Command
Akron-Summit County Public Library, Akron, Ohio
Reed Memorial Library, Ravenna, Ohio
The Randolph Historical Society, Randolph, Ohio

To all of the World War II veterans, Rosie-the-Riveters, home front workers, and farmers.
"Bless 'em all."

CHAPTER ONE
"YOUR TOUGHEST SON"

Part I
Once Upon A Time

Prior to the war, Cerasuolo may have been an idyllic little village, which nestled in the picturesque mountains of Central Italy. About 800 inhabitants once occupied the 8-10 clustered buildings and the other twenty scattered structures in the vicinity. That was before the advancing allied army blasted the area and the retreating Germans responded in kind. Now on January 12, 1944, Cerasuolo presented a drab, pitiful sight. Although the seasonal temperatures were mild in the lowlands, there were freezing nights in the mountains until the sun rose above the horizon. Between the combat action and the winter season, the countryside lacked color. The gray clay brick buildings were reduced to rubble. The villagers' chatter and their children's laughter were replaced by deafening explosions and vibrations of incoming German shells and the outgoing blasts of American mortar fire. Permeating the onetime fresh mountain breezes were the smells of cordite, explosive charges, airborne cement and brick dust, wet earth and mud, foul body odor, and sometimes the stench of decaying flesh. The opposing forces were engaged in the serious business of killing or being killed; and the civilians were caught in the middle.

In the distance, the German-occupied ridges of Monte Dellameta at nearly 7,000 feet loomed over Cerasuolo at 2,532 feet above sea level. Around high noon, the 6-man mortar squads worked like smooth-running machines as they pumped their 4.2 diameter, 11-inch long, 21-pound shells nearly a mile into the German positions on the high ground. The shell-burst destruction zone was about a 50 yard circle with shrapnel from six inches to a pinhead, and the latter particle could kill you if it hit the right spot. At a distance of 100 yards, the concussion could lift you off the ground. Of course, the Germans were throwing everything they had right back at the Americans. It had been 125 days since the allies came ashore at Salerno on September 9, 1943. With the advantage of excellent defensive positions among the mountains and behind numerous fast-coursing streams, the Nazis made the Americans pay dearly in blood for any small gains. The 3rd Chemical Mortar Battalion had come ashore on October 29, 1943, and for 75 consecutive days they had been on the firing line. However, the scuttlebutt today was that the mortar squad was going to be relieved from the line and to receive a long overdue R & R.

At the nearby battalion headquarters, 28-year old Staff Sergeant Robert H. Hillard could hear and feel the explosions. Bob had always been a well-groomed young man; in fact, the spit and polish of training and camp life never bothered him. Thus amid the dust and grime, the prospects of a hot bath, close shave, clean uniform, and some decent grub were quite appealing.

Coming from a large close-knit family, Hillard had a lot of letters to write home. Bob's mother had died in December 1939, and his respected father had passed away just eleven weeks ago. Yet, there were eleven siblings eagerly awaiting news of his safety and well being. What memories and stories they could all tell when this war ended!

Sgt. Hillard came from good fighting stock. His grandfather, John McMillian Hilliard [sic], served in the Union Army during the Civil War. John Hilliard remained in the militia and was called up at different times to quell Indian uprisings. Somehow, John found the time to sire fourteen children by his wife, Eliza Jane Jamison, who stayed at home, ran the farm, and raised her family. One of their children, John Lincoln Hilliard, acquired the ruggedness of the Indian fighter and the gentleness and industry of the farm wife, traits that he would pass on to his children. [1]

John Lincoln Hilliard recalled that his mother taught him everything he knew about farming and beekeeping. When his mother died at the age of 53, her bees all died or left the hives. In later years, her son discovered John Greenleaf Whittier's poem, *Telling The Bees*, which became his favorite. The poem was about a young gentleman who was in love with a girl named Mary. He had been away for a year; and as he came in sight of Mary's home, he saw the hired girl draping each beehive with a black cloth. At first, the young gentleman thought that Mary's grandfather had died. As he drew closer, he heard the hired girl singing:

"Stay at home, pretty bees. Don't fly away. Mistress Mary is dead and gone."

Perhaps, the first six stanzas reminded John of his childhood on the family farm and enhanced his appreciation for his own farm.

"Here is the place; right over the hill
   Runs the path I took;
You can see the gap in the old wall still.
   And the stepping stones in the shallow brook.

There is the house, with the gate red-barred.
   And the poplars tall;
And the barn's brown length, and the cattle yard,
   And the white horns tossing above the wall.

There are the beehives arranged in the sun;
   And down by the brink
Of the brook are poor flowers, weed-o'er run.
   Pansy and daffodil, rose and pink.

A year has gone as the tortoise goes,
   Heavy and slow;
And the same rose blows, and the same sun glows,
   And the same brook sings of a year ago.

There's the same sweet clover-smell in the breeze;
   And the June sun warm
Tangles his wings of fire in the trees,
   Setting, as then, over Fernside farm.

I mind me how with a lover's care
   From my Sunday coat
I brushed off the burrs, and smoothed my hair,
   And cooled at the brookside my brow and throat..." [2]

John Hilliard also enjoyed Joyce Kilmer's poem, *Trees*, which was penned in February 1913. The poem was often cited or sung at Arbor Day celebrations across the land. Most Americans were aware of Kilmer's sad fate. The poet sailed to Europe with the AEF to participate in the War to end all wars. A member of the 165th Infantry (the old Fighting 69th of New York Irish fame) and the famous 42nd Rainbow Division, the 31 year-old Kilmer died on July 30, 1918 – shot through the brain by a German sniper's bullet. Kilmer is buried in Oise-Aisne Cemetery in France. [3]

John Hillard's youngest child, Norie Hillard Foster, wrote the following. "My dad was a strict disciplinarian. He had certain rules, which you didn't dare break or you suffered the consequences. One rule that he enforced was that we cleared the table and did the dishes after every meal. Another rule was that we had to be dressed to come downstairs in the morning (no robes or pajamas). To this day I get dressed the minute I get out of bed and keep my dishes done up, so I guess he taught me something. He allowed no swearing in the house. He said that was barn talk. He loved growing roses and kept a beautiful lawn. It was the best kept up lawn in the neighborhood. My dad had a mind of his own. When he moved from Pennsylvania to Ohio, he changed the spelling of his last name from "Hilliard" to "Hillard." He also decided that he didn't like his middle name Lincoln (he did not admire President Lincoln), so he changed his middle name to Lawrence. He loved to read anything he could find. He read the *Bible*, Mark Twain, and Shakespeare. He had sets of these books for us kids to read. He was self-educated, since he only went to the sixth grade…

My dad told a story about when he worked on the oil wells away from home in Pennsylvania. He roomed with a group of men. They took turns cooking for themselves and made an agreement that when one man was cooking, anyone else who said anything negative about his cooking had to take over the job (which they all hated). During one mealtime, one man sat down at the table to eat and said, "These potatoes are all burned to He--." He caught himself just in time and added, "but that's just the way I like them."

Another story I heard was about the gypsies who stopped at the Wilson house. (It was a house where the Wilson family lived on New Milford Road across from our home and where Mays' lived for a long time afterward.) Dad had bought it from the Wilson family, and my brothers used it as a garage and a place to hang out. We girls weren't allowed to go over there. Anyway, one evening in the summertime, a whole group of gypsies stopped over there. Since gypsies were known for stealing, most people chased them away. Dad went over to do just that; but when he got there, he saw that their children were tired and dirty. He changed his mind and told them they could stay and use the water and have vegetables out of the garden. He also warned them that if they stole anything from him or his neighbors, he would have their hides. They left the next day saying, "God bless you, Mr. Hillard!" Nothing turned up missing, and they were rested to continue on their way.

[With such a large family], we never had enough chairs for everyone, and we used to fight for them. My dad made a rule that if you got up and left your chair, it then belonged to the person who sat in it next. It cut down the arguments, but it also made you appreciate furniture more. We learned to get comfortable sitting on the floor..." [4]

Harriet Holmes Moorhead was born on February 13, 1876. At age 21, she married John Hillard on December 29, 1897. Norie and her sisters fondly remembered their mother. "My mother was a quiet woman as I remember her. My older sisters told me that when she was young, she was really pretty and got her work done in a hurry. As I [the youngest child] remember her, she was sick and really tired. She liked to dress up and always kept her hair long and put up attractively. She was a beautiful woman so people told me and so I remember. She was a good cook and could make a good meal out of whatever she had on hand. She loved all her grandchildren and took an interest in them...

I also remember the benches we kids sat on to eat meals. We all had our special places, and the neighbor kids all thought it was a treat to sit on the Hillard benches. I also remember that if we had friends visiting us, Mom always asked them to eat; and there were always a few extra neighbor kids at our table. They were always welcome.

...We had to stay at the table, we couldn't be excused until everyone was finished eating. I remember being so tired listening to everyone talk, I used to crawl under the table and sneak out without anyone noticing. If one of the other kids saw you, you were liable to feel a foot kicking you; but if you cried out, you'd get caught and made to go back and wait until everyone was finishing eating. We were also made to eat whatever we put on our plates. When Mom would move the table, hunks of fat and crusts of bread would fall out

out of the ridge under the table where we "stored" unwanted food. Imagine being forced to eat fat greasy meat!

We always had lots of magazines at our house. *The Farm Journal*, *The Ladies Home Companion*, *The Grit*, and *Ohio Farmer* were a few of them. The salesmen always stopped at our house to eat since restaurants were few and far between. They liked Mom's cooking and would give her free subscriptions in exchange for a good meal.

Mom used to make the best doughnuts. She made a big crock full of them. My brother Bobbie ... would always help to bake them. Since he didn't like them hot, she allowed him to put some away for himself. The doughnuts would all be eaten up, and he'd always have some later, which he wouldn't share with us. Mom also made her own bread. It was delicious too. I remember the boys would come home from school so hungry and eat the insides out of a loaf of bread. Sometimes, when she started to cut a loaf, it would be just a shell. I think she baked bread everyday until a bread man finally came and delivered bread. She really must have worked hard because she had to build a fire in the old coal and wood stove to bake it. Having a bread man was really a help to her. We had our own cows and chickens and our own eggs. She churned her own butter; we kids took turns turning the churn. We always had buttermilk, which I hated but everyone else loved. We butchered our own meat. Dad always had pigs to eat and would kill a steer or two every fall. The neighbors always came to help when we butchered, and it was like a big party. The kitchen would be full of big kettles of meat fat, which were cooked and rendered into lard, which they put through a lard press. They had a sausage stuffer and grinder and all kinds of equipment for the butchering.

Another time I remember is threshing day. Bob and Elmer Loomis owned a threshing machine and went around to different folks' farms to thresh their oats, wheat, and rye every year. The ladies in the neighborhood cooked for all the men that worked on their farms on threshing day. Ladies went out of their way to cook the best they knew how. It was sort of a competition among them to see who was picked as the best cook. I remember Mom made three or four kinds of meat and potatoes, salad, desserts, and all kinds of pies. It was a real feast and a really special day on the farm.

Robert Horace Hillard was born on March 21, 1915, the tenth child of John and Harriet Hillard. Ominous events were transpiring that would foretell the destiny of baby Robert's generation. The Great War in Europe was destroying the cream of the crop in unheard of numbers.

On the morning of March 10, 1915, 48,000 British troops stepped into No Man's Land behind a devastating barrage. They scurried over the desolate landscape toward Neuve Chapelle. When the barrage lifted, the Germans opened up their machine guns on the exposed British soldiers; and by sundown the soil was soaked with the blood of 10,000 killed and wounded British soldiers.[5]

Waiting for favorable wind conditions in Flanders, the Germans unleashed 168 tons of chlorine gas upon the Allies' line on April 22nd. Within ten minutes 10,000 allied troops were asphyxiated. The Battle for Ypres, Belgium continued into May. During the battle, Lt. Col. John McCrae was in charge of a Canadian field hospital. His friend and former student, Lt. Alexis Helmer was one of the many casualties. Helmer's burial inspired McCrae to write on May 3rd "In Flanders Fields," a poem which bode the future for some of Robert Hillard's generation.

> In Flanders fields the poppies blow
> Between the crosses, row on row,
> That mark our place; and in the sky
> The larks, still bravely singing, fly
> Scarce heard amid the guns below.
>
> We are the Dead. Short days ago
> We lived, felt dawn, saw sunset glow,
> Loved and were loved, and now we lie,
> In Flanders fields.
>
> Take up our quarrel with foe;
> To you from failing hands we throw
> The torch, be yours to hold it high.
> If you break faith with us who die
> We shall not sleep, though poppies grow
> In Flanders fields.[6]

(John McCrae died from pneumonia and meningitis

on Jan. 28, 1918)

By the end of 1915, the combatants had been slaughtering each other for five months. In that time a total of 5,145,000 men were dead, wounded, missing, or taken prisoner.[7] No wonder, there was a women's peace movement going on in Washington, D. C. on March 22nd.

Popular music often reflects the feeling of the times in the United States. In 1915, two of the leading songs related to the war in Europe: "I Didn't Raise My Boy To Be A Soldier" and "It's A Long Way To Tipperary." However, the number one recording was Alma Gluck singing "Carry Me Back To Old Virginia." A young songwriter named Irving Berlin busily made his mark by having seven of his songs listed as hits for the year. Two future singing stars were born in 1915: Billie Holiday and Frank Sinatra.

In Robert Hillard's Portage County, Ohio the Ford was selling for $60 **less** than it did the previous year. "The Universal Car" "...is everybody's motor car because everybody can understand and safely operate it. Doesn't take a skilled mechanic to operate or care for the Ford. Less than two cents a mile to operate and maintain the Ford. With 'Ford Service for Ford Owners' your Ford car is never idle. Buyers will share in profits if we sell at retail 300,000 new Ford cars between August 1914 and August 1915. Runabout, $440; Touring car $490; Town car $690; Coupelet $750; Sedan $975, f. o. b. Detroit with all equipment." [8]

However, those car owners and motorcyclists had better beware if they raced through Thomastown, now a part of Akron. The *Beacon Journal* reported on March 22nd: "Farmers War On Auto Speeders." "Irate farmers, armed with pick handles and clubs, lined up along the South Arlington road near Thomastown Sunday afternoon, prepared to stop speeding motorcyclists even if it was necessary to use force. An attack on the speeders was apparently prevented only by the arrival of the sheriff. A number of motorcyclists had been using the highway for racing Sunday, money having been wagered on the outcome of the contests, it was reported by the farmers. Consequently the motorcyclists were 'burning' up the road. Warned by farmers to quit, they merely laughed..." Traffic violators were then stopped and fined.[9]

In the world of sports the big fight for the United States in 1915 was not the war in Europe, but the heavyweight championship fight in Havana, Cuba on April 4. Jack Johnson, the black champion, was defending the title against the white challenger, Jess Willard. However, the March 22 dateline from Havana attempted to downplay the race card.

"...The big cowboy [Willard] is in better shape than the champion, but this is due to the preliminary training he received at El Paso, when it was thought that the fight would be staged at Juarez. But the big smoke [Johnson] is by no means in the poor condition that reports have credited him with. He is a little fat, but with almost two weeks to work it off, there is no reason why the champion should not be in as good physical condition as he was the day he wrested the title from Jim Jeffries.

Interest in the fight is keen. The training camps of both fighters are visited daily by crowds who are trying to get a line on both fighters. There is no racial feeling over the fight. No one speaks of a white man being pitted against a Negro [sic] ... Johnson is a favorite with the bettors, but there is plenty of Willard money in sight."

The April 6 reports out of Havana marveled at the *26 round* fight. The matter of race was duly noted by some of the sports writers.

"Jess Willard, now heavyweight champion of the world, is the hero of the hour. The big Kansas cowboy, who brought back to the white race the biggest crown in pugilistic circles, is being lionized by all. Everywhere he goes, he is followed by cheering crowds, but the champion is taking his honors with the same modest demeanor he showed before the fight. He is as happy as a schoolboy over the prize he has won. But there is no gloating over his victory, no swell-headedness marks his makeup.

'I knew I would win.' That sums up in a nutshell how he is taking the honors he won in the ring at the race track Monday when with a mighty punch to the jaw he sent Jack Johnson down and out for the count of ten in the 26th round..." [10]

D. W. Griffiths' epic silent film, "Birth of a Nation" premiered on February 8, 1915. The three-hour film introduced many innovative techniques, and its Civil War/Reconstruction theme may have been experienced in real life by some of the viewers. President

Wilson thought it was a fine film, but others decried its pro-KKK stance and its "vicious" portrayal of blacks. Some critics claimed that the film boosted the Ku Klux Klan's membership rosters. However, the Klan could be a clever, subtle siren in its own right; and in some circles it appeared to be a normal way of life. For example, *The Ravenna Republican* carried a large, block advertisement on its entertainment page on September 11, 1925 in which the large letters at the top, KKK, immediately capture the reader's eye. In various type sizes the advertisement reads: "The Junior Ku Klux Klan of Portage County will hold a CORN AND Weiner [sic] Roast Saturday, Sept. 12th 7 miles from Ravenna, on the Youngstown Road, 1/8 Mile East of Edinburg Center. Coffee, Sweet Cider, Doughnuts will be served. The Atlas Male Quartette from Cuyahoga Falls will entertain you. Good Speaker. Crosses will be burned. Everyone invited. Show the Junior Boys That You Are With Them." [10]

Over in Niles, Ohio things were not quite so folksy for the Klan in March, 1925. Rival factions were exchanging gunshots. [11]

The *Ravenna Republican* may have seemed indifferent to the Klan, but it certainly categorized intemperance as an evil. The chief article on its front page for March 25, 1915 was: "Some Reasons Why Saloons Should Be Kept Away." [12]

Closer to Bob Hillard's home in Randolph, Ohio in March 1915, the Hillards' neighbors were busy tapping the maple trees and boiling the sap for maple sugar. Several camps had made 50 gallons of maple sugar in February. Due to so much north wind, a good sugar season was in the forecast. The Randolph news writer added: "If I was a bluebird, I would stay another month where it is warm. Time enough for nesting after March winds have stopped blowing."

Yet, many folks braved the raw March weather to attend a variety of functions at the town hall. The ladies of the Christian Aid Society presented a well-attended "All round the world" social, in which various ethnic foods and decorations were featured. Nearly 100 voters gathered to hear strong arguments for issuing bonds for paving the road between Randolph and Suffield. A teachers' institute featured the artistic, vocational, scientific, and musical skills of the youths of Randolph, Atwater, and Brimfield Townships. In other parts of town, A Civil War veteran was laid to his final rest with the help of his G.A.R. comrades who performed the ritual. "George Brockett says that if [President Woodrow] Wilson keeps us out of the war, he will be reelected president in 1916. Bert Hine, the best historian in town, says that Neutrality will probably be preserved, for the United States government does not declare war until war is demanded by the people." And at Brockett's hall, the folks were dancing to the music of the Wise Orchestra.[13]

Whether demanded by the people or their elected leaders, the American Doughboys were sailing to France in 1918 to fight the Hun. Fears, some real and others imagined, affected the children of the era. In Melrose, Pennsylvania thirteen year-old Mathilda Keil was shepherding her little sisters to the German-speaking Catholic school, when in a fit of anti-German hatred the English-speaking children of the neighborhood hurled sticks and stones at them and ran up to spit on them. In Randolph, Ohio three year-old Bobby Hillard was headed to the Randolph Fair in charge of his sister Rose. "He had a good time at the fair. They stayed all day, but Bobbie wouldn't eat anything at the fair. He came home as hungry as a bear, and Mom asked him why he didn't eat all day. He explained that he saw a man putting 'Germans' on the food. He had heard the talk about germ warfare and really took it to heart; so even back then, the people were worried about germ warfare. (The man at the fair was only shaking pepper on the food.)" [14]

In 1920 Bobby Hillard trotted off to the first grade, an event that probably never daunted the five-year old, because he was a bright and determined lad. Bobby also had developed a temper to go with his determination. The Hillard children were expected to take turns going to the coal shed to bring in the coal for the stove. On one occasion when Dad Hillard asked whose turn it was to fetch in the coal for the stove, the older kids ganged up on Bobby. They all piped up that it was the younger Bobby's turn. In spite of his denials that it was not his turn, Bobby was assigned the chore. Stung by the injustice, he kicked the coal bucket all the way to the shed. But by no means was Bobby a surly kid. He was beginning to learn to whistle, and like all whistlers, it became a lifetime pleasure. His favorite whistling tune was "Donkey Serenade."

Around this time, the Hillard home was struck by lightning. It was soon put out and all was safe, but thereafter Bobby was scared to death of thunderstorms.

This first grader's world extended from the familiar farm-house and its surrounding fields to the elementary school and back, so it is unlikely that the 1921 events made an immediate impact, perhaps never. Nevertheless, it was an up and down year for Ohio. Cal thumped the Buckeyes 28-0 in the Rose Bowl to start out the year. Good things were to come however, because Otto Graham, the great Cleveland Browns QB and Hall of Famer, was born on December 6. Much was expected of the Cleveland Indians since they won their first World Series Championship in the previous year. In 1920 the Tribe went 98-56 to finish two games ahead of the notorious Chicago White Sox, who threw the 1919 pennant for the gamblers. The Cleveland team then defeated the Brooklyn Robins five games to two in the World Series,. Stan Coveleski had hurled a 3-0 shutout, Bill Wambsganss pulled off an unassisted triple play, and Jim Bagby was the first pitcher ever to hit a homerun in the world series. This triumph was darkened by one of baseball's greatest tragedies. The Tribe's star shortstop, Ray Chapman was beaned by a Carl Mays spitball pitch on August 16th and died the following day, the only major league baseball player to ever be killed in a game. (In the same year a handsome young man from the adjacent Summit County, George Sisler of the St. Louis Browns batted .407. Cleveland's manager/centerfielder, Tris Speaker, batted .388.) But alas, in 1921 the Tribe ended in second place two games back of the New York Yankees. Still, kids in northern Ohio could run out to the nearest sandlot or cow pasture and pretend that they were Speaker, Coveleski, Sisler, or even Wambsganss.

    The general appropriation bill for the state amounted to 91 million dollars. Over one-fifth of that amount went to the public schools. At the time, Ohio had only three state colleges; Ohio State received $1,678,724, Ohio University $268,625, and Miami University a mere $261,922. "Next to education the biggest items are $4,275,370 for the policing, patrolling and maintenance of highways, and $5,854,692 for care of the unfortunate wards of the state in the insane, blind, deaf and criminal institutions." Warren G. Harding of Marion, Ohio was in the White House.[15]

    Perhaps the biggest story on the national scene was the Sacco and Vanzetti trial in Massachusetts. On July 14th a jury found the two anarchists guilty of the murder of a shoe factory paymaster and a security guard in a payroll robbery. Nichola Sacco and Bartolomeo Vavzetti were electrocuted in 1927. [16]

    Over time, some news stories are the same, only the dates and some of the names are changed. On March 21 (Bobby's birthday) news out of Dublin, Ireland was that the Sinn Fein bombed a military lorry, a Sinn Feiner was executed by the British, and "Twenty-nine persons are known to have been killed in the bloodiest weekend in Ireland since the present 'campaign' began." On May 1-7, riots occurred in Palestine; and on June 1 a race riot in Tulsa, Oklahoma resulted in 85 deaths.

In Randolph there were still some Civil War veterans who could hoist themselves in to the saddle and ride up the road to the town hall for the Memorial Day ceremony. Over in Akron a new generation of veterans was organizing the Rainbow Division Veterans Association. Over 100 men of the renowned 42nd Division lived in Akron, and all were expected to enter the association.

On Bobby Hillard's 6th birthday, the Akron movie theaters were doing good business. The Realto, The Waldorf, and The Allen were packing them in thanks to some clever advertising.

At the Realto, William S. Hart, the leading western actor, starred in "The Cradle of Courage." "Square Kelly, portrayed by Mr. Hart, has been a safecracker who is reformed in the crucible of war at the fighting front and who becomes a policeman in furtherance of his plan to live straight. Of course, there is a pretty girl who inspires this lofty sentiment in Kelly and strengthens his purpose to relinquish his criminal career."

The comedian, Buster Keaton, in "The Scarecrow," is an added feature..."

Charlie Chaplin was also riding high in popularity. "A cow paraded the streets of Akron Saturday afternoon with a sign on each side reading, 'This is no bull, 'The Kid' is the best show in town.' This animal caused much merriment along the route taken by the animal. Chaplin in "The Kid" is still pleasing the crowds as is evidenced by the crowds seen in front of the theaters. [In this case, The Waldorf] Jackie Coogan is winning the hearts of the theater-goers as one of the best child actors in the universe. The childish love for the tramp who picks him up on the streets is little short of marvelous."

"The Nut," starring swashbuckling Douglas Fairbanks, was showing at The Allen. Fairbanks was still recuperating from injuries received in some of the stunts that he performed. "Fairbanks was required to jump through a window in this scene, landing on a man passing by on the sidewalk outside. In making this leap, he caught his toe on the window sill and fell to the cement sidewalk, breaking the third metacarpal bone in his left hand and severely wrenching his back." [17]

Three of the top recordings in '21 were "Wang Wang Blues" by the Paul Whiteman Orchestra, "Look for the Silver Lining" by Marion Harris, and "All By Myself" by Ted Lewis and His Orchestra. [18]

Also in 1921, the twelfth and last of the Hillard family, Lenora (Norie) Belle Hillard, was born on August 29th. Norie's "Memories" paint a word portrait of the family in the 1920's and 1930's.

"My brother Lawrence George Hillard (b. May 20, 1905) was a really interesting person. He quit school in the seventh grade and went to work. My mother said he had a speech problem, and the other kids made fun of him. The schools didn't have speech classes then so no one helped him, and he grew to hate school. Anyway, he used to tell us he wished he had gone to school one more day so that he could have found out who ate the Gingerbread Boy... One day Lawrence (called Tony) took me to Ravenna and gave me a dollar to buy Mom a present for Mother's Day. I found a pink depression glass candy dish which cost 50 cents... It is worth much more than 50 cents now... Tony had a wild horse, and it got scared of the threshing machine. Tony tried to hold it, and the horse bit him. When a horse bites, it doesn't open its mouth; and it takes a chunk out of you. Tony's arm was bleeding real bad. Luckily, Savalla (a sister b. Oct. 7, 1898) was a nurse; and she got a tourniquet around the arm to stop the bleeding. They took Tony over to Dr. Silberger, and he had to have shots and had a sore arm for a long time. He was lucky they saved his arm. That was quite a bit of extra excitement for threshing day."

Hunting was a passion, and hunting season became a ritual for the rural lads. In Bob Hillard's later correspondence, he often inquires how the boys are doing with their hunting. It was a manly endeavor that held bragging rights for the most successful marksman, and it could put meat on the table during rough financial times. An important adjunct to the sport was the hunting dog, whether it was a beagle that could circle rabbits, a setter that could point a pheasant, or a coon dog that could tree a raccoon. Lawrence and David Deloss Hillard (b. June 25, 1900) had that hunting passion and an unusual sense of humor. "Dad always worked away in Pennsylvania, and Mom and we kids stayed back in Ohio. Mom told Dad that Lawrence

L. to R. - Johnny Hillard, Stanley Hillard, Bobby Hillard, Lester Jobe and his brother. Early 1920's.

The Hillard house on New Milford Road.

and Loss went hunting, which they loved, and were neglecting their chores. Dad told them they weren't allowed to hunt for a month. One morning after that, Loss came into the kitchen carrying a gun. Mom said, 'Where do you think you're going?' He informed her that he was going hunting; and she said, 'Oh, no! You aren't! You heard what your dad said.' ... Before all this happened, Lawrence and Loss had made a deal that Lawrence would go out and sit on a rail fence which was in back of our house; and Loss would tell Mom that if she wouldn't let him go hunting, he was going to shoot Lawrence. So Loss shot toward Lawrence. Lawrence fell off the fence, and Mom fainted. Lawrence was fine, but they didn't get to go hunting again for a long, long time."

Another hunting story involved Norie, who at one time had occasions of crying in school. "One time during a later school year, we had a boy named Bob White in our room. One morning he burst out crying, and all the kids in the room wondered what was wrong. Our teacher told us that he had a reason to cry since his little sister had died. We felt sad then and cried too. That afternoon there was a gathering of my brothers and their friends in the kitchen when I reached home. They were talking about a hunting law being passed allowing quail (or bob-white) to be shot. My dad was against it, and he was arguing with them. I got off the school bus and came into the kitchen. My dad noticed my red eyes and thought I had started crying in school again. He asked me what was wrong now. I told him that Bob White's little sister had died. My brothers and their friends took that as an omen and vowed that they would never shoot quail."

"The first pet I had that I can remember was a red rooster which I named Reddy. He would come to me out of a flock of chickens if I called his name. I dressed him in doll clothes and swung him to sleep on a swing outside; but all good things come to an end. One day my brother Stanley (or Peanuts as we called him [b. June 6, 1909]) and a neighbor boy were walking down the dirt road which ran in front of our house on New Milford Road. They were picking up stones to see who could throw them the farthest. The neighbor boy hit my Reddy with a stone and killed him accidentally. The boys gathered Reddy up and brought him to my mother who dressed him and cooked him for dinner. No one told me this, and that night at the dinner table I was sitting there eating my favorite piece of chicken (which was the neck) when someone asked Mom where the chicken came from. She told them about Stanley and the neighbor boy killing a rooster on the road. All at once it dawned on me what had happened. I asked, 'Was it a red rooster?' She said, 'Yes.' I ran out to the chicken coop calling 'Reddy! Reddy!' and Reddy never came. I was broken hearted, and I wouldn't eat chicken for years after that."

Norie thought Stanley was" a dreamer. He was always thinking of ways to get rich and not to have to work so hard. My dad would send the boys out to hoe corn and find 'Peanuts' (as we called him) lying in a row and reading a book! He was named after Mom's dad, and I think he was her favorite. He was really bright in school, and some of the neighbor ladies with sons his age were sort of jealous of him."

"My brother John Mack Hillard (b. Nov. 6, 1912) was really a character... He was really laid back and nothing much seemed to trouble him. He never worried about how he looked, and my brother Robert Horace Hillard was really neat and fussy. Johnny used to drive him crazy. One morning Johnny couldn't find any socks to wear to school so he just wore his shoes with no stockings. Bobby was horrified and came home and told Mom and Dad that if they didn't make Johnny dress decently, he wasn't going back to school with him any more. Dad got after Johnny (which he did quite often), but the next day at school half the male students came with just shoes and no socks. Johnny had started a new fad! My sister Harriet Jeanette Hillard (b. Sept. 19, 1908) told me she was also ashamed of Johnny when she went to school and was in some of his classes. Johnny never opened a book to study, but the teachers liked him and he got better grades than she did. The teachers thought he was interesting and always added something to their class discussions. Harriet told me a story about one day when they were studying about Napoleon, and the teacher called on Johnny. He got up and told a story about Napoleon being really short and that Josephine was so much taller that Napoleon had to stand on a stool to kiss her. Harriet said, 'I was mortified and wished I could have fallen through the floor.' Johnny's teacher, however, said he had done well by telling a good story and helped the class by bringing history to life."

"...Johnny was my favorite brother. He would spend time with my sister Mildred Ruth Hillard (b. Sept. 4, 1918) and I. He would take us on nature hikes and tell us all he knew about trees, plants, and herbs.

He also read to us a lot. He liked poetry. I remember one peculiar poem. It was about Irish leprechauns and fairies…"

One Easter my sister Harriet, who was really pretty and had a lot of admirers, received a decorated chocolate Easter egg from one of them. It was big and really pretty, and she said it was too pretty to eat. I remember Johnny, Bobbie, Ruth, and I all coaxed her for it; but she wouldn't give it to us to eat. Mom said she might as well eat it because it wouldn't keep. It would get all green and fuzzy and spoil. But she saved it, and sure enough, in a month or so it did. Too bad we didn't have freezers then, wasn't it?'

"My dad used to tell a story about Ruth and Bobbie when they were young. Ruth liked to tease Bobbie. One day she was writing a letter to Santa Claus while Dad was sitting in the kitchen with them. She read the letter she was writing out loud just to torment Bobbie. It went like this: 'Dear Santa, I've been a good girl. Bring me a red sled and Norie a baby doll, but don't bring Bobbie anything 'cause he doesn't want anything.' Dad said Bobbie jumped up fighting mad and told her he did want something, and he'd write his own letter to Santa Claus, and she should mind her own beeswax." [19]

Bobby Hillard entered his teenage years in 1928. Mrs. Hillard never made much of birthdays by having parties, but she would make the birthday child's favorite food for dinner. On Bobby's 13th birthday he could look forward to his favorite food, which was any kind of cake.

If the teenage lad was into hero worship, he wouldn't have to look far in the Roarin' Twenties. On Bobby's birthday (March 21st), Charles Lindberg received the Medal of Honor. On June 17-18, Amelia Earhart became the first woman to fly the Atlantic Ocean. In the world of sports, Gene Tunney and Jack Dempsey dominated the boxing scene; Babe Ruth and Lou Gehrig led the Yankees to a 4-0 sweep of the Cardinals in the World Series (the Indians finished in 7th place in the 8-team American League). Bobby Jones, an amateur, was defeating all comers in golf, and the Providence Steam Roller won the NFL with a 9-1-1 record.

In the entertainment world, Mickey and Minnie Mouse made their screen debut on May 15. Emil Jannings ("The Last Command") was voted best actor, and Janet Gaynor ("Street Angel") was the best actress. It was a time when movie houses had several features in one week. One of the top recordings was Ruth Etting's "Because My Baby Don't Mean Maybe Now", to which one could dance the one-step. Another hit tune was Helen Kane's coquettish "I Wanna Be Loved By You."[20]

In March 1928 the Havre Chevy dealership in Ravenna, the county seat, advertised five makes of cars and two trucks. At the top of the line was the Imperial Landau going for $715, at the bottom was the Chevy Roadster at $495. Billed as the "world's most luxurious low-priced automobile," it sounded like quite a deal. However, the annual income in 1928 for industrial workers, including farm labor, was $1,384.[21]

Besides his farm chores and hunting, the thirteen-year-old Hillard began to hone his skills as a basketball player. Throughout the area, many farms sported an iron hoop inside the barn so the boys could play basketball in the worst of winter weather. The family also loved to play cards, especially euchre and 500. Bobby also played tic-tac-toe with his youngest sister.

In the summer, many of the Randolph youth worked on the muck farms in the Hartville area. The labor required young supple backs to plant and harvest the vegetables, which would be shipped to the urban open-air markets and grocery stores. Work hours ran from sunrise to sunset and the hourly rate was a whopping $.10 an hour. To meet the demand for cheap labor, orphans were shipped in, and their treatment was often not pleasant.[22] In the fall, it was back to school on the 'kid-hack," a horse drawn wagon, which took the kids over the rough and often muddy dirt road to the main road where they could then board the school bus.

On the international scene a ray of hope burst from the social and political upheavals in Europe. On August 28th the Kellogg-Briand Pact was signed in Paris. It was the first treaty to outlaw aggressive war. Yet, there was plenty violence to breed an epidemic of pessimism. A bomb attack against the king of Italy killed 17 bystanders in Milan on April 12th. Seven weeks later, another bomb attack at the Italian consulate in Buenos Aires killed 22 people. Closer to home, the Republican primary elections in Chicago on April 10th was preceded by assassinations and bombings. The Okeechobee Hurricane of September 16 killed 2,500 Americans. The great social experiment of prohibition saw increasing gangland violence. Two men in Cleveland were gunned down in a bootlegging feud, prompting the headline in the Ravenna newspaper: "Gangland Haunts Are Searched." [23]

For better or worse, Herbert Hoover won the presidential election in a landslide over Al Smith, whose Catholicism was a factor in his November defeat. In the same month, Hirohito became the Emperor of Japan. Jack Kevorkian, "Dr. Death," was born on May 26th. James Earl Ray, the assassinator of Dr. Martin Luther King (born January 15, 1927), saw his first light of day on March 10th. [24]

However, a safe haven existed on the Hillard farm in Randolph, Ohio; and the folks around town were involved in doing good works. The Sunday School class of the Methodist Church (26 members) held a party where the decorations and entertainment favored St. Patrick's Day. "Delicious refreshments were served. This is an up-to-date organized class, abundant in good works at home and abroad, supporting a little brown boy named Merriam in the baby fold at Kolar, India, where Mrs. Ethel Wheelock, one of our high school graduates, is engaged in the work of the Master." Elsewhere, the ladies of the Cemetery Society were preparing for the annual Easter supper at the Town Hall. [25]

After the stock market collapse in 1929, the Great Depression spread gloom, despair, and misery across the land. Norie Hillard Foster: "I remember during the Depression how tight money was when Ruthie and I took Home Economics in high school. A teacher called Miss Helming taught it, and we had to baste everything before we sewed it permanently. After we sewed a seam permanently, we used to have to pull out our basting and then carefully roll it on an empty spool so that we could save it to use over again. Sometimes that basting thread was reused so much it became actually dirty and not too pleasant to work with. That's how tough it was to buy supplies then, and we had to learn to do without and save..

I remember we used to wrap our school lunches in newspaper and save the bread wrappers to wrap our sandwiches. Those wrappers were precious, and we used to fight over them. I also remember I was ashamed of my lunch. I had homemade bread and big slices of ham which made a huge sandwich. Other kids had neat sliced store bought bread and lunch meat. I'd trade home-cured ham for baloney! Anyway, those baloney sandwiches made me feel better, even if I was naïve and simple.

In the summertime we picked beans and strawberries for Mr. and Mrs. Roundy. We made two cents a quart for strawberries, and on a good day we could make a whole dollar (picking 50 quarts of berries) which was a lot of money in those days. (A nice pair of leather shoes cost about $1.98 for children's sizes.) For beans we got fifteen cents for each half bushel when Mr. Roundy could sell them at market. We used the money we earned for school clothes. One time I really recall is when one of the neighbor boys, Walter Goodyear, worked with us. He was a really nice boy, and he was saving his money to buy a suit to wear to church and Sunday School. He went to church with Mr. And Mrs. Roundy, but his family was poor and couldn't afford to buy him a suit which he really wanted. My sister Ruthie and Helen Anderson (my sister-in-law Louella's younger sister) used to help him fill up his baskets with beans so that he finally earned enough money to buy a suit. His dream came true for him. He was as proud as a peacock in his new suit, and we were all happy for him.

Ruthie and I used to go to Mr. and Mrs. Roundy's house to listen to the radio before we had electricity. We didn't have a radio at home and it was really a treat. We'd listen to Jake & Lena & Gene & Glen. They were the same people, but played two parts. We'd also listen to Gene Autry & Pie Plant Pete sing cowboy songs.

During the Depression we couldn't sell our garden produce so dad allowed people from town (if they could get to our house) to come and help themselves to vegetable and fruit which was going to waste. He helped a lot of people like that."

As Bobby Hillard progressed in high school, he became one of the taller good looking boys with a keen intelligence and wit. "He was really good looking and looked like a million dollars when he dressed up... Bob liked clothes. He liked to dress well and look 'sharp' . He had a few girl friends in high school (all the girls thought he was handsome) but no one really special... He was really smart, and I [Norie] wouldn't have got algebra or math in high school without his help. He was very neat, and my brother Johnny embarrassed him all of the time." He was always very particular and even liked his work shirts ironed just so. (Many of his clothes were probably his favorite colors blue and green.) On occasions Bobby seemed like a parent to Norie as he told her to wash her face and clean up.

Perhaps the only major setback was when he got the mumps. Norie Hillard Foster: " ...When they [Bobby and Johnny] were in high school they both got the mumps. I was just a little girl then, but I remember that they were really sick; and Dr. Cummings was really worried about them. He made house calls then, and I remember him telling Mom she would have to keep them in bed for a week or so or they could get something more serious. I heard the doctor talking to Mom, and I really got concerned about them and thought they could die. I decided I'd pray for them, so I snuck into their room. It was the bedroom downstairs in our house, and after I got into their room, I climbed up on the rail of their bed. Johnny said I started saying something about Adam and Eve and fell off the bed. Mom caught me then and that ended my prayers, but I really loved my brothers and meant well."

To the teachers and principals, over the years some classes in school are more endearing than others. These students are the ones whose personalities and successful efforts make the profession worthwhile, and one wishes that they could stay longer. Bobby Hillard's Class of '32 appeared to be one of those.

"The past year has been one of great activity at Randolph school. With probably the biggest enrollment in the history of the community, it was found necessary to expand, to some extent, the seating facilities, and consequently the senior class was given a room by itself. The large study hall was practically filled, so that no room is being wasted." [26]

With Mr. Bunker as coach, the football team opened with a victory over North Canton on the Randolph Fair Day. This was followed by a triumph over Freedom, but then the Randolph boys ran into the powerful up-county team from Garrettsville, which was too powerful for the "local aggregation." Perhaps due to injuries and the lack of enough players, the rest of the season's schedule had to be dropped.

Led by Coach Bunker, apparently a coach for all seasons, the boys basketball team put up a valiant effort, but frequently came up on the short end of the score. "Although the team did not win as many games as usual, it did win the respect of its opponents through clean, fast playing, and by fighting to the finish." Bobby Hillard played guard on the team.

The girls' basketball team was a different story. "Coached by Miss Margaret Russell, a Wooster graduate, it seemed for a long time that the Randolph girls would finish the season undefeated. After having run up a string of six or seven victories, the break came, and successive defeats by Paris and Rootstown cost us the chance we might have had of winning the county title. The three Anderson girls, Lida, Luella [the future Mrs. Stanley Hillard], and Grace scintillated as they had the previous season. Gladys Brunner played an outstanding game at guard." [Lida, Luella, and Gladys were in the class of '32.]

"... At the present time, we are in the thick of musical-contest activities, with Luella Anderson, Paul Wise, Grace Anderson, and Alice Schmitt as our representatives." Three other students represented the school in a one-act play contest. Fourteen juniors and eleven seniors were hard at work for their class plays to be staged in April. Baccalaureate plans were being made, as well as the Junior-Senior banquet and the athletic teams banquet.

"Band and orchestra work has been going on as usual. We have been very fortunate this year in having Miss Russell (obviously a multi-talented teacher) with us to hold extra rehearsals, and much of the success of the music work here is credited to her. Mrs. Bush's work with the glee clubs and vocal music showed its worth when Paul Wise, vocal soloist, won first place in the district contest. He also won first place in instrumental solo."

Robert Hillard authored the senior class' satirical Last Will and Testament. The eighteen seniors bequeathed various humorous thoughts and jibes to the faculty, the other classes, and each other. Of the many "words of wisdom,' was the following by Bobby Hillard: "Just one word of warning, don't think you can put anything over on the faculty members, that you can hoodwink them, or get away without studying, you can't do it, we tried and we know whereof we speak. In conclusion we will give you three rules that we guarantee will bring success. The first is Study! The second is Study! And the third is Study!!" On the 21st article of the Class Will, Bobby Hillard wrote: "As for myself I will leave you my appreciation of the torture you have undergone in listening to such trash." [26]

In conclusion, "To sum up the year's work, we [probably Principal Espenschied] might say that it has been more than satisfactory, both from the student and teacher standpoint. We hope

Bob Hillard's senior picture, 1932.

Lucille and June Anderson.

that next fall we will be able to do as well." [28]

However, that spring things were not going well in the nation's capital. Tensions from several previous protests and riots heightened as veterans from WW I descended upon Washington, D.C. from May to July. Congress had promised the former "doughboys" a bonus for their service in the Great War; and with unemployment so high and expectations so low, the men and their families needed the bonus now. Opinions of the "Bonus March" varied. There was the law and order crowd who viewed the protest as unpatriotic and unbecoming behavior for a veteran. Some, including Army Chief of Staff Douglas MacArthur, went so far as to decry the movement as a communist conspiracy against the United States government, although the actual percentage of communist participation was around ten per cent. In other circles the raggedy Bonus Marchers drew great sympathy. To them it was not a revolutionary situation but a cry for help from people "who were out of luck, out of money, and wanted to get their bonus -- and they needed the money at that moment."

On July 28th the protest came to a climax. Fisticuffs and brick throwing erupted among the Bonus Marchers and the police. President Hoover then ordered the area to be cleared out at once. Army troops led by MacArthur, including his reluctant aide Dwight D. Eisenhower and Maj. George S. Patton, began to drive the veterans and their families from their shanties. By evening, hundreds had been injured by gas, bricks, clubs, bayonets, and sabers. One baby died. A fire of unknown origin erupted in the camp, and the sights and sounds of the people fleeing the inferno and mounted Army troops were not forgotten when the November elections arrived. [29]

For the graduation class of 1932, prospects were as bleak as those for the Bonus Marchers. If one was inclined to go to college, money was scarce for tuition and room and board. To stay at home often meant further financial pressure on the family because employment of any kind was scarce. Consequently, Bobby Hillard headed to Pennsylvania to work on the farm of his Aunt Val Brunt (his mother's sister) and Uncle John Scott. Peculiar circumstances had forged the family bonds into even stronger ties. Bobby's older brother Jimmy was raised by Aunt Val and Uncle John. Jim was born with crossed eyes, and his mother could not get him to specialists in

Pittsburgh. "Aunt Val offered to keep him and take him for the treatments. When his eyes were straightened, she didn't want to let him come home with us. (Aunt Val didn't have children of her own.) Dad fought about it, but Mom let him stay."

Little Norie Hillard managed to put a little strain on the relationship. "One summer day my sister Harriet took me with her out to Pennsylvania to Aunt Val Brunt and Uncle John Scott's home. Aunt Val lived there with Uncle John Scott who never married. I loved him dearly. He had had a leg taken off, but he was always good to us children. Anyway, Aunt Val was having a Ladies Aid Meeting at her house while we were visiting them. The ladies were in the house ; but it was a hot summer day, and the windows were open. I was outside playing by myself. They had a building which they called a wash house. (It was where they heated water and did their washing.) It had a front porch on it which I was pretending was a stage to dance on. My dancing stirred up a hornets nest which was on the porch. They got after me, and I ran away from them. Uncle John saw me and started to chase me and hit me with his hat to get the bees off me. I thought he was licking me because I stirred up the bees, and I called him all the swear words I could think of. I told him I didn't mean to stir up his old hornets nest, and he could go to H---. The ladies in the house heard the commotion and were really shocked by my language. I had hornet stings all over my body. Aunt Val and Uncle John made a paste of soda and rubbed it all over me. Aunt Val was furious, and Harriet and I were sent home the next day. Uncle John talked and laughed about it for days."

On Bobby's 18th birthday - March 21, 1933 - the disturbing front page news from Potsdam, Germany may have seemed innocuous at the time. After all, to many Americans, especially those of German descent, it was none of the United States' business. Besides, we had enough troubles of our own with the depression, which President Roosevelt was trying to alleviate with his alphabet soup array of social programs. Nevertheless, there was no doubt as to Herr Hitler's hard line attitude; he was as subtle as a poke in the eye with a sharp stick.

"HITLER ASKS HE BE NAMED AS DICTATOR" ... Said the aspiring despot, "We shall strive to unite all those willing to help, but we shall destroy all those seeking to damage our people... Only defeat forced the nation to agree to the war guilt clause against our better knowledge."... Said German President Paul Von Hindenburg to Hitler: "Your miraculous life is a symbol of the life and power of the whole nation." An estimated half million people witnessed the spectacle. "Endless parades of Reichswehr troops moved through the streets while spectators thundered the chorus of "Deutschland Uber Alles" and other songs of war-time. Brown-shirted Nazi[s] marched beneath the swastika banner..." [28]

Like most of his fellow citizens, young Bobby Hillard also had enough immediate problems at hand without worrying about the disturbing events across the wide Atlantic Ocean. After spending about a year on his aunt's and uncle's farm in Pennsylvania, he returned to live at the Hillard farm in Randolph, Ohio, where the family situation was gradually changing.

Norie Hillard Foster: "My mother was always sickly, and I used to worry about her while I was at school so my school days were never too happy and carefree... Christmas was always a sad time at our house. Mom never did much about it, and we never had a Christmas tree." The older girls pitched in to help. "... My oldest sister Savalla Elizabeth was like a mother to me. She raised two daughters by herself, but she still had time for me and the rest of the family. She was the oldest and sort of bossy, but she loved us all. She was a wonderful nurse and worked many years at Butler Hospital... My next sister Alice Audrey was really a neat, fussy person. Nothing ever was clean enough. Mom said she was her best worker, and Mom was really close to her. Mom always said we other girls should follow Alice's example. Alice always came back and helped Mom can and clean even after she was married and lived away from home. She was always afraid of germs and was a constant hand washer. Anywhere she lived had to be spotless; and sometimes it was hard for the rest of us to go along with her, but she really was a well-meaning person."

Bob and two of his neighbors, Charlie Anderson and Waldo Wolff, were then fortunate in gaining employment at a bathtub manufacturer in Alliance. While the 1930's passed by, the country's economy very slowly improved, and as the troublesome decade dwindled down, there was one area of Bob Hillard's life that quickly improved -- his romantic life.

LUCILLE

Bob's sister Rose worked as a secretary for the First Central Bank in Akron. One of Rose's friends was a beautiful, blond, Swedish, secretary whom she figured her brother should know. Bobby was duly impressed with Lucille Anderson - no relation to his buddy, Charlie.

Bob's parents were not church goers; and although his sister Norie attended the Methodist church with her neighbors Mr. and Mrs. Roundy, Bob had not been interested in church, but Lucille changed that. He began to attend church with her. He also took her to meet his brother Stanley and his wife Louella who lived in Akron. Louella recalled that Lucille "was a very lovely girl and Bob was crazy about her."

Lucille's parents, Esther and Henry, had immigrated from Sweden to Chicago, where Lucille was born on December 11, 1919. Her brother Roland was six years older than she. Her younger sister, June, was born in 1925 in Akron, Ohio.

Henry, a skilled mechanic, decided to move to Akron where employment in the rubber shops was booming. He worked the 6:00 to midnight shift at the Goodyear Tire and Rubber Co. Even when the violent union strikes occurred in the 1930's, Henry maintained an adamant non-union stance. He preferred to be an independent, hard-working family man, who knew how to do his mechanic's job well. Once when a meddling supervisor interfered with his work, Henry peevishly referred to him as a "yumping jiminy yerk."

In his younger days, Henry was not active in the church, and on Sundays Esther stayed home with her husband. However, Lucille and June attended the Swedish Baptist Church by riding a bus downtown and getting a transfer to another bus. For Lucille, the association with the Baptist faith would last a lifetime.

On the Akron city streets, kids were expected to play and entertain themselves until the street lights came on. Various games of tag, kick the can, and bike riding were the favorites. Indoors, the family enjoyed board games like Monopoly and Parchesi. They would also gather around the radio to listen to the Luxe Radio Theater. June's favorite broadcast was "One Man's Family," which was the saga of the Henry and Fanny Barbour family. The popular program aired from 1932 to1959. Once a week, Esther and the kids would walk to the Liberty Theater on West Market Street to catch the latest double feature and news reel.

Lucille is dressed for Halloween in the early 1920's. Her cousin Raymond Osbeck is in the background.

Left - June, Roland, and Lucille on Oct. 26, 1941.

Right - Lucille stands by the cannon on the square In Vermillion, Ohio.

Every summer the Anderson family pitched a tent for two weeks along the shores of Lake Milton. Henry's refrigeration consisted of digging a hole, putting in a cake of ice, and covering it up. In a secluded spot, he dug a latrine. The kids loved to swim, and in the evenings they would sit around a campfire and sing. Across the dark lake, fireflies and other campfires sparkled in the night.

Lucille attended Crosby and Rankin Elementary Schools, and by the time she graduated from Buchtel High School, she was a member of the National Honor Society. She took the commercial course, which was a common thing to do for high school girls at that time. Her favorite subjects were literature and history, and her love for reading was passed on to her sister June. The two of them often walked the long distance to the library to take out books. However, June did not share Lucille's passion for opera music.

Although Lucille had been somewhat of a tomboy when she was a little girl, as a teenager she was non-athletic. She preferred to do her intricate embroidery, intellectual pursuits, and Sunday School work. She was a well-organized young lady, and everything had to be neatly in its place. Lucille was also very proud of her Swedish heritage. June said that Lucille's favorite color was blue, like that of every good Swede. (The Swedish national flag is blue with a yellow cross.)

When Lucille met Bob Hillard, she was smitten with the tall, handsome, muscular young man, four years older than she. He was not an intellectual lightweight either. As for Bob, he fell head over heels in love with this smart, beautiful, blond Swedish girl.[29]

(Perhaps Bob's interest in religion was also enhanced by the heartrending death of his beloved mother. Harriet Holmes Moorhead Hillard passed away on December 21, 1939 at the age of 63. It was said that Bob "took on awful" when his mother died.)

By 1940, Bob's recent past was shrouded in sadness, but his prospects for the future were brightening. He had a beautiful girlfriend and a steady job.

Norie Hillard Foster: "I remember the summer of 1940. I had just graduated from high school, and my brother Bobby asked me if I'd like to go to his shop picnic... Since his girl Lucille was working, he thought he'd take me, and I could ask a girl friend of mine to go along. At that time I had a three piece suit with blouse, slacks, and shorts. On the day we were to go, I put on the blouse and shorts. When Bobby saw me, he said he wouldn't take me unless I put on more clothes, so I went back and put on the slacks instead of the shorts. When we picked up my friend, she had shorts on because it was a really hot summer day. Bobby never said a word. We had a good time at the picnic. All the rides were free, and it really was a lot of fun. After we dropped off my friend on the way home, I was telling Bobby what a good time we had; but I couldn't resist also telling him that all the other girls there were wearing shorts. He said, 'I don't care what other girls wear. My sister is going to dress decently if I take her some place.' I wonder what he would think of how girls dress today [in 2006]."

By 1941 Bob Hillard was employed by the Ohio Transportation Department. The manual labor consisted of pick and shovel work and cutting weeds and grass along the roads, but at least it was in the outdoors, and there were hopes of becoming a surveyor for the department.

PART II
You're in the Army Now.

In the late summer of 1940, a phenomenon was sweeping the nation -- marriage licenses were selling like hotcakes. In Summit County, "Exactly 510 licenses were issued to Summit couples during August, an all-time record that eclipsed even the best mark of June, traditionally the month of brides. The previous high was last June when 479 licenses were issued... Court attaches said they could give only one explanation for the unprecedented activity in the license bureau -- the impending conscription law. And they added, the situation here wasn't any different than in various other parts of the country. They pointed to Brooklyn as an example, where officials kept the license bureau open all night to handle the rush of applicants." In Portage County, the *Evening Record* reported the same phenomenon in "Conscription Helps Cupid." This article mentioned the important fact - and perhaps a leading reason for the increased marriage applications - that married men were exempted from the draft. [30]

It was a time when one could take his sweetheart to the air-conditioned, beautifully ornate Loew's Theater on Akron's Main Street to see "Boom Town" with the all-star cast of Clark Gable,

Spencer Tracy, Claudette Colbert, Hedy LaMarr, and Frank Morgan. Out at Summit Beach Park the lovebirds could roller skate or dance to the music of Benny Jones and His Orchestra for only thirty cents. A Walt Disney Festival, including "Snow White," was featured at the "scientifically cooled" Falls Theater. Next to their advertisements was either a strategically placed or coincidental ad for baby carriages, which were selling for $2.98. The young couple could pay 25 cents a week at no interest!

By September 5th, the draft bill still was not a done deal. Front page news described the hot and furious action on the floor of the House of Representatives. "A grim house, weary of debate, stirred by a vigorous fist fight on the floor of congress last night between Rep. Martin Sweeney, democrat of Cleveland, and Rep. Beverly Vincent, democrat of Kentucky, began its final drive today for a decision on the Burke-Wadsworth compulsory military training bill. The fight came after an impassioned defense of the conscription bill by Rep. Dow W. Harter of Akron, the only Ohio congressman who is an outspoken advocate of compulsory service.

... Frayed nerves of congressmen, embroiled for days in the conscription battle, snapped last night at the end of a speech by Representative Sweeney, in which he assailed conscription and accused President Roosevelt of trying to embroil the United States in war. As Sweeney returned to his seat, Representative Vincent, who sits beside him, moved away and muttered "traitor." He repeated the epithet, and Sweeney swung a punch at his face. Both congressmen exchanged hard blows and kept slugging until colleagues pulled the 55-year old Sweeney away from Vincent, who is five years younger.. One congressman grappled with Sweeney and rolled over a seat with him, crashing to the floor." [31]

Other front page news involved the Lend-Lease deal with Great Britain. "Winston Churchill declared to his parliament today that the British-American exchange of destroyers and defense bases will enable the United States to 'take danger by the throat whilst it is still hundreds of miles away' -- but he warned the British to remember that America is not in the war. The prime minister, speaking for a time during a general London air raid alarm, declared, however, that Hitler 'no doubt will pay the U. S. out if he ever gets a chance.'..." All of this prompted the headline: "U. S. WARNED HITLER MAY RETALIATE." [32]

On September 14th, the anxiety levels were ratcheted up a notch for the eligible draftees. "Peacetime draft legislation, requiring registration of approximately 16,500,000 men 21 through 35 for military training, was finally approved by congress today and dispatched to the White House." The House approved a compromise with the Senate, which also provided for the President "to take over industrial plants, on a rental basis, when necessary to get defense orders filled expeditiously." (If a company owner refused a national defense contract, he could be fined up to $50,000 and get up to 3 years in prison.) Nevertheless, there was considerable dissent in Congress with both houses favoring the legislation by 65 % (a 47-25 vote in the Senate and 232-124 in the House.). [33]

President Roosevelt, who had pushed for the conscription bill, signed the legislation on September 16th. "With the quick strokes of a couple of cheap, scratchy pens, the chief executive signed the nation's first peacetime conscription bill at 3:08 p. m. yesterday... Then laying the history-making law, he put his name to a proclamation which said this marshaling of military strength was 'to fend off war from our shores' to avoid 'the terrible fate of nations whose weakness invited attack.' This new call to arms came as 60,000 national guardsmen were donning uniforms for a year's active duty and the war department announced 35,000 more would join the colors on Oct. 15, the day before the conscription registration." [34]

As the day for registration approached, the authorities expected strict adherence to the rules. "Men of draft age who are planning vacations or trips of any sort were warned today [Oct. 11] that they must be near some registration place during the hours of registration next Wednesday. Men traveling on that day must stop off somewhere and register. When they return home they must report their registration to their local draft board... The home address must be given at which he will most quickly receive communications from his local draft board. For if called before a draft board, the draftee will have to pay his own transportation to that board." [35]

The *Beacon Journal's* front page news for Sunday, October 13th informed the readers of the draft appeal boards, which by law consisted of "a labor leader, an industrialist, a doctor, a lawyer, and an ex-service man." A second story featured a speech by Roosevelt's Republican challenger, Wendell L. Willke, who was concerned with the usual mudslinging. Willke accused the Democratic national committee of distributing "as scurrilous and indecent attempt as ever occurred in American public life to raise religious and racial prejudices." In this particular speech, the draft was not a hot topic. A picture of Tom Mix, "the rootin'est, tootin'est, shootin'est cowboy there ever was," also appeared on the front page. Speeding 80 miles an hour in his custom-built Cord convertible over the Arizona desert, Mix missed the detour sign and rolled his car. Construction workers hauled the body from the debris, "the diamond studded belt still in place, and 10-gallon white sombrero still jammed on Mix's brow. He died with his high-heeled boots on. His cream jacket and cream-colored breeches were not even mussed." Cause of death was a broken neck. [39]

Precinct voting booths, which were often small white wooden sheds, were overwhelmed by the outpour of draft registrants on October 16, 1940. The booths opened at 7 a. m., and by the closing time of 9 p. m. registration supplies were exhausted in many locations. President Roosevelt took to the air waves to declare that today's historic peace time draft is the " 'keystone in the arch' of America's defense program to meet threats of war. At the same time the president gave the potential conscription army a ringing slogan. 'Democracy is your cause,' said Roosevelt." In Bob Hillard's Portage County, 5,758 men registered for the draft. In the adjacent and more populated Summit County, registration soared over 35,000, which included many non-resident truckers who were in the trucking capital of Akron. In New York City, camera flashbulbs flashed as singing, cowboy star Gene Autry took time from his performances to register for the draft. [40]

After registering, the odds of being conscripted were 4.1 to one. Nevertheless, it was the responsibility of the registrant to keep himself posted of his draft status and to keep the draft board informed in "changes in his address, employment, dependents, citizenship, physical condition, etc. and request permission to leave the country... After serving a year in the army, he will become a member of the reserves, subject to call for active duty and re-training, for 10 years or until he is 45. Thus some men registering today may remain under obligation for service for 15 years." [41]

Throughout the formation of the draft system and through the registration on October 16th, the media reported no mass protests or riots, unless one counted the fist fight that broke out on the floor of the House of Representatives. There was no mass exodus of young men to Canada. (Besides, the Canadians were already at war with Germany.) Draft materials and flags were not burned; and the chief proponent of the conscription bill, President Franklin Roosevelt, handily defeated Wendell Willke in the November election. These Americans were a different breed.

Early in 1941 when the first draftees were plucked from their homes for the service, the front pages of the newspapers often showed photographs of the young men before they boarded the buses. Some of their sober faces showed resignation, whereas others were smiling as if they were going on a vacation. By the autumn of the year, thousands of men had been inducted; so the novelty had worn off, the scene was old hat, and the departing young men received a scant mention in the newspapers. Still, the relatives and friends who took them to the departure sites tried to put up a brave front, but the lumps in their throats and watery eyes could not disguise their true feelings.

October 14, 1941 - This Tuesday would be a long day for 26-year old Bob Hillard. Early in the morning his friend Waldo Wolff drove him to the Ravenna bus station, where the efficient Selective Service officials herded the new draftees to their bus. With a belch of noxious diesel fumes, the bus slowly maneuvered from the station with the passengers responding to the waves and goodbye farewells of their relatives and friends. When not chatting with the other draftees, a myriad of thoughts flitted through Bob Hillard's mind as he gazed out the window of the bus -- Lucille, his hopes for becoming a surveyor, his father's health, his future in the army, and the disturbing worldwide events of the past year. In July, one headline read: "U.S. ANNOUNCES JAP AGGRESSION." For some months England was being plastered by the German Luftwaffe. A September headline read: "HOUSE OF LORDS, PALACE STRUCK BY BOMBS; HUGE FIRES RAGE IN LONDON." And on this Tuesday morning, the German blitzkrieg seemed invincible as it overwhelmed the Russians.

From the Cleveland induction center, Bob penned a brief note to his father:
Dear Dad,
Leaving for Columbus at about 6 P.M. Take care of yourself and watch that diet. I guess I am supposed to be a buck private now.

Well, I'll be seeing you. Your son, Bob

October 15, 1941 - From Fort Hayes, Columbus, Ohio:
Hi Dad,
    Will write you a few lines real fast because I just have a few minutes. Well I guess you have a boy in the army now. I don't know where we are headed for but we will probably be leaving tonight or tomorrow. I took out a little bit of insurance and am mailing the paper with this, am going to send my clothes home very shortly and will probably be C.O.D., as they will not take money at the army Post Office, so tell Lawrence to leave money for Alice or you to get them with; but I may get out to a regular Post Office and I'll save you all the trouble.
    Well you want to take care of yourself and watch your diet cause I'll be seeing you and I want to have a good argument.
    Tell Alice, Betty, and all the rest to keep their noses clean or they will hear from me. Well this old army so far could be worse but I don't know much about it yet, but will bye and bye. As I said before, I don't know where we're going but will give you an address then.
    Keep everything under control and I'll be seeing you all...
P.S. Gotta go take about 3 shots of some kind of dope.
    (On this date the death penalty is imposed on all Jews found outside the Polish ghettos.) [42]

October 17, 1941 - Maybe the top brass knows what is going on, but for "buck private" Hillard and the rest of the men at Fort Hayes their destination is still a mystery that is enhanced by rumors. Bob jots two postcards to his Dad. Both are postmarked 11:00 A.M., but the first one may have been written the night before.
    "... Am still at Fort Hayes, Everything's going all right. Don't know where we are going from here. Some of the boys I came with left for Oklahoma and Fort Riley, but I will probably know soon.
    Well, you take care of yourself and don't work. Do like the doctor said. Tell Lawrence to behave himself, also Alice and Betty.
    Tell Lawrence to try; but if he can get my checks cashed, to keep the money. [Perhaps his latest paychecks from the Ohio transportation department.] I'll write if I need it, but not to send it here. Wait till I get where I am going. Be seeing you...
    [Second postcard] Just found out this morning that I am going

to Maryland today some time to work in a chemical arsenal. Don't know much about it but will probably find out, only about 4 of the Company are going and I hear it's a pretty good place. Will give you an address later. In the meantime take care of yourself and I'll be seeing you..."
(Northwest of Iceland a German U-boat torpedoes hit the U.S. destroyer Kearney.)

October 19, 1941 - From Edgewood Arsenal in Maryland, Bob writes to his Dad. Pvt. Hillard is in an upbeat mood and not averse to making the most of his situation

... Will write and tell you that everything is going all right and seems to be a pretty nice barracks. Nice bunch of guys out here in the barracks of about 60 men. I think there's one from about every state in the union. This is the only training base of this kind in the U.S. It is a chemical warfare arsenal, and I guess they send you to school for some sort of trade after the first 4 weeks of training. I don't know for sure so will tell you later when I find out.

Well I suppose that you are all pretty busy around there, but you want to forget the work. Tony [brother Lawrence] will get it done or enough of it, and anyway you have done your share so be careful or I'll come home some of these days and give you a good talking to in person. And also watch your diet because after all maybe it is the thing for you to do.

I suppose you are having an awful time controlling those snots out around there, such as Tony, Bettie, Ruthie, Malon [his favorite brother-in-law], and all the rest, but make them listen; and when I get there, I'll really put them through their paces and after I get a few stripes on my arm which will kind of give me poise.

Will try to give you a few ideas of the land and location around here. [Strict army censorship apparently has not kicked in yet.] We are about 25 miles northeast of Baltimore towards Philadelphia right on the inland side of Chesapeake Bay and across the peninsula of Rhode Island. [Across from that location is a small peninsula that is still in the state of Maryland.] About 25-30 miles out is the Atlantic Ocean. This really is a busy place, not exactly here, but over at the "Martin Bomber factory" just a few miles in towards Baltimore. There is the Aberdeen testing ground for aerial bombs, anti-aircraft guns, flares, and so forth. At night they say it beats any Fourth of July celebration you ever saw. Malon [a truck driver] has probably been up through this town of Edgewood on his way from Baltimore to Philadelphia. [All of these locations are clearly seen on a Maryland road map today.]

Well, I want you to tell Lawrence to get Earl Duke to get my checks cashed and keep the money. In fact, I owed him $5.00 when I left. He'll know about that, but if he can't, he will have to send the check. I don't need it now so tell him to do the best he can because I'll have to have it signed by the company commander to get it cashed. Also I wish you would tell Stanley (because maybe I won't find time to write to him) to try to pick me up a pair of brown bedroom slippers and low brown shoes. They're the best things a fellow can have around here, and I can't get out of the grounds for a month. They don't handle what I want, and [he] can get the money from Rose to get them with. No big rush. I can wait.

The grub around here is pretty good or at least so far, so I will probably get fat and sassy after a while. So you better keep in good shape or you won't be able to handle me when I get back.

Tomorrow we start in on our training and drilling, and so I suppose will have a pretty busy day or days, but I guess after you get used to the routine it isn't so bad.

I hope you get that bunch of clothes I sent home and I'm sorry about the C.O.D. but the Army P.O. won't take any money. They will just deliver and send them from a regular Post Office for you, so I couldn't do much else.

They really make a fellow keep clean in the old army, and it's sure making a difference on most of the boys. And after all, it's to their own advantage.

I can see out over the bay from my bunk here, and I just see some of the fellows out in motor boats fooling around, even some of them fishing. I walked over there this morning with a fellow, and he was taking some pictures heading right out to the Ocean, so maybe after a while I'll send you some pictures of this layout if I can borrow his camera and equipment.

Well, I think I'll sign off now as it is about noon and I want to drop a card to Dan Sausaman [another brother-in-law] and a couple more so I will close. Take care of yourself. Your son, Bob.

(*Moscow is under siege. Stalin gives the Order of the Day: "Moscow will be defended to the last."*)

October 21, 1941 - It has been a week since Bob left home. Today he writes a brief note to his father.

Hi Dad,
 Everything here is going okay, had first drill and it didn't go so bad, don't know what it's all about but will probably find out. Hope this finds you and everybody else okay. You take care of yourself because I'm coming home and challenge you to a duel and I want you in good shape. Make the rest of them kids behave, especially Betty. Don't work so hard...

 (*Five waves of British bombers drop incendiary and explosive bombs on Naples, Italy. In Nantes, France the Nazis shoot 50 people in retaliation for the assassination of a German lieutenant-colonel.*)

October 23, 1941 - From Edgewood Arsenal Bob writes to his Dad.

 ...Just a few lines on this card to tell you everything is going okay. Just finished KP tonight so maybe I'll be out of it for a while, I hope. Sure a lot of dishes to wash for 240 men, but it could be worse. Hope you are all okay and you take care of yourself. Tell the rest hello for me and tell Tony to keep the roads in shape [for the Ohio Transportation Dept.] and watch [that] his dog don't bite him. How is all the work going? I'll bet you're pretty busy around there, but you be careful. Let Tony and Peanuts [brother Stanley] do the work. Tell Malon that when I get out of here, I'll be able to lick any brother-in-law I've got. Lights are going out. Hope you can read this...

 (*The Germans are having spectacular success against the Russians. The Italians are bombing the British on Malta. The British bombers strike at Benghazi and Tripoli in Africa.*)

October 26, 1941 - In a letter to his dad, Bob covers a variety of topics, but like many a draftee he is concerned about events and the people back home. What about his car (a Plymouth) and his brother's hunting dog?

 ...Got your letter or the one Ruthie wrote for you yesterday - the one with the check in it so I may wait until tomorrow before I send this and have it registered as they don't pick up mail till tomorrow morning anyway, but I just may sign it and send it. I have to go about 3 miles on the bus to get to a regular P.O. and I may not be able to get there before it closes, but anyway thanks a lot.

Glad to hear you are okay and everybody else. I suppose you are pretty busy right now, but take it easy.

Everything is going okay here, getting along fine. Haven't learned much yet and don't know what outfit I am going to be in, as I have not been classified yet. Course it doesn't mean much anyway. Had a day of K.P. on Thursday. Just my turn is all, really washed a lot of dishes from 6:00 A.M. - 8:15 P.M. so maybe I'll get out of that for a while, about 1 time every month, because in Co. C there is about 210 fellows in the Co. and it takes 5 a day. All in all, it isn't bad. Maybe it will do me some good.

This outfit trains four or five different branches of service, Signal Corps, Telephone Operators, Chemical Gas Outfits, both for and against and etc., but we won't be actually classified till after the first 4 weeks.

May send you a picture of a few things around here when I get them developed, so don't know how good they are going to be. Tell Stanley about those shoes and things when you see him, because they would come in handy at night and Saturday and Sunday. Did the package of clothes come that I sent from Columbus? Ruthie didn't say in her letter and that is the only one I have got from out there except one from Waldo Wolff [his friend].

Write and tell me how Lawrence's dog is doing. I like to know, and how he is getting along with his work. Tell him to run hell out of that Plymouth and keep it so the wheels will go around.

Well, I can't get out of the camp for 4 weeks, but there is a lot in here to see, mules, co. of Negroes [the service was segregated at the time], field artillery, and a lot of stuff. May take a picture or two today so you'll know what this place looks like.

I wrote a card to Carolyn and Gail but haven't got a return yet. I don't think there is very good service on this end, so be sure and make plain, even print it in letters and be sure of the Co. C part.

           Pvt. Robert H. Hillard
           Co. C 1st C.W.S. Tng. Bn.
           Edgewood Arsenal, Md.

(The Russians continue to retreat. The RAF makes a heavy night air raid on Hamburg, Germany.)

October 27, 1941 - Bob is quite fond of his sister Ruthie and her husband Malon. However, in a family of some peculiar nicknames,

Bob refers to his sister Ruthie as "Snots."

Hi Snots:

Couldn't think of nobody else to write to so thought of you two. Well, everything is going okay, had a big dinner yesterday, turkey and all the dressing. Am really getting sassy and tough so Malon you had better keep in shape because I am going to show my brothers-in-law a thing or two. Got your letter with the check in it and am going to send it back. I don't need it around here. Write and tell me some of the news and how Dad is behaving. I may get home over the Holidays but am not sure, cause we are the last Co. that got in here, so we may have to wait. If your car ever breaks down, don't hesitate to get the Plymouth because it is better for it to be running anyway. Did a package of clothes get thru from Columbus? I had to send them in a hurry. Write and tell me the news and give me Nora's address.

Bob

(After ten days of fierce fighting, the Germans now occupy all of the Crimea; however the Russians are counter-attacking near Moscow.)

October 28, 1941 - It's been two weeks since Bob left home. In a letter to his father, it is evident that this soldier receives many letters and much needed support from his family and friends back home.

...Thought I would write and tell you I got Alice's letter and glad to hear that you were all okay.

Everything here is the same as usual, going okay, keeping plenty busy, even after supper with shaving, writing, pressing my pants, etc., so may be a little tardy in answering your letters, but will do the best I can. Had a letter today from Loss [his brother David Deloss Hillard]. He is working on a building in Philadelphia and said he is doing all right, staying there and only gets home for weekends, so he didn't know much news. Also, Dan [his brother-in-law] wrote me today. Said he is doing okay, going to ship radishes in another month. He was saying he was up to see you and the rest. Harriet wrote me the news out her way, said everything was the same.

Well, how is the work going by now? I suppose pretty busy, and I suppose Lawrence has coon hides tacked all over the corn crib by now. Write and tell me how the dog is doing.

Hope that check gets there okay. Tell Lawrence to handle that

job for me, and I'll argue with him sometime to keep him in practice.
Tell Betty to make Alice behave herself; or if not, just write me and I'll handle that from this end. Also for Betty to study that Algebra because I want her to be at least half as smart as her youngest uncle, meaning me.
This, so far, is a pretty nice place. Nice bunch of officers, etc. Boys are from all over every state in the Union.
Haven't learned much yet, have had a few lectures on gases, what they smell like, etc. Mustard [gas] especially, we all got a little whiff of that, just smells like garlic. Something to know. How it is used and what in, and some others.
We aren't being trained with rifles, etc, just pistols 45 Colts - really a nice little gun.
Had a lesson with a 4.2 machine mortar mounted and a demonstration used to shoot gas within shells.
Make those brats listen to you; and when I come home, I'll take over to relieve you cause I'll be good at grilling them by then.
We have a pretty good time schedule here. 6:00 in the morning till 5:00 P.M. Retreat 9:00 P.M. Black out.
Up the bay at Aberdeen they have a testing grounds of bombs, sky flares, etc., just like the Fourth of July some nights.
Rather cool here today. Don't know whether the ocean has anything to do with it or not. [I] don't believe they have had a killing frost yet like Alice said you had there.
Must do my other work so will close. Keep everything under control and take care of yourself. Write. Will try to answer....
P.S. Also had a letter from [sister] Rose.
(*The German attack south of Moscow is brought to a halt by stubborn Russian resistance and the deep mud that halts the German Panzers. The Nazis move to within 75 miles of the Russian capital on the northwest side.*)

November 2, 1941 - Bob's positive attitude is making his adaptation to army life go smoothly. In a letter to his father on this Sunday, the complimentary closing - "Your toughest son" - exemplifies this attitude, a blend of bravado and wry humor. Besides, it would not look good for a Hillard to complain, and he obviously does not want his ailing father to worry.
... Well everything is going okay here. Same old stuff, it will

be two weeks yet before we get our special drilling in what we are going to do, so I don't know yet what I will have to do.

This army life isn't so bad once you get the swing of it, but it's all so much different. Sometimes you almost have to be in two places at once, but at least it keeps a person in good shape and feeling good. They have pretty good eats here. They cook up in pretty good shape, so a person shouldn't starve in here unless he is too choosy.

Really have a nice bunch of Noncoms here in the barracks. They will help a fellow out most of the time, and ain't so tough.

Went to church this morning and really it was all right, so I hope to keep going. Can't do me any harm and should do me some good.

Already have had a day of K.P. and one of Table Waiter in the mess hall for about 240 men, so I really know my stuff in that line, [and I'm] coming back and give you all some lessons, so get all set for it.

Am going to put a couple pictures in here, one is for Lawrence to pick himself out the team of mules he wants and I'll get them for him. There really is a lot of horses and mules around here. The barns in this picture are only a small part of them, [they] use them in the Field Artillery and Cavalry.

The other is a shot of the bay with the piers sticking out from the right and the four army yachts out from it.

The other is some snot I don't know very well and isn't very plain, but will try to send you a good one of him later cause he is the youngest and toughest son you've got. It was kind of windy that day as you can notice by the waves.

This really is a pretty nice country around her. I believe it is a warmer climate here than around home, but it has been raining on Friday and Saturday.

We had a hike on Friday in the rain, had to set up pup tents, display all our equipment outside, in just such an order as the army wants, so we got everything all wet and dirty and had inspection Saturday morning, so it really was a busy barracks Friday night, but everybody did all right, rated the best floor in all of the Co. by the Co. Commander. They really make you keep yourself and all your clothes in perfect shape, especially on Saturday morning at inspection, or if you don't it's K.P. for as long as they see fit, that includes haircut, teeth, fingernails and clothes, bunk, shoes, and everything you possess, even your foot locker and how your clothes are put away and in what place. Every locker and etc. must be the same.

Well, tell all the rest hello for me, and take care of yourself because I'll take you for a hike when I get there.

Had a letter from Johnnie and everybody is okay out there, said he was kind of busy, Gail and Carolyn wrote and Gail wants me to get her in the army.

Tell Tony to take it easy and try not to do every thing in one day and tell me how his coon dog is doing. Elmer should be here hunting ducks and geese. Write and tell me the news. Tell Alice thanks for the stamps.

Your toughest son.
Bob

(On the previous day, a German U-boat torpedoes and sinks the U. S. destroyer Reuben James west of Iceland. There are about 100 casualties. A popular song is soon written about this U.S. "peace time" tragedy. "What were their names, boys? What were their names? Did you have a friend on the old Reuben James.")

Nov. 4, 1941 - It is 7:00 this Tuesday evening as Bob writes to his brother Stanley, who at 32 is six years older than Bob. For the most part, there is less brashness when writing to his older brother, and Bob allows a rare soft admission in closing.

Hi Peanuts,

Got your letter and the package about 11:30 today. Was shore glad to get the stuff and it really fits, both shoes and slippers, really appreciate what you have done, and I want you to see Rose and get the money for the stuff. Also I have been thinking that I owe you for a suit I had cleaned in that big bunch of stuff you got right after you came back, so figure out this stuff and square up with Rose, and thanks.

These shoes and slippers are really what I need, a little bit more to keep shined, but the shoes are better when not on duty Sat. from noon till Monday 6:00. Also I started to church since I got here and them big old shoes look like hell; as yet I have only one pair but have two more pairs coming. They really give us a hell of a lot of clothes to take care of - 2 suits of wool, shirts and pants, 4 pairs of cotton summer wear pants and shirts, 6 pr. of underwear that's 3 cotton and 3 wool, pair of arctics [boots], rain coat, overcoat, field jacket, blouse, 3 suits of yard bird clothes, and a few more things, and they all have to be kept in order, as you probably know.

Been learning to march and drill, also getting a lot of lectures on chemical agents, gases, but as yet haven't learned very much. They also teach Signal Corps, Telephone, Motor Squads, and etc. here so I don't know yet what I'm going to do or why I'm here. I got a good grade on my I.Q. I guess, but as far as knowing chemistry, I don't. Made 133 on a possible 161 in I.Q. but it was right down my alley, not bragging...

Really have a pretty nice bunch of fellows here with the exception of 2 or 3, which is always the case. They are from about every state in the U.S. Nice bunch of Non. Coms....

I'd sure like to be home for a couple days of hunting and show Elmer [Loomis] up, really a lot of duck and geese around here, could go hunting if I had a stamp and gun, but I still haven't very much time. They even announced it to our Co. the other day...

Your toughest Bro., Bob

P.S. The girl friend is really doing all right with her letters and also sending me stamps. I'm really pretty lucky with a girl like her...

November 6, 1941 - It's Thursday evening in the noisy, bustling barracks at Edgewood.

Hi Dad and the rest,

Received your letter today and will try to drop you a few lines real fast as I got quite a bit to do tonight, which is generally the case, just keeping busy till 9:00.

Everything is going [the] same as usual, same old routine, eat drill, listen to lectures and sleep, also keep stuff in shape, but it isn't so bad.

Really is a lot of noise in the barracks at this time, can't hardly hear yourself talk.

Been raining all day, is kind of muddy around here, been a pretty nasty day.

How did you like that picture of your toughest son, boy wasn't that something, may send you a good picture after while. Ask Tony to pick out his team of mules to run with his new dog.

Tell Tony to leave the corn go and I'll come home and husk it out some day at noon. How is the steers doing and has he sold them yet? Ask him how the work is going and if Earl Duke ever said he got a card from me.

I also wrote Joe Pinney a card last night and told him how to run his men, especially you.

Haven't been learning very much. In fact, it's kind of out of my line this chemistry stuff. Some of the boys in here with me have 1-2-or 3 years college on general chemistry, so I don't know how I will make out. Nobody does for a couple of weeks yet.

Soon [I'm] going to have to try out for marksmanship with a 45 and then it will mean guard duty for the ones that make out.

Had a letter from Mary Ann yesterday. She said everybody out there was okay and sassy as ever. Savalla is still working, etc.

Got that package from Peanuts. [Probably the slippers and shoes that Bob requested] Everything fits all right, really handy around here at night and Saturday afternoon, and sure much more comfortable.

Did I tell you I started to go to church, really it is all right and hope to keep it up.

This camp has a pretty nice list of entertainment, shows 20 cents, day room, library, etc. if you can find the time to get there.

Well, I'm glad to hear that you are all okay and still able to kick around. As for me, I'm getting just as tough as a pine knot, and tell Ruthie especially I am going to challenge all my brother-in-laws when I get back.

Some of us are going to parade in Baltimore on Nov. 11 [Armistice Day] Boy, that will be something to see. Bands playing. President Roosevelt there to shake hands and all that sort of stuff -- only fooling around about the last.

Write soon and tell me what the hell day they are celebrating Thanksgiving out there. Be positive about it. Ask Rose. I can't get no answers out of these guys around here as yet, but will try before I send this.

Tell Peanuts they are starting to holler about the General Orders which all good soldiers must know.

Well, everything is kind of quiet around here, so I haven't much to say or write about.

By the way, I should have another check coming from the State. I don't need it down here, but I wonder if they had forgot.

Tell the boys, Elmer and Waldo, to save me a pheasant to shoot at when I get home. I bet Elmer has them all tied up by now.

So, Alice and Norie cheat at cards, so Ruthie writes. I never would have thought that.

I suppose that Malon is still pushing that truck around. Tell him to keep it between the ditches.

So, be good Dad, and take care of yourself.

Your toughest son,
Bob

I haven't got any stripes on my sleeve yet, but I take a long shirt sleeve and have lots of room for them. Just give me time - a long time...

Remember, Dad. Make them Brats behave themselves, especially Betty till I come home to take over.

(*Japanese special representative, Sabaru Kurusu is on his way to Washington to try to heal the breach between his country and the United States. It is merely a smoke screen; the Japanese military plans to attack Pearl Harbor have already been made.*)

November 13, 1941 - It is Thursday evening at Edgewood Arsenal, and Bob writes to his dad and the family.

...just doing about the same old thing, but will soon know what I'm going to be trained for in a week or so.

About half of our outfit had to go to Baltimore for a parade on Armistice Day, really a gala affair. Quite a few different outfits there from different camps, sailors, veterans of other wars, Red Cross, etc. Quite a few in the parade, so of course I had to be one of them to go in there and show my ignorance.

Had my first practice with the 45 revolver yesterday and done fair to middling. Shot 50 shots all different ways, fast and slow, and at stationary and moving targets in about an hour. Really shakes your arm up when you aren't used to it. Shoot for record next week.

Also had another I.Q. test on Monday. This one was pretty tricky. They're getting worse all the time, but I believe I did all right in it, though it doesn't mean very much anyway, I guess.

Hope you haven't gotten that check back by now. I don't think I'll need it for a while, at least I haven't needed much money so far as I couldn't leave the post and haven't got much business in Baltimore anyway.

This was payday today. Line up for 2 hours to get $10.52. Boy, I'm really in the bucks.

I'm going to put a picture or two in this, and the small one is for Betty, providing she writes to me or does she think she's too uppi-

ty to do that. I'll attend to that young lady when I get home.
Well, I suppose by now Lawrence has all the animals on boards around there. Is his dog any good or just a dog? How are the steers doing? I suppose you have them in by now. Means more work, more chores to do. How are you getting along with the corn husking? By now, I suppose Lawrence has husked it all out in one day.
Did Joe Pinney or Earl ever say anything to Lawrence about the cards I wrote them? I'd like to know just what they thought of them.
Does Lawrence still lie and argue as much as he did or has he reformed?
I suppose Alice still cheats at cards as she always did. She'll stand watching too.
Ruthie I suppose is still the same as ever, still bragging about that husband of hers [Malon] or at least she always did so to me.
You can also tell Malon to keep himself in shape because President Roosevelt said that this army was the hardest and fastest hitting army in the world, and he should know because him and I know everything between us.
Well, I hope this letter finds you in health, and so take care of yourself, and don't forget that hike you and I are going on when I get home.
Tell Alice to take good care of that picture in the front room. Maybe you better tell Ruthie and Betty too...

                                        Your toughest son,
                                        Bob

P.S. Be good and take care of yourself.
I'm still the toughest damn guy in here when the chips are down. And I ain't bragging. Still haven't got any stripes yet.

(In the Mediterranean Sea off Gibraltar, a German U-boat torpedoes and severely damages the Ark Royal, a British aircraft carrier. The battleship Malaya is severely damaged by another submarine.)

November 24, 1941 - On this Monday, Bob writes a letter to his sister Ruthie and her husband Malon Spangler, which has a more carefree tone than the ones he writes to his father. At the time, Ruthie is age 23 and Malon 32. Bob comments on a brief visit to Edgewood by his sister Rose and girl friend Lucille. The intensity of training appears to be increasing.

Hi Malon and Ruthie:

Received your letter today and will try to answer at least a little bit.

Rose and the Girl Friend [Lucille Anderson] wrote me a card that they made connections all right on their buses going home, so they should have been back Sunday eve.

It was really nice to see them, though I didn't get to see them as much as I'd have liked to, as we had to drill Friday and ½ day Sat. I don't know what they thought of this place. They were here about 5 hours on Sat. and took a few pictures, and Rose will probably tell you all about this place and how it is run.

You know Ruthie, I still have the nicest girl friend, though you are always making wise cracks about her and calling her a Swede and etc., but I still say the Swedes are the most aristocratic people there is, and I don't want any back talk.

You said in your letter about the boys getting so much game - hells fire, it must be tied. None of them boys could hit anything that had any life, this includes Malon too.

So the dog pack Lawrence has got isn't so good, huh. Well, your pappy knows how to train dogs, so let him hunt with them a while and he will make real killers out of them. Just ask him the next time you are down home. His youngest son is very smart too, though you probably already know that, and he also is too tough for the rest. Well, everything is going okay here just about the same, got everything under control and right in there pitching.

We started this morning eating outside of our mess kits, going to do that for a week. Boy, the stuff is really mixed up in that pan. Can't tell beans from butter and etc. But it isn't so bad and anyway it's just for a week.

Well, [they] have been giving us more steady marching the last couple of days, getting us toughened up, had about 7-8 miles this afternoon in 2 hours with full pack on and had to wear our gas masks part of the way. Those gas masks sort of slow you down, makes it harder breathing.

Also went by the range where the mortar squads were laying down a smoke screen. You can see them shells going through the air after they are fired. No fooling, there are 4.2 inch shells and about 18 inches long. We will probably get into that later.

Bob and Lucille at Camp Edgewood, Md.
Nov. 25, 1941.

Bob Hillard (second from the left in the front row) stands at attention.

We have a couple of practices in the gas chamber with our masks, and we will probably get some more. It's a good thing to know if one gets in a stink some time.

This is a pretty nice bunch of fellows here. Most of them, just like myself, got caught in the draft. Don't mind it so bad and figured might as well make the best of it now they're here. Really whoop it up in here on occasion, especially over the weekend. If somebody has got something to eat or read, everybody helps him out gladly.

Lucille and Rose brought me some fruit and cookies on Sat. Boys really did go for them.

Picked myself up one extra K.P. so far for just a minor little detail I missed for inspection, but I've been pretty lucky.

Well, I've got to be closing this up soon, have to shave, polish shoes, and maybe press a pair of pants before 9 o'clock, some times pretty busy at night, so tell Dad and the rest down there hello for me and glad to hear they are all okay...

                      Your toughest bro
                      Bob

P.S.... I wrote to Fritz Niles a letter on toilet paper last nite and told him he was on my personal shit list. So when you see him, he will probably tell you about it; listen to him swear.

Well, be good and I'll probably be seeing you. Don't know for sure. You never know until the last day around here. So long.

(*The British and German forces are engaged in North Africa. Today, the Germans receive air reinforcements in Libya.*)

November 26, 1941 - Bob sends a postcard to his dad, in which he briefly describes some previously mentioned items and concludes with: "I've got some good arguments thought up for you when I get home, so you had better keep up on the news. Don't work too hard, and tell the rest to keep their noses clean. So long. I've got a load of work to do.

        Your toughest son,
        Bob"

(*While negotiations with the Japanese representatives are taking place in Washington, the Japanese fleet has already left the home ports for attack locations.*)

November 29, 1941 - Bob begins this letter to his father on Saturday morning.

...Will start this letter and finish it between times the rest of the day.

Our outfit just finished up our inspection for Sat. by the Co. Commander and all of us in our barracks got by okay both inside and a barracks inspection, really a lot of foolishness, but that is the army for you.

We just had mail call and I received Ruthie's letter, so I know all the news around there. She was telling me of your butchering one pig already and that you had been not feeling so well for a day or so. Listen to me now, you better take it easy on this working and stuff, leave the boys do that butchering or hire someone to do it. Anyway I will probably be home for a day or two around Xmas or New Year's I hope. Don't know for sure though, so save me a lot of work and if you can catch me, if I do get there, maybe I'll get it done. So take it easy. Hells Fire you done your share of work.

Ruthie says Lawrence's dog is a real killer so I bet he is really bragging about it.

Have just finished dinner, so we have the afternoon off to ourselves to catch up on some of our work. Tomorrow I got a K.P. so that is the reason I'm writing this today., though it probably won't be mailed out till Monday unless I get someone of the boys leaving to mail it for me if I get it written in time.

I see that Ruthie is still bragging about that husband of hers, so if you want to you can show her this letter. Also tell her thanks for the stamps she sent me.

After inspection they took a picture of our Co. C., about 250 of us and the officers, so I may get a chance to get one if they let us buy them. That is about the only picture I would really want out of this place.

Am going to send you a couple of pictures that Rose sent back to me, a couple of them especially for Lawrence.

How is Lawrence making out with his work? I suppose he is pretty busy, and did he ever get his well down over by at the barn now that he has got his cattle in it.

Well, everything is going just the same, and Rose will probably tell you all about this place though she didn't get to see much of it.

Things are getting pretty quiet around here. The boys have

already started to leave, so by tonight we will really have room in here.

I suppose, Dan, by the time you get this will be going back South. If not, tell him to write and I will probably drop him a line soon.

And whatever you do, make them snot noses behave themselves or they will have to take their medicine when I get back there cause I will be in a good frame of mind to give orders to them.

As yet, I haven't got no stripes on my sleeves. The only stripes I have are the ones the pack straps put on me as I probably told you before. We have been getting our marches with full pack and also with a gas mask on part of the time, just getting us used to it.

Next week, we are going on a day or two overnight, stay in our tents somewhere around here, so that will be some more marching with packs, but so far I haven't minded it so much. These marches haven't been so tough, they are all done according to rules, march for 50 minutes, go about 3 or 4 miles, then a 10 minute break to smoke and etc. So we march 50 minutes out of every hour.

Well dad, I'm going to stop this nonsense, so be good and take care of yourself.

Your toughest son,
Bob

P.S. Tell Alice and Ruthie to quit making remarks about my girl, even you will admit that she is very nice. So long.

(Yesterday, the defenders of Tobruk broke out to join the British 8th Army. Today, the remaining Italian soldiers in Italian East Africa laid down their arms. South of Moscow, the Red Army launches a bloody counter-attack to force the Germans to retire.)

December 14, 1941 - It has been two months since Bob left home and one week since the Japanese attack on Pearl Harbor, which resulted in 2,330 American dead. On this Sunday, Bob takes considerable time to write several letters. One is a respectful letter to his Aunt Val in Pennsylvania. In the letter to his father, he knows that his dad has not been keeping on his diet, but Bob tactfully inquires about it. In the letter to Ruthie and Malon, Bob briefly mentions his thoughts on last week's attack. However, one notices that weekend passes are greatly reduced, and Christmas furloughs are doubtful. Surely, everyone knows that the one-year draftees now have an open-ended arrangement with Uncle Sam.

    Letter #1 to Aunt Val.

    ... Received your letter on Friday and was glad to hear from you, but sorry to hear Bob and you haven't been feeling well. Why don't you two forget some of that work and take it easy for a while, after all it will keep and tomorrow is always another day.

    Had a letter from both Ann and Betty and they say everything is the same at John's, both getting along good in school and both bragging about their basketball team. Also that Savalla has been busy lately and probably will be for a while.

    Alice also wrote last week and said everybody was okay out there at home, but she was having one <u>helluva</u> time keeping Dad on his diet. That is quite a job to do that, and that Dan had been home for Thanksgiving for a week or so but has already went back south to finish up his crops for the winter and then get a start for the spring season down there.

    I suppose you folks have already started to get winter out around there by now. The weather here has been pretty nice except for being a little cold up till last night, and then it started to rain and freeze on everything and is still doing it tonight, so it has been very icy around here yesterday and today, but I still think it is a slightly warmer climate than what we are used to out home or what you get there in Pa.

    I just happened to think of Charles Hillard now. How has this draft affected him or is he exempted from it from being a teacher? I don't imagine that Johnnie will be reclassified again, do you? He is just as well off if they don't.

    So you still claim to have the smartest dogs around, "huh?" Well, you may be right, but as far as I'm concerned I wouldn't have any use for Spike here as we have several already around camp and one is a kind of mascot.

    Well, everything is going okay with me, Val. This army life isn't so bad although one is pretty busy getting his work done and about the only time you have to ans.[wer] letters is on Sun.; and if you catch extra duty then on that day, you just have to postpone them , so I'm sometimes sort of tardy with my answers. But anyway, this life really makes you keep your stuff in shape, shoes shined, pants pressed, clothes clean, and also your own self, barracks, locker, and etc. So, it may learn us something useful.

Well Val, I have about 3 or 4 more letters to write yet and don't know any more news, so [I] soon must be closing this up.

You mentioned about sending something to eat, Val. Really I appreciate your thoughtfulness, but it doesn't hardly pay for you to go to all that bother and work and then have the stuff smash up in the mail; so I'll say thanks anyway, but if I were you, I would just forget it and someday I'll come out in person and eat you out of house and home.

Don't know when we will get off to go home, but will sometime. So long, and I've got everything under control and I'll be seeing you. Be good and take it easy both of you.
Love.
Your Nephew
Bob

Letter #2 for this date.
Hi Dad,

Will drop you a line or two to say that everything is still going okay, and I've got everything under control.

By the way, how have you been feeling lately? I hope all right, still going to the doctor and sticking to your diet I hope. Well anyway, take it easy and behave yourself, and I'll be seeing you, although I just don't know when, but may even on the Holidays.

How's the livestock coming by now? I suppose you shot away that box of shotgun shells of mine and didn't get anything. I'll have to give you a lesson or two in marksmanship when I see you again.

Did the bull calf grow any or is he just a bad buy? He should be looking pretty good by now. Also, I hear you have some feathered watch dogs around your pump now. [Geese] You're really doing all right.

Lawrence I imagine is pretty busy now having all his cattle in the barn and working besides. Has he got all his corn husked by now?

Well dad, I got to write a couple more letters and do some work, so will close for now. Take care of yourself and make them snots listen to you... Your toughest son...
Letter #3 to Ruthie and Malon Spangler.
Hi Snots,

Have just finished writing to Dad and Alice, Val, Mary Ann, and Betty. I have one more to write after this one; course you probably wouldn't be able to guess who. [He was saving Lucille's letter for last.] So I had a couple minutes spare time and decided you two were worth at least that much of my valuable time, so you can consider this as a compliment in getting this letter.

Well Malon, I suppose you are still kicking the semi around. I imagine your outfit is really busy now and probably will get busier now that the lid has blown off the pot and let the smell out. Oh well, that was bound to happen, so it really didn't surprise me much.

Everything is going here just the same with me. Had a pretty busy week. [We had a] camping trip and it really was colder than hell sleeping out, but we did have some fun, found a little whiskey on the sly to doctor up for snake bite and etc. [We] had a few tents kicked down with the boys playing, and some of them had about ten guys sleeping in them in the place of four to keep warm, but everybody is still living even after our hike of about 20 miles getting out there to camp with full field pack; and I am still the toughest damn guy in here and I'm not bragging.

Had K.P. the day after we came back and really done a helluva lot of pans, stoves, and dishes that were left over, besides the ones of the mess hall.

Then on Sat. [I] had table waiter and also had to stand inspection besides with everything, so I've really been busy and no fooling; so that is one reason I'm tardy on my answers to your letters though you possibly hear what little I write home anyway. This old place is really strict on keeping stuff in shape. That is what makes up for most of our week when we are off on our own.

Malon, I want you to do me a favor if you can find some time Sunday. I'd like you to get Waldo W. [Wolff] to get me [the] total of what money I made down at the Alliance Porcelain the couple of months I worked there in 1941 and also get Abbie Brockett to find out the same at Byers Machine Shop if they can, and tell Lawrence to do the same on the State. I may never need the sheets, so just keep them at home for me if you get them, and I'll shit in your mess kit sometime in payment.

Ruthie, I want to say thanks for the stuff you and Alice and Betty sent. Everybody said it was very good, no fooling, and even I'll say it wasn't bad. So thanks.

They have cut down on the weekend passes around here. Only 10% can leave on a weekend. That is only 4 out of each barracks and 2 non com officers each week. Even the boys with the class "A" cards had to turn them in, so it is just like any other day around here. Most of the boys are here and raising hell, shooting craps, playing poker, etc., so it is pretty noisy.

Still don't know if any of us will get home for the Holidays or not, and won't know till the last minute, but I hope to get home before I'm shipped out of here, which I think will be the muddle or the first part of Jan., so I'll probably be seeing you; and I want a big chunk of chocolate cake and a whole pie to eat, although we have been getting pretty good grub most of the time, nothing fancy but good enough so I haven't been starving. In fact, I think I've gained a couple of pounds though I haven't weighed myself.

I suppose winter has set in there by now. We have had cold weather here, but no snow. Friday night it started to rain and freeze. And Sat. was really a slippery day, but today it is just kind of cold. I'd say about 20 degrees above or 25.

Write and tell me what Rose thought of this place and what she told you folks.

Did Waldo ever show you the letter I wrote him? You ought to ask him for it if he didn't.

Fritz wrote me yesterday and also sent me a Xmas card, a really nice one. Told me he was out home and still pouring on the weld.

I had heard before of this and lately have heard rumors that I am going to be Uncle again. Well I'm glad to hear that, but I bet that a Spangler and a Hillard combination will be a spoiled mean little urchin, though you two would be hard to convince of that. I'm only fooling about this last as you should know, so I'm wishing you luck, and in the meantime Ruthie take it easy.

How is Peanuts behaving now? He sure was dumb for getting in the Army in the first place, although he may not get recalled, at least I hope not. Besides there is only one war so all it takes is one Hillard - that's "me." [Stanley had been drafted, served three months, and then sent home due to the changing age requirements.]

Well, [I] must close as I may write Rose and I have to write "Lucille" and no wise cracks out of you two about the last. So write and tell me all the news and "be Good" and I'll be seeing you. Keep everything under control, as I have always done.... Uncle Sam's Toughest Draftee...

P.S. Does Lawrence still lie as much as ever and by the way how is he doing with his cattle and stuff and Ferdinand the bull? So long.

(*The Red Army and the Russian winter force the Germans back on the Eastern Front. In North Africa Gen. Rommel counterattacks. In the Far East the Japanese move at will through Southeast Asia and the Pacific islands.*)

December 21, 1941 - On this Sunday, Bob writes a teasing letter to his dad.

... Just a few lines just to let you know I'm all well and just as sassy as ever, and hope you are okay.

I suppose you have been pretty busy lately with butchering and all and the work around there, but you want to remember to take it easy.

Well, the way Alice said about your hogs - the size of them - you must have finally "found out this year how to feed them" or did Lawrence do the feeding? Anyway, she said it took 4 fellows on the blocks to pull them up and down in the scalding barrel or did Waldo W. give you his formula for feeding them?

Well Dad, as I said before [I] am getting along fine here, don't need a thing. As I have everything under control and as you know me being so damn mean and sassy I'll always keep it that way.

I won't be home for any of the holidays. I don't know when. Also, I think we are going out of here on Jan. 11 so [I] may or may not be seeing you then, but anyway take care of yourself and be good and don't eat much of that pork, save me some, as I'll be seeing you sometime....

A second letter of this date is to his sister Alice, who is called Al or Audrey, her middle name. It appears that prosperity and tranquility have settled within the Hillard household this Christmas season.

Hi Audrey,

Received your letter of Thursday and while reading it and all of your letters, I usually almost go into hysterics thinking of what a funny and fat looking person that done the writing, but they do have a good side to them. They really help to break the monotony.

No, really Audrey I'd rather get a letter from you than most any other person except one. Course you probably wouldn't know who I was talking about. Anyway, your letters are just like you. (That is what makes them so funny.) So really and seriously, keep up your writing if you can find time, and I will try to answer them.

Well, I suppose you are as busy as ever around there keeping them hoodlums straight. You really stepped into a hard job there, Al, but some of the bunch, meaning the rest of us, really appreciate what you have done, that also includes me. Well, that is enough of that stuff.

Now that Dan is back, I bet Dad is really happy. I suppose the two of them play pretty often and argue most of the time, and of course it wouldn't be on politics.

So they finally got the bathtub set up. Well, I'm sure glad to hear that. Something I probably never would have got done.

Somebody was saying that Tony was going to get the telephone put in. That would be a nice thing to have around there. Just think of all the gossip you could pick up by listening in [on the party line] and then you probably would be able to learn some new things. That way it would make you smarter and you could call up the Girlfriend if you were ever in doubt of anything, because she knows everything just from being real smart and also from going with me, "but don't go reversing the charges."

So you are still bragging about that daughter of yours. Well, I guess you always will, though I don't blame you any. Tell Betty to drop me a line or two if she finds time away from her algebra. I will try to ans. soon.

I suppose you are all getting fat and sassy on that pork that you say you have butchered on Wed. But I am not doing so bad myself in the eating line, been getting plenty of grub and lots of sleep as usual, and everything is going okay and I'm still the toughest damn draftee at Edgewood Arsenal, Md. And always will be... Tell Dan to write also and tell me about his farming because after all I'm just a farmer at heart too... Your toughest Bro.... Keep the fights down when you are playing cards.

(Japanese troop transports lie north of Manila in preparation for the invasion early the next morning. They are set to overwhelm Gen. Douglas MacArthur's American defenders.)

Christmas Day 1941 -
Hi Folks,

Will write this to all of you and it will probably be sort of short, but I just want to thank you all for sending what you did. You really showed some sense in picking out what you did, as even last night I lit up the pipe and tried out the pants creaser and it really works, so the boys are even saying thanks when they use it. So Betty, you really done all right, though I won't get a chance to repay you, but maybe some day it will be my turn. So, thanks again all of you and I may be home some time to really thank you in person.

Everything is just going the same here. I've got to start getting cleaned up for dinner as we are going to have a very gala affair. Some of the 2nd Louies and their wives are going to be here and we are really going to have a slam bang affair.

Well, I suppose you are all getting ready about now to sit down to a big dinner and then get a good sleep afterwards, so I think I'll do the same if I get caught up on some of these letters - the reason this is going to be so short. But I will try to write more the next time. So until then, be good all of you and write and thanks again.

Love, Bob.

Well, I've got to go shave and shine a pair of shoes extra special, so so long. And I'm still the toughest drafter down here and always will be.

In another Christmas letter, Bob thanks his sister Ruthie (Snots) and Malon for the four gifts that they sent to him. "Uncle Sam's Toughest Draftee" also adds the following.

... I really did all right. Received 3 cartons of cigarettes from Lucille, Tony, and Loss, a box of stationary and toilet set from Savalla and the rest. Package of eatables from Rose, and besides a few more things from Lucille. She also sent me a pipe, etc., so you see I really did all right. In fact better than I should of for it has been all one-sided.

Well everything is going okay here with me and the rest, having a little fun, and we got a little Christmas cheer for today on the sly, just enough to make the boys sort of happy so they don't give a damn.

Only 25% of the boys get passes at one time and some of these fellows are really shit asses in messing up passes for the boys that live close to here. You see if you once had a pass since Dec. 6 when they quit giving them out, you can't get any till all the rest have had one that wants one. Well, there are four or five in our barracks alone that live in Baltimore or closer that can't go home because of

that sort of shitty deal for them. One fellow lives just outside the gate and he can't go....
(*The British garrison in Hong Kong surrenders to the Japanese. The Americans in the Phillipines retire to the Bataan Peninsula. In a Christmas address to his nation, King George VI states: "Never did heroism shine more brightly than it does now, nor fortitude, nor sacrifice, nor sympathy, nor Newbury kindness."*)

December 27, 1941 - Bob writes to his Aunt Val to thank her for her Christmas kindness.

... Received your letter and card yesterday and also the stamps and the postcards and really want to say thanks for everything because things like that do come in handy around here.

And [I] also got the things that Savalla sent including the candy that you made and it really was very good. It only lasted about ½ hour as the boys really go for candy like that, so thanks ever so much.

Well, I wasn't starved a bit over Christmas. In fact, we all had too much to eat, so all in all with all the things you and the rest sent, I done all right by myself - much better than I deserved.

Hope you didn't feed John and Johnnie and the girls too much for dinner, cause I do remember that you are a good cook, and I'm not just fooling when I say that...

Charley [Hillard] is away ahead if he can stay the hell out of here. There is enough without him, although it isn't tough or anything; and this little stink will be all over soon, but it just breaks up the routine for awhile is all...

(*In "the little stink," the American and Phillipino forces are being pushed back on Luzon. On the other side of the world, British commandos raid German bases on Norway's coastal islands.*)

December 28, 1941 - On this Sunday, Bob hurriedly writes to "Alice and All."

"... Lucille said in her letter about receiving a card from Al and Dan and Betty; and she said she felt rather bad about not sending any in return and asked me to say thanks for her when I wrote you....

Al! Ruthie wrote back and told me about the expected brat. I suppose she is crazier than ever, if that is possible, but she still is all right even at that....

Must be closing this up as I took a fellow's turn at table-waiting today just as a favor to him, and I've got to get over there soon. I want to send this with a fellow into Baltimore at 1:00...."

Bob also jotted a note to his father, which included the following.

"... May get home to see you any time, so don't be surprised if some morning Alice may have to set another plate and bake a dozen or so extra pancakes for breakfast just for me alone...

I just happened to think we got a dog here as a mascot for the Co. C just like Pat. Looks just exactly like her and that son-of-a-gun is really a hunting fool, goes with us everywhere...."

(*The Japanese continue pushing back the Americans and Phillipinos toward Bataan and Manila.*)

Part III
The Battalion Moves South.
Fort Benning, Georgia

December 29, 1941 - Pvt. Hillard was correct when he noted that the Army was good at quickly springing surprises on the lower ranks. On this Monday, the outfit is apprised of the move to Fort Benning, Georgia; so Bob dashes off a postcard to his father. "Everything going okay, but I'm pretty busy. Reason for the card, packing my stuff up, and going to move tomorrow so will write later and give you the address, just found out at noon today. Keep everything under control there at home and I'll be calling you some of these days..."

December 31, 1941 - The Fort Benning Military Reservation is on the western border of Georgia near Columbus. Thousands of troops with varying military functions descend on the area, thus making it a bustling city in its own right.The puffing, chugging steam engine made reasonably good time in transporting Company C to the sunny south. This Wednesday evening, Bob lets his father know his whereabouts in a postcard. "Arrived here this afternoon, so everything is sort of messed up and have a lot of work to do tonight. Got everything under control down here and will tell you all about it later..."

(*As 1941 comes to a close, the Russians are gradually pushing the Germans backward in the bitter cold and leaving a vast* *trail of frozen bodies behind. The Japanese enter a burning Manila on the 31st and prepare for the final thrust on the ill-equipped American forces on Bataan.)*

January 1, 1942 -
Hi Dad:
    Wrote you a card last night as I was pretty busy last night, so will drop you a line or two throughout the day. Got here about 3:00 yesterday and on the way down had a pretty nice trip though we rode during the night so didn't see much of N.C. or S.C., but we sure seen a lot of Georgia pines and red clay and that is what we have here at camp.
    So far, this camp is just like all the rest of the camps, although I haven't got to look around here yet, so I'll tell you all about it later.
    The weather down here is quite a bit warmer than Maryland, although at night it gets sort of chilly and right now it is raining like hell, so maybe that is the kind of weather we get around here.
    Don't know what we are going to do down here, but I imagine we will get a little better training, at least more practical.
    I am having a fellow send home a package from Baltimore, so you should get it soon, all that is in it is a pair of shoes, some little things that Savalla sent me which I didn't need and I didn't have room to bring along, although I did take the stationary and stamps out of one gift. And then some old letters that I had, so keep Ruthie and Alice out of them letters. I really had a helluva lot of stuff, so I couldn't carry it all.
    Well, everything is still going okay, and I keep it that way because I'm just that mean. This is a much bigger place. Somebody said 75,000 men [are] here, although we can't see much of the place from here. And it is only about ½ mile to the Alabama line from here, so we can get away from the State Police if we have to. That makes it nice, don't it? ... Your toughest son...
Pvt. Robert H. Hillard
Co. B 3rd Separate Cml. Bn.
Ft. Benning, Georgia
    A second latter is written on the same date and goes out to Ruthie. It covers the same information except for the following.
    "... I just read the last letter I got from the bunch of you, the

one with the $2 in it, so tell Tony thanks a lot, and you asked if I needed any more. Well, I don't need any as I've got everything here that I need, and don't have much need of money, but if I ever do, don't worry I'll let you know....

They brought 240 of us down here, part of Co. B at Edgewood and our Co. C, but they have got us all mixed up from the way we were back there, although we are still all right here in a bunch..."

(*Representatives of 26 nations at Washington sign the Atlantic Charter, which strives to "ensure life, liberty, independence and religious freedom and to preserve the rights of man and justice." Even the USSR signs the charter. Meanwhile, the fighting still rages in Russia, the Philippines, and North Africa.*)

Januarty 3, 1942 - Bob writes to his Dad:
"... Well, I suppose you're all filled up with pork and stuff now, as I've been hearing about your butchering. I suppose you set the hair on all of them, being as how I wasn't there to supervise the job.

Everything is going just the same as the other place although a helluva lot bigger, and we still are not on the main posts.

I haven't even gotten around here yet, as we are restricted to our grounds for a while at least till they get things in order.

I've been hearing that you have two real dogs there now. I suppose you and Elmer have hides tacked up all over the buildings....

Your toughest son, ... P.S. You know something, a good Republican down here wouldn't have a chance in this Democratic south..."

In a letter to his sister Alice on the same date, he included the following. "... Decided to use a pencil today for it makes the writing much easier, and anyway I figured that this was good enough for you.

Am starting this just after inspection this morning, so will probably be interrupted by chow call.

Well, this is a part of the sunny south that you and the rest are acquainted with, and so far since I have been here, all we have had is thunder and lightning and rain [which] seems sort of funny for this time of year, but it is fairly warm, gets sort of chilly at nights, and believe it or not, they give us more bedding here than we had at Baltimore, more than I would need at home on a helluva cold night.

Since we got here, [we] haven't done anything but just cleaning up the barracks and all around the building. We sure had a dirty mess when we came here.

This place is more like the army than the other place, so maybe I'll learn a few things here that will do me some good, if I ever have to use them later.

I thought maybe on the way down that I would run into some of that southern cooking, the kind that you are so fond of, but so far it has been the same as before so I'm eating like a horse and still fat and sassy and awful tough.

There really is a lot of equipment scattered all over this place, not just here where we are at, for we are by ourselves, but have seen tanks of all kinds, jeeps, etc. One of the fellows that was here said that somewhere close to here, he knows all about the place, that there is a parachute outfit here so maybe I'll get to see them fellows in action and I'll write and tell you all about it.

Been reading your last letter and you said you were saving me some pie. That's a good idea. And also I heard that you were also singing carols from indulging in too much Christmas spirits... Your smartest and toughest Bro...

Bob also took time to write a short letter to his 14-year niece, Alice's daughter Betty.

"... Will add a line or two for you.

You say your basketball team is pretty good, but not good enough for the Ohio nine, and look what it would have been if I had been there - just think of it...

Hope you get as good on your report cards as I did because I still bet they tell the kids about me even yet.

Well Betty, the army life isn't so bad at least so far for me, but I guess I'm just too mean to be affected by it, but that is the only way to be, so I'll be right in there pitching....

(*Gen. Jonathan M. Wainwright takes command of the beleaguered American troops in the Phillipines. German and Italian aircraft continue to bombard the island of Malta in the Mediterranean.*)

January 11, 1942 - From the "Land o' Cotton," Bob tries a little southern lingo on his sister Ruthie and her husband Malon.

Hi Ya White Trashes,

    Since I have a few minutes to kill, I decided to drop you two a letter and then not write home till about the middle of the week, so if you see them, tell them I'm still keeping them flying down here in the sunny south with the pine trees a swaying and the hound dogs a baying, and Georgia peaches running hither, and see this here and there and there, mostly there in the hills of that thar red clay, so you see everybody is happy and everything is under control with the hill billy music and the honky tonks having the controlling hand, but the sun still shines and the stars still come out at night, and the moon does shine even when one is walking guard, just a southern Utopia for us Yankees.

    No, all in all this isn't such a bad place, just as good as the others, good eats or good enough, and I even believe the cooking is better. We even get home made bread.

    This morning they issued us our equipment, enough to go anywhere with everything but our guns, 4 pairs of gloves, mask, pack, tin hat and etc., so we really, or at least, will look like soldiers.

    Big old place down here and as yet I haven't got to see hardly any of it. As yet, I have been busy just messing around, time off for chow. Boy, I'm really learning my bugle calls, especially chow call, you know the one that says, "Come and get your beans boys and etc." I think there are about thirty calls altogether, though we don't use them all.

    Well, we don't have to keep dressed up all the time here, just for supper and inspection and haven't had to stand retreat yet, but they will be getting around to that later, though I hope not.

    You know I want you to write and tell me if a big picture gets home of our Co. C at Edgewood. That is about the only thing I want out of that place, and if you can [I need] that list of wages if you can get them boys to get them. And I'll send you a list of the boys' names on that picture in rotation and where most of them is from.

    ... I have to write to the girl friend yet. "That is the most important thing to me." No remarks there Ruthie...

P.S. If you two ever get low financial[ly], and need some dough fast, see Rose for I think she has a little of mine and you can have it with no if or ands. And don't go getting mad at me for suggesting this or I will beat hell out of both of you....

Menu for chow - Chicken, mashed potatoes, stuffing, gravy, coffee,

bread, cake and ice cream, not bad, huh.
(*The Americans launch a counter-attack on the Bataan Peninsula and regain some ground.*)

January 14, 1942 - Bob writes to his brother Lawrence (Tony), who farms and also works for the road department. His particular interests are how his former working buddies are doing, the Company C picture that he sent home, and Tony's draft status. Bob and his fellow soldiers must have had a few laughs with the gas outfit's "motto."
Hi Tony,
Well, how is business and tricks by now. I suppose you are right in there pitching on the road gang and probably pretty busy plowing snow and etc. Tell Jack and Earl and Gilly I said hello and that I have got this army life well under control.

In Nora's letter I hear you are in the beef business now. Write and tell me how they weigh out and how Ferdinand the bull is growing.

Also, I got the $2 you sent me. Listen fellow, I don't need any money and If I ever do I'll write and let you know, but I'll keep the 2 and you just write it down on the books that I-O-U.

I even went and bought myself a regular army watch, just a cheap one. In here a watch is a pretty handy thing, can't hardly get along without it.

If you're ever around and can get or have a frame built for the Co. C picture, I wish you would cause I would like to keep that; but before you do, tell Rose I wish she would take it into Akron as Lucille wanted to see it. So I'll write later and tell Lucille that Rose will bring it. But keep that picture frame in mind if you can find the time or even get Bob Loomis to make one. Someday maybe I'll pay you off for these little things.

Nora said in her letter that you had to be classified 1-A, that is not good. Anyway, they just need one Hillard, that's me, so tell them that; but if you ever have to go, remember if you want to join a tough outfit, join the gas outfit, that's us. We smell.*

...I had to haul coal all day today, but we don't work too hard, in fact, that is what I need - a good day's work.

Well, I have to go on guard tonight at 2 till 6 tomorrow, so I must be closing this up and get some sleep, or they will shoot me if I fall asleep on post, so be good and write and send me them wage slips

as soon as you can, as I have to fill out an income report and pay just like the rest...
P.S. Tell Elmer there is more and bigger rabbits down here than you can shake a stick at...

[* The Chemical Warfare Service "prepared to conduct and defend against chemical warfare, with chemical mortar battalions and defensive teams serving in all theaters of war. Fortunately, both Allied and Axis forces observed policies against first use of chemical weapons, leaving the Army's Chemical Mortar Battalions to serve in their secondary role, providing conventional indirect fire support to front line troops." [39]

The 3rd Chemical Battalion's motto, "We Cover," appears on the unit insignia, which shows a genie emerging from an Aladdin's lamp. The genie is in dark gold with a light gold background. The motto is in a cobalt-blue ribbon. The insignia was not officially approved until September 22, 1942. "...The story of the genie and the Aladdin's Lamp is symbolic of the functions of the organization, in that the former could fulfill any wish desired when requested of the Magical Lamp. The motto, "We Cover," alludes both to the "modus operandi" and to the spirit of the personnel of the organization in the fulfillment of their allotted tasks."

The unit's coat of arms shows the same genie in blue on a dark gold background, however, it does not contain the motto. [40]]

(On January 14th, the Anglo-American Arcadia conference comes to a close in Washington. A joint Chief of Staffs Committee has been formed to co-ordinate the Anglo-American war effort. Top priority is given to the campaign against the Nazis, and the strategic importance of North Africa is recognized.")

January 18, 1942 - On this Sunday, Bob writes to his dad.
...Will drop you a line or two and hope you are feeling as good as I am, for I'm getting along the same as ever, right in there pitching and just as tough as a Georgia pine knot; and this southern sun is really a difference than what you are getting up there, just like summer down here.

Well, I suppose they are keeping you pretty busy now with the butchering of beeves, but you want to take it easy and just be the boss of the job and give them hell if they don't do it right.

Had a letter from Loss and Johnnie, and they are okay. Loss is working on steel construction and says it has been cold as the devil and that they had to lay off for a day or two, and Johnnie is still working at the refinery and pretty busy.

Well, there isn't any news here of importance, just the same old routine, 3 meals a day and keep busy in between times.... Your toughest son .. Make them snots behave or tell me about it in your next letter. [Due to Army censorship, it is quite likely that Bob is purposely omitting any training details to anyone.]

(The Red Army penetrates the German lines and are pushing back the enemy no matter the cost. The Americans are still battling and waiting for help on Bataan.)

January 25, 1942 - On this Sunday, Bob writes to his sister Ruthie and Malon.

"... Don't know where we are going or why, but just between us, yesterday we all had our blood typed, mine is A, and the other day we got the rest of our equipment including a mosquito net, so business is maybe picking up.

Ruthie, you wrote something about going down to John D. Kline and getting a birth certificate. If you do, ask about mine and if you can get one for me too; and you ought to get Nora one because that little fart won't think to get one herself and she may need it. I had a letter from her on Fri., so if I find time, I am going to try to write to her, but I have a helluva lot of letters to write today, and this is the first one and I may write to Fritz too.

Malon, how are you and Tony making out with a frame for that picture I sent home. You know, why don't you make one for it? That would be the best thing I would think, and isn't that some picture that my friend took - the gas house gang - and we are really tough, you can tell Peanuts that, much more so than the cavalry.... Well, news is as scarce as hen's teeth, so I will be closing...[From] The toughest soldier below or above the Mason-Dixon Line."

A second letter goes out to Bob's father, in which the son as usual tries to downplay the seriousness of his situation and to alleviate any worry on the part of the elder Hillard.
Hi Dad,

Just received your letter about a half hour ago as we have mail call here on Sunday, and [I] was really glad to hear that you're feeling okay and hope that you keep that way; so, not to be giving orders or anything, take care of yourself and take it easy. And I want to say thanks for the stamps, although I am not broke or anything. Stamps are one thing that come in handy to one here, for we are out here all by ourselves 9 miles from the main posts and they don't sell stamps here, so we have to wait till we get a chance to go down there, which can't be very often as they are keeping us busy as hell, but not working too hard. So, I'm in good shape and getting along the same as ever. In fact, I am the toughest draftee in this damn army and you can tell Stanley I said so. I'm just a 160 lb. fighting machine, have put on a little weight since I have been here and can really step off with a 70 lb. pack with the best of them. You know that I am just so damn mean that I don't give up, and any more I am used to these hikes. There I go bragging again, but I'll be in there pitching, you can bet your flock of pigs on that.

I sure hope Lawrence and Stanley don't have to get into this, and I doubt if they will be called for a long time yet, for they have lots of guys in here now, and anyway it will soon be over probably just as quick as it started.

As for getting a furlough, that is pretty hard to do now for we can't get a whole weekend pass any more, just one evening and [we] have to be back for reveille the next morning, but if I get the chance I will get home to see you and help you eat some of that ham.

Now I say you're really using your head by going into the pig business by keeping both of them sow pigs. It will be something that you can probably tend to yourself or at least see that it is done right without too much work, and you will hardly miss the amount of feed that it takes.

Lawrence must have had pretty good luck with his beef cattle. [He] should have made some dough on them. I suppose he is a pretty man right now on the road and at home with his wild eyed team of horses....

Well, dad, I must be closing this up and do some work. I have guard duty starting tomorrow night for 24 hrs, the third time since I have been here, so I must do my tomorrow work tonight.... Your toughest Son by far...

(*It has been fourteen weeks since the attack on Pearl Harbor, and the Japanese continually have been relentless and successful. American and Filipino troops retire to the southern end of Bataan.*)

February 13, 1942 - It is Friday morning at Fort Benning.
Hi Dad,

Have about 30 minutes before I have to go on guard duty again, so am in the guard house at the present time and thought I would write you a line or two.

Well, everything is still under control down here, and I am right in there pitching still, just as mean as cat shit and the toughest guy in this army. (That's what I think.)

One thing, they have really been keeping us busy with work details and guard duty, so haven't had very much time to write, but have been hearing from around there pretty regular, had a letter from Rose yesterday and maybe will find time after while to answer it if I don't fall asleep.

Hope you and all the rest are feeling okay and still able to kick around in the cold weather and snow [that] I hear you're getting up there. While down here it has been pretty nice and warm but gets sort of chilly at nights and especially on this guard duty.

Have really been getting into some real demonstrations since I have been down here and have seen most everything in action, especially on Wed.; and we have a part in all of them in our kind of work. Have even seen the parachute troops jumping as they have a big outfit of them over at the main posts.

Talking of being busy, I imagine all of you there are just as busy taking care of things; Lawrence is probably trying to do two jobs as usual. Tell him I said I could handle him easy now and always could.... Your toughest son, Bob.

(The American and Filipino troops are still putting up a valiant fight on Bataan and waiting for help. The British have the same situation at Singapore as the Japanese have them trapped.)

February 14, 1942 - Bob writes to his sister Ruthie and Malon. Alice, who had been running the household, has moved back to the farm with her husband Dan. Ruthie, who is now pregnant, and Malon move in to assume Alice's duties. Temporarily casting aside his usual bravado, Bob reveals his true feelings on being drafted and going on furlough.
Hi Snots:

Received your letter today Ruthie, and really I should be kicked in the rear end for not writing you sooner, but I can honestly say that I have been busy as hell, not just me alone but all the rest of the boys in this Co. B.

We have been pulling guard duty at least every 3 days for 24 hour stretches and sometimes oftener and then K.P. and D.R.O., which is just about the same thing only you have to set the tables and clean out the dining room instead of just washing dishes and pans, so it is the same difference, but all in all [I] have been busy; but I have still got my chin up and I'll kiss anybody's rear end and if this thing gets it down [sic], that is just because I am so <u>damn</u> mean as you two probably already know, so I am right in there pitching, and will keep on doing that.

Have just finished up a day of K.P. today and am on D.R.O. tomorrow on Sunday, my own time. That makes me mad, but it is all in a day's work. So will make this short, as I should write Alice, for I also had a letter from her today from Laurel Hill, N.C. Hope you can read this as I am trying to get it done before lights out.

You didn't hate to see Alice and the rest leave any more than I, but I can understand her leaving. Dad ought to have his rear end kicked and etc. He doesn't know when he is well off.

As for a furlough, just between you two and I, I doubt it very much, although I won't say yes or no for I would like to see you all up there, but maybe if I did come back, I wouldn't want to leave again any more than I did at first, so maybe it is just as well. But I still will if I ever get the chance. You can bet on that.

[I'm] talking of selling my car, and I believe I might as well if it could be arranged, only if Malon and you or Lawrence doesn't need it, and I really mean that either one of you can have it just as it is. No money involved at any time. If you decide you are not going to need it, Malon why don't you and Lawrence look around and maybe sell it for me if you can. Set any price you two decide on, but only if you won't need it yourself.

Glad to hear you got your raise in salary, but that is as it should be, so keep up the good work and keep them rolling and between the ditches, also your tarp tied down.

And Ruthie take it easy and write and tell me when I become uncle again and good luck both of you... Bob.

(*Food, drinking water, and ammunition are in short supply for the British at Singapore. Gen. Rommel has the German army on the offensive in North Africa.*)

February 26, 1942 - From Fort Benning, Bob writes to his Dad.
"... Am going to write you a short letter and also one to Nora in the same envelope...
 I am going to send a package home one of these days of some things that I don't need and thought I might as well get rid of instead of hiding it on inspection day.
 A leather writing case, a package by itself that I wish you would get Nora to put up for me, a camera and 1 roll of film that has been taken but hasn't been developed, and another that already to use. I want Nora to have it anyway, so I'll tell her about the camera. And also that pants creaser that Betty sent me, which would be all right at home but isn't much good here so tell them to use it if they want to.
 I have to fall out now for CO duty... Your toughest son, Bob...
 (*Four days ago, Gen. MacArthur was ordered to leave the Philippines and to set up his headquarters in Australia. The Japanese are also pushing into Burma. Rommel's Afrika Corps is digging in on the Egyptian frontier, and the Axis bombers are still plastering Malta.*)

March 7, 1942 - Bob writes to Ruthie on this Saturday evening.
 ... I have been really busy, being as how we moved into tents last weekend and had all this framing up to do, and still we aren't quite done; for in here the old saying is never do any more today than you can help, leave something for tomorrow. So everybody leaves a little bit and skips all the details he can.
 As far as the weather goes, we had a couple of cool days with snow, and it has been raining pretty regular, but yesterday and today it has been nice.
 I had a detail today, so I got out of inspection, had a Ration detail. Go down to the main posts and get all the grub for all 4 kitchens for 2 days, so we had 2 truck loads - 1 ½ ton trucks at that, so we had a busy day dividing it up after we got back. That is just one of the many details we get on.
 I just received a letter from Nora today, so I guess everybody is okay up there as she mentioned all of you.
 Had a letter from Johnnie, and I did answer him after he was out home.
 This tent life isn't so bad although it is really back in the

woods on a mud road, and things are not quite as handy, but being as how I am the toughest guy from here, I can really take it, and this is really a tough outfit and plenty gassy, especially after a good meal of beans. We even eat mustard.

We also have been busy on demonstration, about 4 a week, but some of them are kinda fun, especially taking our future officers thru the gas chamber. They really come out crying like they lost their best girl. They go thru first with it [the gas mask] on, and then the 2nd time they have to take it off in there for just an instant and get out, but we all had to do that too at Edgewood....

U.S. toughest soldier, Bob

Tell Tony to keep the road between home and Akron in good repair as I might want to use it some time. [to go see Lucille]

(The Japanese control Java, are ready to occupy Rangoon, Burma, and are set to invade New Guinea.)

March 15, 1942 - On this Sunday, Bob writes to his dad.

...Have finally found time to write as we really have been busy as hell and will be after Wed. [the] 18th, when some big shot general of this area inspects us. They do that once every year so they are really making us clean up outside as well as inside.

But outside of being busy, everything is going okay; [it's] getting warm down here just like summer most of the time except for a raining day or so and chilly at nights.

Well, I suppose all of you are keeping busy up there and waiting for spring to get there.

I had a letter from Dan and Al, and they have had some raining weather and etc., but I guess he is getting started [farm work] by now.

News is scarce here as we have been too busy to think up any development. And I am going to drop Nora a letter in this too, so I will say so long for now and take care of yourself and be good.

Uncle Sam's toughest Draftee
Your son - Bob.

(In the Bay of Manila, the Japanese artillery is pounding the Americans on the off-shore islands. In Germany, Der Fuhrer blames the Russian winter for their setbacks, but he promises to annihilate the Red Army in the coming summer.)

March 28, 1942 - On this Saturday evening, Bob sits in his tent and writes a pensive letter to his dad. He has been in the army for over five months and at Fort Benning for almost two months. The routine, though bearable, has become monotonous.

Hi Dad:

    I will bet by now that you will think I am a helluva a guy for not writing sooner to you, but I never say much, so I guess it doesn't make a lot of difference, and I have been pretty busy just doing nothing but putting in a lot of time doing it.

    Have been getting along the same as before, can still say I'm just as good a soldier as the next one and just as tough and mean as they come.

    I hear from Nora that Lawrence has gone into the horse business again. Well, he should have a good team in a year or so.

    Was glad to hear that the mad dog scare was over and nothing around there got bit, kind of a bad thing to have around.

    We are still tenting around here, and as I said before it isn't so bad, pretty warm in the daytime but cools off considerably at night.

    How have you been feeling these days. I hope all right, and you better keep yourself in shape for we will go on some hikes when I get home.

    I suppose people around there have started thinking about gardens and etc. by now, as it won't be long now till that time gets around.

    I am going to write Norie a line also in this letter so will say so long for now. Be good and behave and I should be seeing you, only [I] don't know when. Your son, Bob.

    (*With dwindling supplies, the Americans on Bataan await the final Japanese offensive. The island of Malta in the Mediterranean has suffered an incredible 1,600 bombing raids by the Axis.*

    On April 9th, the American and Filipino troops on Luzon are surrendered to the Japanese. On the following day, the 100 km Bataan Death March begins. Eventually, around 70,000 prisoners begin the trek under the broiling sun.. Soldiers are beaten and denied food and water. Prisoners are being shot, bayoneted, or beheaded for the least trivial offense.)

    On January 1, 1942, Bob's outfit was designated: Headquarters and Headquarters Co., 3rd Separate Chemical Battalion. On April 1, 1942, that was changed to Headquarters and Headquarters

Detachment, 3rd Chemical Mortar Battalion.

Fort Bliss, Texas

On the far western tip of Texas lies El Paso on the Rio Grande River and the Fort Bliss Military Reservation. A short distance north is the Arizona border, over which the reservation extends. Perhaps the troops sent to Fort Bliss' climate and terrain are preparing for the conditions in North Africa. Nevertheless, the change of scenery puts Bob in a far better mood - at least for now.

April 14, 1942 - From Fort Bliss, Texas, Bob writes to his sister Ruthie on this Tuesday evening.
His Snot:

Been hearing things about you, the fact that I'm uncle again. Had a letter from Rose and she told me all about that boy and [I'm] glad to hear that you're both okay. So, be damn sure you take it easy for a while before you start doing your work again or I will beat h--- out of you when I see you again.

Well, I moved a short distance since I last wrote you, quite a ways, but distance don't seem so far anymore, so all I need is a furlough and I'll be home to see you and that smart family of yours, but can't say when that will be.

I guess you know I'm at Fort Bliss just two miles from El Paso and it is right on the U.S. Mexico border, just the Rio Grande River divides it and Juarez, Mexico (pronounced as Waras). So, I was across the line on Sunday afternoon and Eve. and I'm telling you it is really a wooly place if you know what I mean.

I even went to a bull fight there just to see how it was done, and it is a pretty gory mess, although it was exciting at times and something I had never seen before.

I bought 3 aprons for souvenirs while I was there, also the fellow I went with did too, but he left his in a place down there when we went in to get a glass of beer, which I can assure you I don't indulge in too much. Anyway, he talked me out of one, and I was going to send to Lucille, you know who I mean - the one and only, that beautiful blonde - one of them and one to each you and Nora. So, hope you don't get mad, but I'm going to skip you this time and just send Nora's as it might pep her up. I haven't sent either one as yet, and they're just old cheap things, so you are not missing much and it might pep Nora up a little. Anyway, I'll be thinking of you. [At the time of this writing, Nora Hillard Foster still treasures that decorative, yellow, Mexican apron that her brother sent to her.]

El Paso is a pretty nice town, pretty tough as 85% of the 202,000 are Mexicans, but it does have some nice places, parks and etc.

As for this camp, well it is about the same as any other, so I'm still in there pitching and will continue to do so. I'm just that mean and stubborn, best damn soldier down here, "So there" too.

Pretty doggone hot here and the sun really shines down. I and about all the rest have peeled noses and faces, and we did have a pretty good tan when we left Georgia, but will get used to it in time.

So Ruthie, I must be closing for you, so take it easy and be good, and [I] will have to send this to your old address instead of the hospital as darn if I know the name of it, and anyway I hope Malon picks this up in time. So long for now, Your smartest Bro....

[A letter to his dad on the 25th covered the same information.]

(The Americans on Corregidor are undergoing intense Japanese shelling. The British Chiefs of Staff approve Gen. George Marshall's plan for a second front against the Germans.)

April 27, 1942 - In writing to Ruthie, Bob's only concern is how things are at home.
Hi Snots,

Well, I suppose you think you are somebody now since young John has arrived on the scene. But [he] will probably be just another spoiled urchin, or maybe perhaps he will be different than all the rest. Anyway, Ruthie take it easy.

I wrote Dad yesterday so perhaps you will hear all the news from here from him, as there isn't any news anyway.

By the way, how does Dad like his namesake? Rose said in her letter that he was sort of tickled about the whole thing and was bragging about it though of course he probably wouldn't let you know, or did he.

And how is he behaving since Peanuts left, you know there is one guy that should have had his a-- kicked right up around his shoulders for getting mixed up in this before he had to.

Did Nora get her apron that I sent and how did she like it, pretty funny, huh! And also high priced. Tell her to keep that in mind and get her to answer for you when you see her, of course, for I realize that you are probably busy.

 Lawrence I hear has went back to the sod and the plow for a month or two, he should do all right and I believe he done the smart thing.

 I hear Malon that you have changed jobs, so how do you like it, and what are you doing?

 Tell Fritz that I am going to buy him an earthen pot so he can just melt his metal and pour it on, [as a welder?] for that's all he ever done before, and also that I am the toughest soldier down here and I don't want any back talk from him.

 Well, everything is going okay with me as usual, and I don't have any news so will have to stop for now and will try to write to that beautiful blonde if you know who I mean, before it gets dark, so so-long and be good. Bob
Malon, you better keep in pretty good shape for our 10 round bout we agreed upon. Brother-in-laws is my dish. So long.

 (Yesterday, Hitler proclaimed, "I will ruthlessly eliminate everybody who does not stand up to this task.")

May 5, 1942 - On this Tuesday evening, **Cpl.** Bob Hillard writes to Ruthie.

 ... Just received your letter today and was glad to hear you're all okay and still as sassy as ever.

 Well, if young John L. just turns out to be as good a man as his youngest uncle, then I'll say you have something to brag about.

 I too have been pretty busy these last few weeks and especially since these new fellows came in last Sun. a week ago.

 Also, I think somebody made a mistake when they made me Corp. and I'm even sending home the proof, so wish you would give it to Dad, and he can lay it up for me, financially it is all right but [I] probably will catch a lot more he--.....

 (The Japanese are preparing to invade Midway Island and the Aleutians. Air raids and artillery shells pound Corregidor. Tomorrow, Gen. Wainwright will sign the unconditional surrender.)

May 9, 1942 - It's Saturday evening at Fort Bliss.
 Hi Dad:
 Will drop you a line or two to tell you that everything in

Bob Hillard smokes his pipe on a mountain overlooking Camp Bliss. Other soldiers are "Kreyson (Minn.) and Taylor (Tenn.).

Top - Johnson, Hillard, K. Kitchen, Goodwin
Bottom - T. Maragda, L. Kellenberger, F. Igalson, L. Kavawer

Bob and Lucille. Home on furlough and sporting Sgt. stripes.

Texas is all under control. Things are going just the same as ever so can't kick a bit.

Well, [I] suppose Lawrence and you are really going into the farming business by now as it is getting along about that time.

Weather has been hotter than hell and I imagine in a little while later it will get hotter still, but have got sort of used to it by now.

Had a letter from Ruthie and she said everybody was the same. Also had a letter from Betty and she gave me all the news in N.C., so have heard from all over.

How's the world and everybody treating you and how are you feeling these days? You want to take it easy and don't try to do all the work in one day.

I think I'll send you home a pet rattlesnake or two just for a playmate for your dog and perhaps a few other of these reptiles running around here in the fields.

How is the namesake doing by now? I'll bet you think you're pretty smart. Well, if he is just as good a man when he grows up as his youngest uncle (meaning me) then I'll say you have something to brag about.... Your son, Bob.

               The best _damn_ soldier here.
               Believe it or not...

(The Japanese are mopping up smaller resistance groups on the other Philippine islands.)

May 13, 1942 - Bob says goodbye to the old Plymouth.
Hi Dad:

Will write you a line tonight saying the same old thing, everything [is] as usual so I am still going strong.

Was in town last night and had that bill of sale signed over to Lawrence as you will see, so am giving him a little work to do for me. So, you can tell him he is now the proud owner of one _damn_ good car, tho he probably will have to go to Ravenna, but he can get that done.

Well, the weather here is pretty warm and the old sun really beats down, but am getting used to it by now, and we also have a good old stiff breeze coming down off the mts. from the west.

Have been pretty busy here of late, but I can imagine that you and Lawrence and the rest are busier than that....

May 17, 1942 - From Fort Bliss, Bob writes to his sister Ruthie.

"... Since I have quite a bit of time to waste today and not much to do except write, I thought I would scratch you out a couple of lines and give you an account of what has been happening here, of which there is nothing.

Things have been going about the same here. We have been pretty busy, get up at 5:15 in the morning and thru at 5:00 retreat, then supper, and as we have no light in our tents we have to keep pretty busy even in the evening, especially on Friday night for inspection Sat.

Had a letter from Peanuts yesterday, so will try to answer it today, but I guess he is getting along okay, [he was] just telling me of getting ready to go on an overnight hike when he wrote.

Just been listening to a guy who was in town last night over in Mexico, who really must have thrown a time, and over there is one place if a fellow wants to he can do just that for that is the darnest horniest place I ever seen. Even El Paso is plenty tough, between the soldiers and M.P. and civilians, they have a helluva time.

Well, the week after next I think our Co. is going over to the Carlsbad Caverns to go thru that place and the Co. that has already been there says it really is some place worth seeing.

That boy John Tony, as Gail wrote and said, must really be something and anyway I'm glad Dad has taken to him for even you will admit that it is better that way for all of you to have him in that mood. So, keep the old boy cheered up and sometime I'll be back and start him off in a good argument...."

(In bitter fighting the Germans stop the Red Army advance.)

May 24, 1942 - Bob writes to his dad.

"... I had a letter from Alice and she was telling [that] she had started to cooking and was busy as a cat covering shit on a tin roof, so tell her I will answer one of these days.

Well, Tues. we are going up to Carlsbad Caverns and look it over for a day or so.

I have a few pictures that we took up on one of the mountains when a bunch of us climbed it, so will send along a couple. Some that Woody and I developed ourselves, or rather he did yesterday in town at the U.S.O. club, as they have a room for soldiers in which to make them, and it really is quite interesting.

Well Dad, news is scarcer than hen's teeth, so will be saying so-long for now so keep everything under control and don't work too hard, and be sure and make a man out of young John L., tho I know he never will be as good as his uncle (meaning me) for Ruthie will probably make a sissy out of him if you don't watch her close...."

(*Having broken the Japanese code, Americans forces are headed for Midway and the Aleutians. Fighting continues in New Guinea.*)

May 30, 1942 - On this Saturday evening, Bob writes to his Dad. Cpl. Hillard was certainly impressed with his trip to the Carlsbad Caverns.

"... Had a letter from Rose and I haven't written as yet, but she asked me what I wanted for that car. (Hell, tell Lawrence or Malon anything is all right, they know how cars are selling and I sure don't.) ... Was up to Carlsbad Caverns this week and believe it or not that place is really worth anyone's time and money. It really is enormous, big rooms 4,000 ft. long and 800 ft. wide, ceiling 300 ft. high and smaller ones with these growths looking like icicles and icebergs, etc, all the different colors imaginable. Café, rest rooms, shower, down in it 829 ft. underground and then the lighting system is very cleverly arranged. I bought a few snapshots taken in there with a flash camera, so will send you a couple. They were bought at the café down in the cavern. Also has about 7 miles of pathways there, and they are fixing more so they are safe for visitors. So all in all, it was quite a trip and had a lot of fun... Right now, I'm in charge of quarters so have to stay here in the orderly room till morning, but I will get caught up with my letters I hope..."

(*Rear-Admiral Fletcher's command leaves Pearl Harbor for Midway. The British launch a "thousand bomber raid" on Cologne, Germany. The city is devastated by raging fires.*)

In early June, Bob received that long-awaited furlough back to the farm in Randolph, Ohio. The monotonous clackity-clack of the train wheels and the frequent stops along the way only heightened the anticipation of seeing his Dad, Ruthie and Malon, Norie, Tony, and the rest of the family. He could show off his neat and trim bearing with those Sergeant's stripes on his sleeve.

And of course, he could hardly wait to see that "beautiful blonde," Lucille. Before his furlough ended, they would be engaged, and he presented her with a beautiful china set as an engagement gift. Sure of her love for Bob and knowing that they would soon be separated for a long time, Lucille was in favor of getting married while Bob was at home. In some quiet location, the two lovers had a serious discussion about matrimony. Bob considered the possibility that he could be killed in a foreign land; and worse yet, he could very well be severely maimed. If that happened, he couldn't bear to burden her if he came back disfigured and a basket case. Their engagement was a strong bond of commitment, but marriage would have to wait until he returned from the war for good.

In the previous correspondence with his father, they had discussed the prized sow pig, which gave birth to a good litter that spring. Norie Hillard Foster: "Dad was showing him the sow pig with little ones that he was raising. Bob picked up one of the pigs, and it died in his arms. [Later], Dad said it was an omen, as all the other pigs lived and were healthy. Dad said that he would never see Bobbie again..."

The difficult part of furloughs is when they end. Often, the second parting is more heart rending than the first. Bob most likely kept his thoughts to himself, as it seemed to be the manly thing to do. In addition, looking at all of his correspondence to the family, it did not seem to be in his nature to reminisce much.

June 20, 1942 - Bob is back at Fort Bliss on this sweltering Saturday evening.
Hi Dad:

Well, I arrived all okay on Wed. night [June 17] after a little delay over in N. Mexico, but everything is going okay. And I did get here in time to go on a problem early Thurs. morning [June 18] and just got back last night, the reason I haven't written sooner. So I have been going since. Then this morning we had another one of those damn inspections, but we have this afternoon off.

It really is hot down here now, worse than before. I am writing this and sweating like the devil.

When you or someone else answers this, I wish you would put in Stanley's address for I have lost it and I owe him a letter.

Everything here is back to its old routine, so I am back in there pitching.

I have to go on guard tonight so will have to be making this

short. I just wanted to write and tell you to take it easy and take care of yourself, and I'll be seeing you one of these days, and as tomorrow is Dad's Day and I can't get into town to get you anything, so will hope you have a good time, but don't get too high on spirits, though I wouldn't blame you a bit... Your son, Bob.
(*The U.S. Navy stems the tide of Japanese success in the Pacific by defeating them in the Battle of Midway, which ends on June 7. In North Africa, Gen. Rommel masterfully has pushed back the British, who lose heavily in casualties, prisoners, and materiel. On the 20th, the German Panzers move into Tobruk.*)

June 27, 1942 - It's been another grueling week of solving battlefield situations in the desert conditions. On this Saturday evening, Bob again writes to his Dad.

"... Well, here goes a line or two just to let you know I'm still here and pitching the same as ever. Things are as usual, busy as hell and [I] have been out also at nights too on problems, so don't have much chance to write very often....

Nothing much doing here tonight, just sitting here listening to the radio of a bunch of Mexicans, so can't understand anything but it sounds all right....

Really hot down here now, about 110-115 degrees and the old sun is really bright, but we did have one shower this week....

I suppose you are getting all set to celebrate the 4th of July. I suppose we will get that day off, but am not sure. Anyway, it doesn't make a helluva lot of difference to me..."

(*In North Africa, the Germans advance into Egypt. The British are retreating to El Alamein. Earlier in the week, Gen. Eisenhower assumed command of U.S. troops in England.*)

July 8, 1942 - From Fort Bliss, Texas, Sgt. Bob Hillard writes to his Dad.

Will drop you a line or two to show you I haven't forgotten [how] to write, but have been busy as hell and that takes in some of the nights too. And [it] will be just as busy from here on in, but it isn't so bad anyway, so can't kick.

Had a letter from Stanley and he seems to be getting along okay. I guess he is in a pretty nice climate there.

Everything is as usual here. [On the] 4th we had a parade in El

Paso, also the cavalry and an outfit from Mexico, so had quite a parade, but to me they are still a pain in the rear.

Weather is same here as always, hot around 110-115 degrees, but one gets used to that.

I sent home a warrant not so long ago to you for my Sgts. and just wonder if it got there, so write and tell me if it did.

I suppose you are plenty busy now and Lawrence too, but you want to take it easy, for you have done your share already and keep yourself in shape for a good argument when I get back, and hope you are still as good a Rep[ublican] as before... Your Toughest and smartest son, Bob.

(The British are stubbornly holding El Alamein. Their air force bombs Tobruk and Benghazi in North Africa and Messina and Reggio Calabria in Sicily. U.S. naval forces in the Pacific are headed for Tulagi and Guadalcanal in the Solomon Islands.)

July 21, 1942 - In the evening, Bob writes to his dad.

"... Will write you a couple of lines tonight, but it will be short. Anyway, I am still mean and sassy and getting along as usual. Had to work over the weekend as we had another DAMN inspection today by some big shots, and we had to get ready yesterday for it, so this bunch is all madder than hell and like a bunch of dogs wanting to fight.

Believe it or not, it has rained all afternoon and still is, so it is quite comfortable.

Had a letter from Stanley today and he is doing okay. Seems to like the place out there as far as the weather goes.... Your toughest son, Bob....

(The Germans move on Stalingrad. The Russians admit that the Don River is "running with blood." In North Africa, the British artillery is quite effective against the German panzers at El Alamein. Rommel calls for more troops to cover his losses. He has no faith in the Italian soldiers.)

July 26, 1942 - In a letter to his dad on this Sunday, Bob contemplates a move to Louisiana and a reassignment possibility.

"... Have decided to drop you a few lines while sitting in the guard house, as I am taking Woody's place for a hour or so as Sgt. of the guard, and this gives a person time to get caught up on his writing.

Everything is going as usual here. We are getting ready to leave for La. maneuvers on Tues. and I will give you our address for down there, but don't use it before next Sunday Aug. 2 as there won't be no post office there till then.
    Co. B. Sep. Cml. Bn.
    A.P.O. 201
    Leesville, La.
    c/o Postmaster

I have just been wondering if a warrant that they gave me ever got home in a letter I sent you, the one I got when they made me Sgt. If it did, I wish you would put them up and keep them, that is the Cpl. and Sgt. warrants. I have never heard you mention it getting there so would like to know.

I would like Malon to get me a book on welding, both electric and acetylene, that is, one that covers most all kinds of work. As to different kinds of heat, flame, and etc. Tell him to see Fritz if he can't find it himself. The reason I want it is that I have put in a application for the Ordinance Dept. as a officer and specified any job as a welder, hoping I may get appointed as one in repairing equipment. But before I do, I will have to go before a board, and they usually ask a lot of little questions on your line of work. So would like to study up a bit and not get caught short. For I would like to take a try at it if they give me a chance, cause your toughest son would make one helluva good Lt. Have him send it also to La. if he gets it. That is after next Sunday....

    Your toughest son, Bob.

(In response to the Russians' urgent demands for a second European front, the allies respond that they are not ready to invade Europe. However, Roosevelt and Churchill agree for a large-scaled landing in North Africa called Operation Torch.)

August 12, 1942 - Between Leesville and Shrevesport, Louisiana is the Fort Polk Military Reservation. On this Wednesday morning, Bob writes to his dad.

"As we have a short break and I got Betty's and Ruthie's letters, I thought I would drop you a line or two. It really is quite a problem to find time to write with all of our moving around. So if you don't happen to hear from me, just consider that I haven't got the time.

Well, we have been moving all over the place for about 100 miles in diameter between Leesville and Shrevesport, and I don't know what in the hell we are learning, except to make us mean as hell, but it is the same old thing, so have everything under control.

Had a letter from Rose and she put in a picture of you and her. You really look okay, at least in the picture, so hope you are feeling well.

This country is a pretty wild old place where we are at, lots of woods and brush and a <u>helluva</u> lot of red bugs and these darn little ticks, so it keeps one busy almost during breaks to delouse ourselves.

Dan and Al I believe done a smart thing by getting the Wilson place, considering the road, electricity, water and cellar partly dug, for that to me would mean a lot if I was in their place.

I suppose you think John Jr. is just about the thing now, but let me tell you this, that he will never be as good a man as his youngest uncle, course I wouldn't want to brag.

As to that [welding] book I wanted Malon to get, I would like to have it, but if he can't get it by just writing for it, tell him to forget it, for maybe I will never get up before the board, tho I hope so, and another thing, the boys are really getting broke down to private, so if it happens to me don't be surprised, as they are using a lot of foolish little excuses for that purpose, but it doesn't make a lot of difference to me anyway.... Your toughest son, Bob.

(*The U.S. Marines have landed on Guadalcanal, where today the first supply aircraft land on Henderson Field. Also, Gen. Montgomery lands in Egypt to take over the British 8th Army.*)

August 22, 1942 - From the Leesburg, La. area, Bob writes to his father at 5:00 P.M.

Just a few lines to tell you I am still down here in La. with the red-bugs and ticks, but still in there pitching and just as mean as ever.

We have been kept pretty busy and now [I'm] packed up ready to move out on another problem, as Sunday is just another day here, but have had today off, so have caught up on my writing a little today.

Oh by the way, Lucille wrote and told me about Ike and Harriet's new addition to the family. So, you're a Grand-pappy again. And I suppose you think you're pretty smart.... Uncle Sam's toughest soldier and your smartest and meanest son., Bob."

(*A battalion of Marines reinforce their comrades on Guadacanal. Americans and their allies await the Japanese offensive on New Guinea.*)

August 31, 1942 - It is 7:00 P.M. on this Monday as Bob writes to his father.

"... Tell Elmer L. [Loomis] that he ought to be down here with a good coon dog and his traps. For since I have been here and running around these woods, I have seen a million tracks in the creeks and swamps, and I mean some of them are big, looks like a young bear track.

I wish I could catch you some of these hogs that are running around here wild. They are all over this area as they are turned out just to run wild, and there isn't a fence hardly in all we have covered. Anyway, they are these razor-backs and thin as hell, even worse than the hogs Dan and Stanley bought you from Hartville.

It rained like <u>hell</u> at [the] camp field today. This is the damnest country for to rain in sections I ever seen. I was talking to a lady the other day, and she told me she put a clothes line up on both sides of her house on wash day, so as to keep her clothes dry by changing them from one line to the other. There is a damn fool from California here telling me this, and he expects me to believe it. I just want to show you what I have to put up with in this place..."

(*In North Africa, Rommel's latest attack at El Alamein is thwarted. In the Solomon Islands, the U.S. carrier Saratoga is hit by Japanese torpedoes and must return to Pearl Harbor. In Russia, the Germans are within 15 miles of Stalingrad.*)

September 13, 1942 - It is 12 noon on this Sunday, and Bob writes to his dad.

Have just finished another problem last night, and this happens to be the first Sunday we have had off for quite a while, tho we are going to have to move again soon. So, you see they keep us on the go most of the time, tho we are not working too hard.

Have just read Ruthie's letter and sure hope they don't get Malon, and she said they might. Tell him I said I don't think he could take it here anyway.

I heard from Betty Jane also, so everybody in Penna. is okay and still kicking.

We are over in Texas again, just across the La. line, so from now on my address is the same except my A.P.O. is 308 instead of 201... Your toughest and smartest son, Bob.

(*The Germans are fighting in Stalingrad; the Russians are backed up to the Volga River. On Guadalcanal, the Marines on Bloody Ridge repel the Japanese banzai charges in the night.*)

October 18, 1942 - Bob has been in the army for a year.

Hi Dad:

Well, here we are on another break and waiting to pull one more problem, and then it is back to Ft. Bliss for us, so from now on my address will be Ft. Bliss, Texas.

I am sort of glad these maneuvers are over, but again I don't care much as they were not so tough, and it doesn't make much difference where one is at. So all in all, everything is going the same. I have everything under control and am still the best damn soldier in this man's army.

By the way, how have you been feeling and doing for yourself? Hope all right, and anyway keep swinging and keep up your arguments for when I get back. I don't want to win too easy from you.

I hear your namesake John Jr. is quite a boy, but I doubt if you ever will make the man out of him that his youngest uncle is, "meaning me."

I wonder what Elmer Loomis thinks by now of this army. Write and give me his address and I will write him a card or something.

Tell Lawrence he better start feeding that new horse if it is that hungry. And that he should change its name or the neighbors will be thinking he is a dude farmer calling a horse that.

As to news here Dad, there just isn't any....

(*Fighting continues on Guadalcanal. Three days ago the Japanese tried to land six transport ships, and American aircraft sank or stranded three of them. At Stalingrad, the Russians refuse to yield to the German onslaught.*)

October, 1941 - Back at Fort Bliss, Bob writes a brief, undated note to his dad, which concludes:

"... Lucille was telling me of going out to see you. And [she] was saying that she had a nice time. Also of how nice that you treated her. So, for that I may be seeing you the last of Nov. or 1st of Dec. and we will go celebrate. Be good and I'll do the same."

November 1, 1942 - On this Sunday, Bob writes to his dad.

[I] have today off so will try to get caught up on some of my letter writing. And so you are the first one on the list, tho I don't have a <u>darn</u> thing to write about.

Since we moved in on Tues., they have been keeping us busy as hell. For they really want this place to shine. But it is just the same old stuff. And what I need is some good hard work.

As I said before, I may get home the last of Nov. or first part of Dec. Of course, they can always change that, but anyway that is the time I am slated to go... [The rest of the letter inquires about Stanley, Rose, his friend Elmer Loomis, and the rest of the folks at home.]

(The Marines advance on Guadalcanal against an enemy that fights to the death. The Russians at Stalingrad are fighting with the same tenacity.)

December 29, 1941 - From the tone of this letter and the following ones, Bob did not receive his expected furlough. The gap in letters may be due to his laxity in writing or other factors. At 9:30 on this Tuesday, Bob is in top humor as he writes to his dad.

Just a few lines to say I am still in here pitching and sassier than ever and still the best soldier in Texas. Tell Stanley that when you write him.

Only hope that you are there getting along as well. And as for you, keep your chin up and that bunch in line.

Tell everyone I said thanks for the cards and am sorry I hadn't sent some in return, but I just never get around to things I should do. Just another habit of mine I guess.

Tell Lawrence not to catch all the game up around there, but just to get most of it and to watch that high power team he is supposed to have, better still to put two bridles on them.

I am going to send along a receipt that you can give to Rose to keep. I have had it for a long time now, but never sent it to her.

Well, I will be signing off for now, but remember don't you and Ruthie make a sissy out John L. Jr. and take care of yourself and don't work too hard.

Tell everyone I said hello and for Betty and Norie not to get smart or I will settle them when I see them again. Your toughest son, Bob.

(*The Americans are still on the attack on Guadalcanal.*)

January 14, 1943 - It is 6:00 A.M. on this Thursday at Fort Bliss.
Hi Dad:

Well, here I am bright and early. I suppose right now you are getting up, which would be about 4 back there, but it so happens that I am on guard and so have a little spare time till I am relieved at 2 this afternoon.

I hope everything is going as well up there as it is here for me, and that you are feeling okay and able to keep those hoodlums on line. We have been kept pretty darn busy here, so I have really neglected to write many letters, but hell I haven't anything to write about.

I suppose I could write of the weather and it has been fairly cool, and we did have about 1 ½ inches of snow about a week ago, but it just stayed on till noon except up on the mountains where it hangs on most of the time.

On Sunday, I did see a two man Jap submarine that they captured some where and brought into the post for people to look at. And they use it as a specimen of what the enemy has [in order] to sell war-bonds and stamps. It really was quite a weapon, only it had its disadvantages as to speed, range and etc.

Have you heard from Stanley lately? I wonder how he likes Texas by now. [What does Stanley (Peanuts) think when Bob calls himself the toughest soldier in Texas?] ...

Your son, Bob

(*The Japanese continue a stubborn resistance as they withdraw on Guadalcanal and New Guinea. Roosevelt and Churchill begin the Casablanca Conference today.*)

February 7, 1943 - It is 10:00 on this Sunday at Fort Bliss
Hi Dad:

I suppose by now you will think I am a helluva guy for not writing sooner, but I guess you can put it to one of three things. (1) Nothing to write of (2) Too darn lazy (3) I have been sort of busy doing nothing... I have been just sitting here thinking of all the changes that must have come about there at home, thru all this rationing of food, gas and etc. And who knows, maybe it will help.

Anyway, there is nothing to be done about it by any individual except take it... As always, Your son, Bob.

(The Japanese are gradually evacuating Guadalcanal on the "Tokyo Night Express," which is attacked by aircraft from Henderson Field.)

March 20, 1943 - It is Saturday night at Fort Bliss, and Bob writes to Ruthie. He is thankful for the birthday cake (his 28th birthday is tomorrow), and he humorously twits Ruthie and Malon about the latter's draft prospects.

Hi Snot:

Well, as I am staying in tonight and have a few minutes to kill, I decided to write you in answer to your letter I received on Thursday. And also to thank both yourself and Rose for sending me the cake which arrived today. And it really was good. And so the fellows also said thanks a lot. And so you tell Rose the same thing, for I may not get to write to her, for hell I haven't anything to write about.

Harriet's kids sent me some cookies yesterday, so I must write them for sure.

I hope you are wrong about Malon getting drafted in May. But if he does, he could do a helluva lot worse than getting under me, tho I don't think I would want him for he couldn't take this racket, he is too puny. And [he] would be crying or gold bricking all the time. But by using force and etc. on him over a period of time, I could perhaps make at least half a man out of him tho that is da-- doubtful, for you have henpecked and pampered him the last couple of years, so I can't blame him too much for what he is.

And you of all people talking of my appetite and also of the blonde, as you want to call her. People would think I was a hog, but I do pretty well at that....

Did I tell you about the new Co. of W.A.A.C.s that moved in here. Boy, are they some steppers when it comes to this army stuff. Perhaps you had better not let Malon read this or he might enlist...

(The New Zealanders in Tunisia valiantly advance against the Axis. A spring thaw in Russia halts any vehicles. Losses on both sides are over a million dead at this point.)

March 29, 1943 - Army censorship must have become more strict for the 3rd Chemical Mortar Battalion. Bob's letters are fewer, and they contain vague sentences as to what he is doing.

Hi Dad:

Perhaps by now you will think I have forgotten how to write, but I guess you will have to put it down to just plain laziness on my part, and of having nothing to write about as is always the case with me.

I had a letter from Loss a while back telling me of the new boy. Stanley Eugene [born on Feb. 28] I think he said his name was. Also heard from Maggie and Val and they are struggling along as always. Bob is the same as ever - still contrary as only an Irishman can be... Your son, Bob.

(The British are now pushing the German army back in North Africa. The RAF bombs Berlin in a night attack.)

The 3rd Chemical Mortar Battalion arrived in Boston on April 20th and were soon on board the USS Orizaba and headed to Oran, Algeria. The Orizaba had made six trips to France in 1918, carrying over 15,000 troops. Now, in its second war this transport ship left Boston with a capacity of 2,938 troops plus its crew. When the ship arrived at Oran on April 28th, the British, with allied assistance, had the German army cornered at Tunis. On May 9th, the Germans unconditionally surrendered to the allies. Meanwhile, the Orizaba headed for the United States with German POW's, and then headed back to Oran. [41]

Sgt. Hillard's outfit was attached to the U.S. 3rd Infantry Division in the area near Bizerte and began to train for the invasion of Sicily. Bob jotted a brief note to his father on May 14.

"Just a line to let you know I am okay and still in here pitching. Am in North Africa and it seems to be quite a interesting place. Tell the rest I said hello and to write when they find the time. Take care of yourself and don't work too hard and I'll be seeing you sometime. So long for now. Your son, Bob."

July 5, 1943 - For over two months, Bob's mortar squad prepared for the invasion of Sicily, called "Operation Husky." There are "Problem" rehearsals, practice in boarding and unloading from ships, working with the infantry units to which they were attached, and learning more about Sicily's geography than they ever dreamed existed. Five days before the launch, Bob writes to his father.

"Well, I suppose by this time that you are thinking I must have run out of paper and ink. But that not being the case, I will just have to blame it on my being too lazy and also too busy to write.

Everything is going okay with me here, and so that means I am as sassy and mean as ever, only of course you don't know a thing about that.

Tell Betty I received her letter and was really glad to hear from her, and for her to write again even without no answer.

By reading the letters, I gather that everyone is doing okay over there. At least all feeling well and getting around.

Tell everyone I said hello and take care of yourself and don't work too hard. For I'll be seeing you some of these days. So long for now. Your son, Bob."

On this same day, the USS Orizaba and other transports leave various ports in North Africa to form convoys of ships. By early light on July 10, the United States transports lie off Gela, Sicily and are disembarking the troops into the landing craft. Operation Husky is underway.

Sicily is shaped somewhat like a pork chop with the bone on the right (east) and the meaty part on the left (west). The plan was for the British under Montgomery to land on the southeast side of the island and to proceed up the "bone side" to Catania, pass the huge volcanic eminence of Mt. Etna, and take the port of Messina - about 111 miles in a straight line. Only about two kilometers across the Strait of Messina lies the Italian mainland.

Gen. Patton's 7th Army was to protect the British left flank. In the process, it was hoped that the Germans and Italians would be cut off and destroyed. The aggressive, competitive, and glory-seeking Patton had no intention of letting his Americans play second fiddle to the British, especially the pompous Montgomery. The 7th Army headed for Palermo on the northwest coast of the "pork chop" - about 83 miles to the northwest of Gela. In spite of poor roads, hilly terrain, mine fields, German panzers, and good defensive fighting by the enemy, Patton's troops moved into Palermo on July 20.

Meanwhile, on the road to Messina, the British became stalled by the German resistance and the massive Mt. Vesuvius. The twisting, rugged coastal highway from Palermo to Messina is about 138 miles. The 7th Army swung along the coast to the east. The race with "Monty" was on.

July 23, 1943 - On this Friday, Bob Hillard finds time to write to his dad.

Hi-ya Dad,

Just a few short lines to let you know I am still okay and as mean and stubborn as ever, as only you should know.

I am now in Sicily and did help take part in the invasion, so perhaps [I] am not so useless after all in this game.

Tell Ruth I received her letter and was glad to hear that you and the rest are okay and feeling fine, but for her to quit bragging about that boy of theirs for he couldn't be as smart as she writes of. And tell the rest I will try to write some time, especially Johnnie and Stanley.

As there is nothing to write of, I will close. So take care of yourself and tell everyone I said hello and I'll be seeing you some time. So long for now, and I will write whenever possible.

Your son, Bob

(Also on the 23rd, the Italian government deposed Benito Mussolini as their Duce. Three days later, this event caused the allied command to order Eisenhower to make plans for the invasion of the Italian mainland at Salerno.)

With dogged fighting, excellent engineering, and amphibious end runs, the Americans moved toward Messina. On the morning of August 17, elements of the 3rd Infantry Division entered Messina, and Brig. Gen. William Eagles humorously remarked that reinforcements of the 7th Army were sent in "to see that the British did not capture the city from us after we had taken it." It was Patton who accepted the city's surrender. [42]

In 38 days the allies have overrun the island, killed or wounded 29,000 enemy soldiers and captured over 140,000 more. On the negative side, the Americans suffered 2,237 dead and 6,544 wounded or captured. The British losses were 12,843 casualties with 2,721 dead. Worse yet, the Germans skillfully escaped across the Strait of Messina to the mainland and German reinforcements were streaming into northern Italy.

August 18, 1943 - One day after the fall of Messina, Bob writes to his father.

Hi Ya Dad:

Just a note to let you know I am still okay and still in here pitching. Only hope that you are feeling as well as I.

Tell Betty and Alice that some of these times I will try and answer their letters, but to write anyway. Also for Alice not to eat too many of the vegetables out of her victory garden or she will lose her girlish figure.

I must close for now as I know nothing to write of. So take care of yourself and try not to work too hard, and I'll be seeing you. So long till next time. Your son, Bob.

From the outset, the Italian Campaign was hampered by conflicting strategies. The invasion of France - Operation Overlord - was still the top priority of the high command, thus the demand for men and materiel was allocated there first. If Italy and its airfields could not be easily wrested from the Germans, at least their divisions would be tied down and unable to fight in France.

The Italian government signed a secret armistice on September 3 and officially surrendered on the 8th. However, the political and military situation was in a state of chaos, since the Royalist Government had fled Rome and left a leadership vacuum. The Italian Army was split. Some troops and officers favored fighting for the allies, others for the Germans. Yet, the Germans distrusted their former Axis partners, and thousands of Italian soldiers were sent to the Fatherland to be detained in factories and work camps. In some cases, the SS massacred the officers of Italian units. In addition, Royalist and communist partisans fought the enemy and each other.

Nevertheless, aided by the rugged terrain, the German Army was able to establish several nearly impregnable defensive lines across the Italian peninsula. Many rivers course from the Apennine Mountains to the sea; and when the Germans blew up the bridges and mined the roads, each allied crossing cost many casualties. Along the coastline were several extensive marshy areas, which prevented movement. Inland lay mountains 6,000 feet high with steep, rocky slopes, cliffs, and ridges which the Germans expertly fortified. Barren rock prevented soldiers from digging foxholes, and if a shell exploded on the rocks, the flying stone fragments were as deadly as the steel shrapnel. Should the allied advance take a mountain or ridge, another steep valley, river, and mountain awaited them on the other side. Inland from Salerno are some hills ranging from 140-400 feet. Eighteen miles to the east is Mount Cervialto, which rises to about 6,000 feet, and on the road north to Naples lies the 4,202 feet mass of Mt. Vesuvius.

In the early morning hours of September 9, 1943, Gen. Mark Clark's Fifth Army assaulted the beaches in the Gulf of Salerno. Some hills up to 400 ft. in elevation had to be wrested from the Germans. As the Fifth Army sent men and materiel and the British advanced slowly over the rugged terrain at the bottom of the boot, the Germans withdrew their troops and panzers from the southern end of the peninsula and concentrated on the Salerno beachhead. A strong German counter-attack on the 13th had the Americans on the ropes. During the night two battalions of the 82nd Airborne Division dropped into the beachhead. American artillery, naval and air support, and the landing of the British 7th Armored Division stemmed the German advance. [48]

September 10, 1943 - Bob Hillard and the 3rd Chemical Mortar Battalion did not land with the assault troops at Salerno. On this day, Bob surely had plenty to write about, but his sense of duty and army censorship prevented anything more than the following generic letter to his dad. Still, it was his way of checking in and letting the home folks know that he was all right. Also, it has been about a year since Bob has signed his letters with "your toughest son," and now he uses a conventional closing.

Hi Dad:

Well as before, I will try to get in my word or two even if I have to do it in writing and tho I haven't anything to write about.

I am still doing okay as far as I know and feeling fine and just as mean and sassy and also stubborn as only a Hillard can be, tho of course I couldn't ask you to give your opinion of that. Anyway, laying all joking aside, I hope you're feeling better and by all means chin up of course, tho I know you are doing that. "Now look who is giving advice." And just keep in mind that we are going on that "binge."

I must say so-long for now, so tell the rest I said hello and take care of yourself and don't work too hard.

As always, Bob

(A similar letter was written to his dad on September 21st.)

October 2, 1943 - Bob writes to his dad.

"... Just a line to let you know that I am still kicking and as mean and sassy as ever. Was glad to hear that you are feeling better, and so I take it for granted that you must have reformed from your old habits. But you will have to go some to keep ahead of your youngest son. Tell Rose when you see her again that I sent my wrist watch home to be repaired and for her to write and tell me when and if it gets there. Also tell the rest I said hello and for them to write, and by the way let me know how Johnnie and Stan are making out. So long for now and take care of yourself..."

(*The U.S. 3rd Division was advancing to the Volturno River north of Naples.*)

October 20, 1943 - As the 3rd Chemical Battalion prepares to join the forces that are slugging it out with the Germans along the Volturno River, Bob Hillard writes to his dad.

"... It seems as tho I have been sort of forgetting you in my letter writing, and of course that will never do, for you may decide to put my chair and plate away for keeps and that would be disastrous. So, here goes tho I have no news to write of, I may as well start with telling you that I am feeling okay and only hope that you are feeling as well.

I had a letter from Savalla today, and she was telling me of seeing you and the rest, so by that I understand that everyone is okay and still pitching.

Tell Lenora to drop me a line and give me a hint of the news, and also Betty for I suppose the rest are too much occupied with other things to write. Although my answers are slow in coming. I am going to send a picture along of a couple of the boys and myself, something you can scare the kids with.

Well, I must be saying so long for now, so keep your chin up and take care of yourself and I'll do the same.

Bob.

Oh, and by the way, how is that namesake of yours getting along these days?

October 22, 1943 - John Hillard would not get to read this letter from his son. After supper John retired to another room with his grandson and namesake. After a short time, young John L. tottered up to his mother and said that Papa needed a glass of water. When Ruthie went to check on her father, she found that he had died. After years of congestive heart failure, 71-year old John Lawrence Hillard had a fatal heart attack.

Norie Hillard Foster: "His favorite grandson was John Lawrence Spangler (my sister Ruthie's son), I guess because he was named after his grand dad. The day of Dad's funeral I remember coming home from the service, and Johnny Spangler climbing up in Dad's favorite chair and saying, 'Read to me, Papa.' It was really sad and brought tears to a lot of eyes."

The 3rd Chemical Mortar Battalion arrived in Italy on October 29, 1943 to participate in the Naples-Foggia Campaign, which began on November 1st and lasted a grueling 82 days and cold nights in the mountains of Central Italy. The battalion provided mortar fire for the French Expeditionary Corps, which consisted of the 1st Algerian Mountain Division, 2nd Moroccan Division, 3rd Algerian Division, 4th Moroccan Division. Fighting from one steep ridge to the next, the allies pushed the Germans back to their main defensive line, the Gustav Line, which was anchored on Cassino. [43]

An indication of the vicious fighting at Cerasuolo, Italy is given in the account of Medal of Honor winner, Pvt. Shizuya Hayashi of the famous 442nd American-Japanese regiment. The action occurred on November 29, 1943. "... During an assault on high ground held by the Germans, Hayashi rose alone in the face of grenade, rifle and machine-gun fire, fired his automatic weapon from the hip with the aid of a shoulder sling, and charged the machine-gun nest. He took the position, killing seven men and two more as they fled. After a platoon advance of 200 yards from his point, an enemy anti-aircraft position opened up on the platoon. Hayashi returned fire, killing nine, taking four prisoners and forcing the remainder of the force to flee from the hill." [44]

December 29, 1943 - During a lull in the action, Sgt. Howard Thompson, Bob's good friend, decided to write to Ruth Spangler.
Hello Ruth and family,

I do not know just how or what to write to anyone that I have not met, but by knowing Bob so long it seems that I do know you.

You know how Bob is to everyone, and he has not changed

since he left home, and I don't think he will.

I got a Xmas package from my girlfriend and it contained a cake, and as you could guess I was boasting about it, and he started as usual, that he had a sister that could beat anyone cooking a cake, and we argued and argued, so it ended up by me writing this letter.

Will you write and tell us how the family is getting along. I remain a friend.

Howard

January 1, 1944 - Bob writes to his sister.

Hi Ruthie and all:

Having decided that on this date and all and being on sort of a break, I might as well write a few letters and finally got around to writing this last one. Laying all foolishness aside, how is everyone around there including the Spangler tribe, which reminds me that someone told me I was going to be Uncle again. I see there will be a group of spoilt urchins around home with me not there to teach them. But perhaps a couple of years will not make so much difference. Oh by the way, believe it or not, I was bragging up your cooking ability and Tommy wouldn't quite believe me and said he would find out for himself, so I think he wrote you tho I don't know what he said. But anyway, if it is at all possible, you can't let me down. Good-bye for now and write if you find the time, and tell Betty to drop me a line.

Bob

[*On January 5, 1944, the FEC and Bob's outfit began a push toward the Rapido River north of Monte Cassino.*]

January 12, 1944 - It was about noon, and a bone-tired Lt. Quentin Unger was asleep in his tent, which was pitched next to a house. Unger's unit had spent the previous cold night firing a night mission. About 200 yards away was Col. Edgar D. Stark's company headquarters, where Col. Stark had called all unit commanders to inform them of imminent R and R. Unfortunately, the commanders failed to institute diligent regard for mass parking, and four or five jeeps were clustered around the house. It offered an excellent target of opportunity for the German Luftwaffe.

German Messerschmitt ME-109's zoomed down on Cerasuolo and dropped their bombs on the building surrounded by the jeeps. One of the drops was a direct hit on headquarters, which completely demolished the building. In his tent, Lt. Unger was lifted six inches off the ground by the impact. Hearing the shrieks of wounded men and seeing the smoke and dust, Unger and a group of men sprinted to the HQ site. They began to dig with their hands to remove the debris and found several survivors. Nevertheless, Col. Stark, four company commanders, and 15 enlisted men, including Sgt. Robert Hillard, were dead. The scene was then "turned over to the graves registration people to take care of the dead." For Unger, it was the worst single casualty loss of the war for the group he was with, and the day would be forever etched on his mind.

On the following day, the 3rd Chemical Mortar Battalion was pulled off the front lines for R and R.

Like the eddies from a stone cast into tranquil waters, death often has a rippling effect. The sad news travels in all directions and touches everyone in its path to varying degrees. The watery ripples fade into the tranquil scene again, but in real life the ripples of a loved one's death remain frozen in time. More than sixty years after the death of Bob Hillard, there is still an anguish in the faces and voices of those who knew him.

In January 1944, Norie Hillard was employed in Akron at the Goodyear Aircraft Company as a "Rosie the Riveter." The pay was good, and one had the satisfaction of doing something for the defense of the United States. One cold winter day, the telephone rang. It was her older sister Rose who had some bad news, but she did not want to talk about it over the telephone. Norie immediately took the bus to Goodyear Heights where Rose lived. It was there that she learned of her brother's death. Years later, Norie remembered that she "cried for days."

It also fell to Rose's lot to notify her young friend, Lucille Anderson, of Bob Hillard's death. The hope of having Lucille for a sister-in-law were shattered.

Twenty-four year old Lucille Anderson was devastated. Her sister June remembered that Lucille's "sobs were awful." In time, Lucille immersed herself in her church work as a Sunday School teacher. She eventually left the Central Bank and hired on at the Ohio Bell Company, where she worked her way into a supervisor's position. She lived with her parents and cared for them until Esther died in 1966 and Henry in 1978. Lucille then moved to an apartment.

After the war, Lucille never married. She had a few dates, but there was only one Bob Hillard. One story is that Bob gave her a china set for an engagement present, and that every year on their engagement anniversary she would take the dishes from the shelves for a dinner.

When Stanley Hillard was called into the service, Bob's sister-in-law Luella (Stanley's wife) roomed with Rose. Louella recalled Rose saying that "Lucille grieved and grieved. Finally, one day Lucille's mother was at her place, picked up Bob's picture and said, 'I think we'd better get rid of this.' Lucille grabbed the picture and literally spit the words out to her mother, 'Don't you ever touch that picture again.' She was just furious and that was the end of that.... When Rose came to visit Ohio from Arizona long years later, she and Louella drove to Cuyahoga Falls to visit Lucille who was retired and living in a rather 'stark' (according to Louella) apartment there. She remembers Lucille as being very religious (a large picture of Jesus on the wall) and still faithful to Bob's memory."

For all of the 405,399 U.S. casualties in World War II and their relatives and friends, what if the war had not snuffed out all of their tomorrows, opportunities, hopes, and dreams? What if Bob Hillard had survived the war and returned home an able-bodied man? Lucille would have looked lovely in a white wedding dress, attached to her proud father's arm, and walking down the aisle in some small church. She could have passed on her love of reading and embroidery to her daughters. Her children would have known the majestic strains of Puccini's "Un bel di" or "Nessun dorma." Bob would have taught his sons how to hunt and fish and how to play basketball. He and Lucille could have smilingly watched their wide-eyed children by the Christmas tree eagerly opening their presents. They could have sat on a porch swing, holding hands, and watching the changing pastel hues of a summer evening. In time, Bob could have had a grand-child climb onto his lap for a story, and at the conclusion hear the loving words, "Papa, you're the best."

Lucille was fifty-seven when she took early retirement from Ohio Bell in 1976. She loved to travel, and on one trip she, June, and June's son visited Italy. June asked Lucille if she wanted to visit Bob's grave at Nettuno, but Lucille refused to go there.

Lucille E. Anderson, 78, passed away Monday, March 16, 1998.

Hillard and a friend.

A family friend stands next to Bob Hillard's grave marker at Nettuno, Italy.

Lucille Anderson
Dec. 11, 1919 - Mar. 16, 1998

Bob and Lucille

CHAPTER NOTES
"Your Toughest Son"

1. Lenora Belle Hillard Foster, "Memories."
2. John Greenleaf Whittier, "Telling The Bees," web-books.com...
3. Joseph E. Persico, *Eleventh Month, Eleventh Day, Eleventh Hour.* (New York: Random House, 2004), 236-37, 259-60.
4. Lenora Hillard Foster, "Memories."
5. Francis A. March, *History of the World War.* (Chicago: The United Publishers of the United States and Canada, 1919), 265-279.
6. John McCrae, "In Flanders Fields." en.wikipedia.org/wiki/In Flander's Fields.
7. Persico, *11th Month...* 51-52.
8. *Ravenna Republican,* (Ravenna, Ohio), March 25, 1915. Ford advertisement.
9. *Akron Beacon Journal,* (Akron, Ohio), "Farmers War On Auto Speeders", March 22, 1915.
10. *Beacon Journal,* "Willard To Have Plenty Of Backers," March 22, 1915.
11. *The Evening Record,* (Ravenna, Ohio), November 11, 1925. KKK advertisement.
12. *Ravenna Republican,* March 25, 1915, p 1.
13. *Ravenna Republican,* April 1, 1915. Randolph local news.
14. Matilda Keil Staats, the author's mother, related the anti-German story. Bob Hillard's trip to the county fair is from Lenora Hillard Foster's "Memories."
15. *Akron Beacon Journal,* "Need 91 Millions To Pay Expenses Of Buckeye State," March 21, 1921, p 1.
16. Wikipedia encyclopedia, 1921.
17. *Akron Beacon Journal,* March 21, 1921.
18. Wikipedia encyclopedia, 1921.
19. Lenora Hillard Foster, "Memories."
20. Wikipedia encyclopedia, 1928.
21. *Evening Record,* March 21, 1928. Chevrolet advertisement.
22. Robert Foster interview. Bob worked on the Hartville muck farms as a youth.
23. Wikipedia encyclopedia, 1928; *Evening Record,* March 21, 1921.
24. Wikipedia, 1928.
25. *Evening Record,* "Sunday School Party Is Held At Randolph ," March 23, 1928.
26. *The Speedomter.* Portage County high school yearbook. 1932.
27. Robert Hillard, 1932 Randolph High School Senior Class Last Will and Testament. Courtesy of Lenora Hillard Foster.
28. *Speedometer.* 1932.
29. "The Bonus March (May-July, 1932)," pbs.org/wgbh...

30. *Evening Record*, "Hitler Asks To Be Named Dictator," March 21, 1933, p 1.
31. Interview with June Anderson Buttermore on Feruary 7 and 9, 2006.
32. *Akron Beacon Journal*, "Rush To Wed Still On; Draft Given As Cause," September 4, 1940.
33. *Beacon Journal*, September 9, 1940.
34. *Beacon Journal*, "Harter Fights For Draft Bill," September 5, 1940. p 1.
35. *Beacon Journal*, "Churchill Sees Peril In Ship-Base Trade," September 5, 1940, p 1.
36. *Beacon Journal*, September 14, 1940. p 1.
37. *Beacon Journal*, "Oct. 16 Date Set For Call," September 14, 1940, p 1-2.
38. *Beacon Journal*, "Delay Irks Draft Board," October 11, 1940.
39. *Beacon Journal*, Draft Appeal Board Named," and "Tom Mix Killed In Auto Mishap," October 13, 1940, p 1.
40. *The Evening Record*, October 17, 1940.
41. *Beacon Journal*, October 16, 1940, p 1.
42. Hal Buell, *World War II Album, The Complete Chronicle Of The World's Greatest Conflict*. (New York: Tess Press, 2002), All of the italicized additions to Robert Hillard's letters are derived from this source.
43. Military.com, "3d Chemical Battalion."
44. Tioh.hqda.pentagon.mil... "3rd Chemical Battalion."
45. 1biblio.org/hyperwar/USN/ships... "DANFS: USS Resaca (AP-24).
46. Army.mil/cmh-pg/brochures... "WWII Campaigns:Sicily," p 12-13.
47. *Ibid*.
48. Worldwar2history.info/Italy, "Introduction to the Italian Campaign.
49. 4point2.org/3cmb. "3rd Chemical Mortar."
50. Katonk.com/442nd/news... Medal of Honor awards to members of the 442nd RCT.
51. Lt. Quentin Unger. The account of the action at Cerasuolo on January 12, 1944 as related to his son Chris Unger.

CHAPTER TWO
"YOUR LOVING SON, ROBERT"

Part I
Hello, Frisco

In response to President Lincoln's first call for troops, William Jackson Francisco mustered into Company A of the 2nd Wisconsin on June 30, 1861. The 27-year old Francisco was a diehard Union man and a proud member of the famous Iron Brigade of the West. Of all the 2, 000 regiments in the Union Army, the 2nd Wisconsin would suffer the greatest percentage loss in killed and wounded. At Gettysburg 77% of this brave and patriotic regiment would be gunned down. However, after the bloodbath at Antietam in 1862 and prior to the Chancellorsville Campaign in 1863, Francisco was having second thoughts as he sat in the Quartermaster's tent and penned a letter to his brother Charles. It was a raw March 2nd at Culpepper, Virginia.

"... There was 8 or 10 Rebels brought in this morning. They are coming in every day from the front. I suppose they don't like to hear that we are getting so many men more soldiers coming into our Army. I tell you we are getting a large Army here now.

Now let me give you a little advice. If you know where you are well off, you will stay at home and either go to School or teach School, one or the other. One may think it's fun to be a Soldier, but I tell you, you are better off there [even] if you have to work for a dollar a month than you would here a-Soldiering for $13 per month. You say you was seized with a fit of Patriotism, Love of country, etc. But I think you are some like the rest of the men that have enlisted under the Bounty call. It is for the money [which] induced you to enlist. I think if you had no more inducement than we had when we come, you would not be so anxious to come. Think of the difference in the times now than it was when we come. We come for $11 a month and no bounty. Would you like to come for that? ..."[1]

Robert Edwin Francisco was probably as hardy and patriotic as his grandfather with the Army of the Potomac; and like his grandfather, on this cold, raw day in February 1941, Bob Francisco would have liked being elsewhere. Since registering for the peacetime draft on October 16, 1940, Bob had kept an anxious eye on his draft status. Coming out of the Great Depression, some young men may have welcomed the change of scenery and the $10.52 per month that the Army offered, but Bob was content with his situation on the farm in Randolph, Ohio.

The farm on Laubert Road required much hard outdoor work - plowing, sowing, harvesting, maintaining equipment, etc. for the 160 acres. There was a herd of 60 cattle, 32 of which had to be milked by hand. However, farm life was not all a drudge. A young man could hunt and trap with his friends, play cards and eat popcorn with the family, and during the hard times chow on a farm wasn't bad. Bob's mother raised Plymouth Rock chickens for the eggs and meat. What she sold went for clothes or to make dresses from feed sacks. By 1941, Bob had a car and was employed at Monarch Rubber in Hartville. Army life could not be as good as this.

Bob's luck did not last for long. In the January 28 induction call, seven "conscriptees" were rejected when they failed the physical in Cleveland. He found himself among the seven replacements - one volunteer and six draftees. [2]

On Thursday morning, February 13, 1941, Bob reluctantly appeared at the bus depot in Kent. Nattily dressed in a suit and tie, overcoat, and scarf, Bob jauntily doffed his hat as the newspaper's camera flashed. That evening, the group photograph appeared on the front page of the *Evening Record*. [3]

Due to the events at his birth, Bob seemed destined for this bus ride to the Cleveland induction center. When baby Bob entered the world on September 11, 1915 in Copley, Ohio, the "Great War" was raging in Europe. As deadly and destructive as it was, who could have imagined that this "War to end all wars" would arise from the ashes like the Phoenix and repeat itself in a more virulent form twenty-five years later.

In September 1915 the Russians under Czar Nicholas confronted the Germans in the East, and the allies began a bloody offensive in the West. In the United States President Wilson was trying to maintain a neutral position, and local opinion supported him. "Somewhere between [William Jennings] Bryan's Peace at any price and [Teddy] Roosevelt's Our Rights at any cost, there must be a golden medium. Wilson's keeping right along in the middle of the road seems to satisfy the majority." [4]

Under "War And Baby Killing," the *Beacon Journal* editorialized: "... The Germans in retaliation have again raided London and this time six babies have been butchered. We know in advance all about the arguments that will be used in the vain attempt to justify these acts of savagery, but not one of them can have any weight whatever... Like all wars this one is calling forth intense piety and long and loud are the prayers that ascend beseeching an All Merciful God for His protection. The horrible inconsistency of the thing would appall the bloodiest barbarian that ever cumbered the earth with the corpses of the blood lust. We can imagine the spirit of old Attila hovering over Berlin, listening to the prayers being offered up as the beginning of a Zeppelin raid on London that has at the end of it the mangled bodies of the defenseless babies!..." [5]

Of primary concern for the President was the German U-boat activity. Back on May 7th, off the coast of Ireland the *Lusitania* sank in eighteen minutes after being struck by a German torpedo. There were some Americans among the 1,198 dead. This meant that unarmed merchant ships were no longer protected by the rules of war. [6]

Frederick H. Seymour, a Portage County resident and advertising manager for the Quaker Oats Company in Great Britain, related his experiences to the *Ravenna Republican*. "... He said that if ever the Stars and Stripes looked good to him it was when as his American ship was passing through the war waters and the zone of the submarines, the Captain displayed a very large flag of the Republic and illuminated both sides with electric lights so that the commanders of submarines could see its nationality...

You no doubt have seen in the papers that London was the victim of air raids on Tuesday and Wednesday nights of this week. You will, therefore, be interested in having some of the details based on personal experience.

On Tuesday night I only heard the reports of the anti-aircraft guns, but on Wednesday night I had a front seat for the show. I had dined with Weiner and was taking the bus at Piccadilly Circus about

10:45 when there was a sound of explosions, and a zeppelin was shown up very clearly by the search lights. The night was very dark but clear, and I should say that the zeppelin was about ten thousand feet up. It was really a beautiful sight against the dark sky and looked something like a gigantic goldfish. Guns were shooting at it from various points and we could see the shells bursting all around the air-ship. Most of them, however, appeared to fall far short, although viewed at an angle it was, of course, impossible to say how far the shells came from the ship. At any rate they evidently did not damage it in any way. The ship was a half mile or more east of Regent Street and traveling practically parallel with it. When my bus turned west at Oxford Circus the zeppelin also turned west up Holborn and Oxford Street. All lights were turned out and I must say that I have seldom ridden in a motor car faster than we traveled that night on the bus. When we turned north at Orchard Street, the zeppelin also turned northward and ran parallel with us for some distance and then bore off to the northeast; all the time the search lights were fixed on the ship and shells kept breaking around it. It finally disappeared behind clouds and evidently did not make a return trip over the western portion of the city.

The next morning I saw a great deal of the damage that was done in the city. A bomb had been dropped on a motor bus near Liverpool Street Station and some sixteen or eighteen people killed. The windows had been blown out of all the buildings in the immediate vicinity, in fact, the building immediately next to the United States Consulate Office was badly damaged..." [7]

On the home front, life continued as usual. Thanks to the growing popularity of the automobile, Randolph Township was constructing a concrete road, although much of the work involved teamsters with powerful teams of horses. The new Rio Six was selling for $1,250, but the average income for all industries including farm income amounted to only $633. [8]

Memories of the Civil War were still fresh in the minds of the public. On September 11th, the front page of *Beacon Journal* carried a group photograph of white-bearded and mustachioed veterans. The grand occasion was the 50th reunion of Battery D, First Regiment, Ohio Volunteer Light Artillery, which was meeting in Cuyahoga Falls. Over in Ravenna, another Civil War veteran was struck by a car of the outgoing interurban railway. However, "He is congratulating himself, as well as receiving the congratulations of his friends that the accident was not attended by more serious results." [9]

In Akron, show biz was going strong. "Supreme Vaudeville" reigned at the Colonial Theater. The multi-talented "top liners" on the bill were the Rigoletto Brothers, a set of twins who specialized as "singers, dancers, plastic posers, strong men, acrobats, aerial artists, instrumentalists, necromancers, travesty artists, and illusionists." Second billing went to the Alexander Kids, "a troupe of prancing, dancing youngsters whose merry antics carry you back to happy childhood days." At the Orpheum, the featured silent film starred Theda Bara, "The Vampire of the Screen," who could be seen in "The Devil's Daughter." The slick advertiser referred to the film as "that much talked of film which was twice rejected by the censor board." One could watch the two features at the Strand Theater in comfort. "The air washer, one of the Strand features, is proving its worth these warm days. It changes, purifies, and cools the air every four minutes." In addition, the Strand featured a $12,000 organ, which Mrs. Katherine Bruot played for the audience. [10]

For baby Bob Francisco to reach adulthood, he would have to escape the childhood diseases that still periodically plagued the nation. On September 11th, the *Beacon Journal* was concerned about the "small infantile paralysis epidemic" in the city. In the past few weeks, almost a dozen deaths were attributed to the disease. Not knowing the cause of the disease or the cure, blame for the epidemic was assigned to children ignoring the quarantine signs. Children of the afflicted household were allowed to play in the streets, and others were allowed to visit. [11]

In 1915, Irving Berlin wrote seven noteworthy tunes, one being "Hello, Frisco."

Around 1921, the Francisco family moved from Copley to the farm on Laubert Road in Randolph. There were new fields, woods, and streams for a small boy to explore. For the six year old Robert Francisco it could have been a new world.

The local news touted the Randolph Fair to be held on September 23 and 24. "Efforts are being made to make this the best fair ever held in Randolph. Dinner will be served on the ground." (Knowing the humor of the Franciscos, one of them might have wondered why they didn't serve dinner on a plate.) Robert would soon attend the new school building, which was nearing completion. "There will be two, large comfortable rooms, which will accommodate four grades, fifth, sixth, seventh, and eighth." The Christian Church sponsored a festival in the park by the town hall. "Good music was furnished by the Randolph Orchestra." However, life did not always fill the requirements of a Norman Rockwell setting. One local male "again had the misfortune of being struck by an auto while walking in the middle of the road Tuesday night. This time breaking [an] arm and leg." [12]

In September 1921, one news story that momma and poppa did not want their children to see or ask questions about was the Fatty Arbuckle scandal. Roscoe Arbuckle, the rotund silent screen comic, was at the peak of his career when he became the trailblazer for Hollywood criminal proceedings. Fatty allegedly held a wild party where he raped and killed a young actress. After two hung juries, he was finally acquitted, but the scandal ruined his career. [13]

Whereas "Fatty's" star had gone out, that of Tom Mix, the cowboy, was ascending. In the "Photoplays" section of the *Beacon Journal* the National Theater touted their headliner: "Tom Mix, the Fox star, is noted as a crack shot with rifle or pistol. He certainly hit the bullseye of popular favor in his latest picture, "The Big Town Round-up"... Mix in action is a veritable embodiment of speed..." [14]

Times were certainly changing. The *Ravenna Republican* gave front page attention to the fact that women were now serving on Portage County juries for the first time. [15]

A somber note was struck on November 11th, Armistice Day, when President Harding dedicated the Tomb of the Unknown Soldier at Arlington National Cemetery.

On Bob Francisco's thirteenth birthday President Coolidge was concluding a western trip by boarding a train in Chicago for Washington. Meanwhile, one of Al Capone's gang was staying in Chicago - permanently. "Gangland and police rubbed shoulders today at the funeral here of Tony Lombardo, slain lieutenant of "Scarface Al" Capone. Gangland, including Capone and his picked bodyguard of gun men was present. Police at least 100 strong mingled with the immense crowd that had turned out to witness one of gangland's greatest funerals." [16] One just knew that vendettas and grander funerals were to come.

On September 11, 1928 air races were the rage for fame, glory, and cash. One could only marvel at the progress of flight since the Wright brothers' first flight 25 years ago. Today, news of the national air race came across the wires from Los Angeles. "Earl Rowland, who brought his plane down at the flying field here at 2:30 yesterday afternoon, is in all probability the winner of the $5,000 first prize. [Almost four times the working man's average yearly income.] He led the field practically all the way from New York. He said today that he believed his flying time was approximately 22 hours." In another segment of the national air race competition in L.A., an army lieutenant was not so fortunate. While flying upside down, his engine stalled and the airplane plummeted into a field directly in front of the grandstand. The pilot did not survive the crash.[17]

Erich Maria Remarque was writing the classic *All Quiet on the Western Front*." The book would be published the next year, and in 1930 it would be an Oscar-winning film. Based on his experiences in the German army during the Great War, the graphic anti-war statement did not endear him to the rising Nazi Party. The book was banned and burned in 1933. Even after Remarque left Germany, the enduring hatred of the Nazis for Remarque never flagged. In 1943 they beheaded his sister because of her association with the author.[18]

Bob Francisco loved the movies, and he may have been interested in what was showing in the theaters near him. At The New Kent Theater, Richard Dix and Jean Arthur were featured in "Warming Up," a "mixture of romance and baseball." Also showing was the Our Gang Comedy, "Growing Pains." On this Tuesday evening, the Kent Opera House offered two dramatic films. However, the Ohio Theater offered the slickest advertising. Chester Conklin headed the cast in "The Big Noise," "A different comedy - modern as tomorrow's tabloid - Conklin as a timid soul who was nobody's business today and the Big Noise Tomorrow." At the Ohio, Tuesday night was Bargain Night. "This ad if presented at the Box Office with one paid adult admission will admit two to the Ohio Tonight." [19]

In Randolph, the churches were full of activity and good works. The ladies of the Christian Church were serving "one of their excellent 25-cent suppers." Over at the Methodist Sunday School, two of Bob's peers, Louella and Grace Anderson, sang "It Pays to Serve Jesus." Incidentally, the offering at the service was $7.55.[20]

School life held no special charm for Bob, and he dropped out of high school. Farm life was a different matter; it was a vocation amidst the massive unemployment of the Great Depression. Money was tight, but with planning there would always be food on the table.

Edwin Elmore Francisco, Bob's dad, used the estate money he received from the sale of his father's farm in Copley to purchase the 160-acre farm in Randolph. Edwin had a penchant for homemade wine, and he had been known to buy a round or two at the White Rooster tavern. He was not always a happy drunk, and things could get pretty nasty around the house. At one time he "went for the cure," but he fell off the wagon. Yet, Edwin was a worker, and he knew everything there was to know about Holstein cattle. He kept extensive records on his registered cattle, and he acquired a Massachusetts Holstein to improve his herd. This knowledge was passed on to his sons. He and the kids did their own haying and silo-filling. Edwin owned the silo-filler and filled the silos of neighboring farms. The "big gang," sort of a co-op, only came to the Francisco farm to do the thrashing.

Like most farms in the area, there was the path to the outhouse; and water for cooking, drinking, and bathing had to be carried into the house. Alice Francisco, Bob's mom, shelled corn for the chickens, and then she put a little oil on corn cobs to start the fire in the iron stove. If the fire wasn't hot enough, Alice removed the metal lid and put her skillet directly over the flame. Nothing was thought of some chickens falling asleep near the kitchen table. Every day, either out of boredom or plain interest, Alice counted the cars that came down the road.

In the late 1930's, Bob and his brother Elmore took over the farm operations. Bob was especially proud of his team of work horses.

PART II
THE RELUCTANT WARRIOR

February 13, 1941 - From Cleveland at 6:00 P.M., the War Department sends a standardized postcard to Bob's mother. "This is to inform you that Robert E. Francisco, 35009786, has been accepted for active military service and sent to Reception Center, Ft. Benjamin

Harrison, Ind."

Later in the evening, Bob hastily jots a postcard to his mother, Mrs. Alice B. Francisco, to confirm that he has been swooped up by the military.

Dear Folks,

Well, I guess I fooled the whole bunch of you for I am on my way to Ft. Benjamin Harrison, Ind. I will write a letter a little later. I am riding through Wooster on a train right now, so if you can't read this, blame the train... Yours truly, Robert Francisco.

[* Following each of Bob's letters will be a headline or news story from *The Evening Record*, a Portage County newspaper to which his family and neighbors had access. [21] The front page headline will be in bold print. For February 13th, the headline reads **"Senate Committee Okays War Aid."** Another front page item reads: "Far East Swept By War Alarm." Americans in China are being urged to come home due to the invading and rampaging Japanese army.]

Feb. 18, 1941 – A postcard similar to the one of Feb. 13 from the War Dept., is mailed from Indianapolis to Alice Francisco. "This is to advise you that Francisco, Robert A. [sic] 35009786 has this date been assigned to 5th CASC. His post office address is Ft. Benj. Harrison Ind. This card is to be filled out for each man at Reception Center, upon assignment. He will be required to address the card and mail it to his nearest relative."

Feb. 27, 1941 – From Ft. Harrison, Bob writes a letter on military stationery to his family. The envelope is addressed to his sister Dorothy, and it is posted on the 28th at Indianapolis. A U.S. flag and soldiers appear on the envelope.

Dear Family:

Well, I got a letter from you today and I have got time to answer it now, so I guess it is a good time to do it for I guess I will go to the show tomorrow nite.

Well, I am glad to hear that Elmore got Glenn's milker and I sure would have liked to been there at the sale. Did Glen bid in [sic] the tractor?

I guess Dorothy must have sent back that cold for I feel one coming on again. They had us out rolling on the ground yesterday and it snowed last nite and we had to wade around in it this morning without any overshoes. They got our sizes lost last week one day, then they only got a few pairs & they were all too big for us fellows with a small foundation. We are to get some decent clothes one of these days, but I don't know when.

I guess I am putting one over on you. This time I am having this small piece of paper so I get done quicker.

Today is the first time I have had three good meals since I left the Reception Center, but I have had better [than] they got here.

I may get home a week from this Saturday nite, but I may not. If I do, I will let you know so Elmore can come to the bus station to get me.

Tell Elmore to hold that money for a while and I may send it for a radio because I sure need one. I would like to have you get me the prices on some of the portable battery sets.

Have you heard of anyone yet that wants a good car yet? If I don't sell it, I am going to take it with me, if I don't get too far from home.

I may write a letter to Hazel [his older sister] tonite, but if I don't, tell Delbert [Hazel's son] I said Happy Birthday, even if it is a day or so late.

I am sending a picture home that was taken over at the Reception Center by the barrack that I stayed in the first 5 days. I was on the second floor. The thing is full of negroes now. There was about 25 buildings like this in a square, and they are building more every day. Use it [the picture] to scare all the rats away.

Yours truly, Bob

["**Congressman, 6 Others Die In Air Crash; Rickenbacker Critical"** Eddie Rickenbacker, famous race car driver and America's flying ace of World War I, received extensive injuries in the plane crash near Atlanta. In other news, the Japanese government ordered its citizens out of French Indo China. The negotiations with the French were a prelude to an attack by the Japanese army.]

Mar. 6, 1941 – The novelty of military life and the change of scenery have worn thin for Pvt. Francisco. Like all the other citizen soldiers who have enjoyed freedom, Bob is finding that military regimentation has some down sides to it. He posts this letter from

Warren Pontius   Elmore Francisco
Robert Francisco   Kenny Pontius

1946

In The Army Now Bob

Indianapolis to Dorothy.
Dear Family,
   Well, I guess all my planning on coming home over the weekend all went up in the air, yesterday at noon. They made a new ruling here that no one can leave the post more than 100 miles. So that means that I probably won't be home until the middle of June or the first of July. Though I did hear that we would get three days leave at Easter, but I am not counting on it. The reason for this is just because some fellows went home and didn't get back on time and now the rest of us are to pay for it. Boy, this kind of life sure gets under my skin, especially when they won't let us go where we please when we have our time off.
   I am still loafing with this cold but I guess I will go back to work tomorrow, that is if my temperature stays down to normal, it has been from normal up to 100.3. All the doctors do is take your temperature & ask you what's wrong. Then they give you some asperin and licorish [sic] tablet and tell you to gargle with warm salt water, and that is all they do unless you get so sick you can't walk to the hospital. Then they come and get you and put you in the hospital with the cockroaches and bedbugs.
   Maybe I shouldn't speak but we have had two or three good meals this month. I heard the mess Sargent caught Hell for trying to save on the food bill and that is the reason we are getting fed better now.
   I guess if someone wants to advertise my car for $625 and no sales tax or $212 and the payments or something like that, then you can take out the expenses when the car is sold or I can sign a paper so you can get the money from the bank. Well I bet you are all taking it easy now with the chores since Elmore [his brother] got the milker to work.
   Has Elmore got his new car yet? And do you think you know who got our gas? [With gasoline in short supply, it was a target for thieves.]
   Well Dorothy, you wanted to know if you should get Ethyl's address for me. You can write to her and tell her. If she wants to write to me, I might try and answer her letters. (Ha Ha) [Ethel Meyers lived on a farm about a half mile away from Bob's family.] I guess that will hold you for a while. You might find out why Glen hasn't answered my card yet or maybe he didn't get it. It was sent the 23rd of

Feb. Is he staying at home or some place else. Well it is almost noon now so I must close. Will be hearing from you soon, I hope.

Yours truly, Pvt. Bob

["**Jugoslavs Seek Greek-Axis Peace**" This is a pro-Nazi measure in that its success would allow the Nazis to commit their troops elsewhere. The Germans also have their eye on North African bases.]

Mar. 10, 1941 – Posted this date to Dorothy Francisco from Indianapolis, Bob's letter exhibits his dry sense of humor.

Dear family,

Well I have heard that figures don't lie but I don't believe that any more, because I figured that I would be at home now, but it didn't work out that way.

Tomorrow is the day we move again, but I don't know where. We will be still in the 201st Infantry [Co. F] though. I will let you know my new address if it is changed. After we get moved, we will start our target practice.

How is every one at home now? I finally got back to work last Friday. That was a week of loafing that I got paid for, but I was getting tired of it and finally argued with the quack till he sent me to work. He was going to make me stay in Friday yet. But I still had hopes of coming home then yet and I didn't want to be on the sick list. We may all be shut in for six weeks because there is a few cases of measles in this company. We will know tomorrow.

I have heard that we would get three days off so I could come at Easter but I don't think there is anything to it. This camp is just like Randolph. You can't believe any of what you hear and half of what you see.

Well, how is the milking machine doing by now?

Dorothy, was Warren up last nite (but Mom A [sic]) to take you to a show? I bet he was looking for me because in the last letter I wrote him I said I would be home Sat. nite. I don't suppose I would have had much fun if I would have come home because all the time there I would have to be getting ready to come back. I went to the theater last nite and saw one of Dr. Christen's shows. Boy, it was good. You will probably hear it on the Radio. It is called Cure for Richies, and tonite I am going and see Boom Town, that one I missed back home.

No, I have not got my new outfit yet and I don't know when we will get them, if ever. We did get our footlockers, though. I guess I will send your new suitcase & my clothes home one of these days.

Well this is about all I can think to say now and I have still got four letters to write, but I hate to waste all this blank space. I will sure have lots to tell you when I get home. Don't forget to get that address from Dale, and write that letter.

Well So Long   Privet [sic] Robert Francisco

["**French Threaten Sea War To Break British Food Blockade**" Also, the Nazis resume their air blitz on London.]

Mar. 15, 1941 – Posted this date to Dorothy Francisco, Bob uses his best military stationary.

Dear Folks,

Thanks for the candy. I haven't had time to open it yet because I am getting ready to leave for Ft. Custer Mich. in the morning at 6:00. I can't tell you my correct address and I don't even know for sure if I am going to Michigan. Boy, the weather is sure swell here this week. It snowed a little but not much. I have been rolling around on the ground and playing like I used to when I was a little kid like Howard [His nephew, four year-old Howard Mangold].

Maybe if I get to Mich., I will be closer to home than I am here. I am about 350 miles from home now, but I think it is closer from Mich. Ft. Custer is to be 75 miles from Detroit.

I have been here a mo. now and didn't get paid yet, but I got a book with tickets in it and it isn't good at any other place but at Ft. Benj, so I guess I will buy a pipe and some tobacco. That will be one way to get a little good out of it.

They told us the other nite that we had been the best bunch of men they had yet. They also said that they had saved $175.00 on our meals this mo. and they was going to give us a chicken dinner and ice cream for our supper tonite, but we got roast ribb [sic] mostly bones and mashed potatoes. Well I must close because I have to finish packing and shine my shoes. That is one job I will learn to do before I leave here.   Yours truly, Bob

['**British Defy Nazis In Middle East**" The British are rapidly shipping men and materiel to Egypt. They also send an expeditionary force to Greece, a move which is certain to trigger Nazi retaliation.]

March 29, 1941 - Bob settles in at Ft. Custer, Michigan.
Dear Folks:
    Well I got today off and I wonder what I will have to do today. Yesterday afternoon they gave us off and we had to have an examination. Then we had to move again. We moved from a barrack to the one next to it. Then we had to mop and clean up the one we left. That gave us about a hour off for the afternoon.
    I don't know if I told you about the deer they have here or not, but last Sunday they left her out of the pen and you should have seen her run. She went down over the hill like a big rabbit. I thought that was the last we would see of her, but in about five minutes she came back just as fast as she left. She run around the yard a while and finally went back in her pen.
    Well I guess you might as well not look for me home before the middle of May, because they won't give us time enough off to get that far away. We have to be back 11:00 Sun. night, that wouldn't give me time enough to say hello and goodbye. It takes 10 hours to go from here to Warren, Ohio.
    Well I guess I will go to Battle Creek today and look around. I haven't got any money to spend but I can see what I could get if I had some. I guess we get paid Tuesday. If we do, I am going to try and buy a camera and take some pictures of this dump. Tell Dorothy to send me those pictures of the mink and us that she took last winter and the ones that I have of the fish up at that dam near Penn.
    Well the army hooked me out of another $1.76 yesterday. I got a new overcoat and it was too long and my jacket were [sic] too long, so I had to take them to the tailor and have them made to fit. My blouse is one of them 1920 models and I am trying to trade it in on a new one, but they won't take it as long as it is fit to wear. It is a little tight so I think I can make it so it isn't fit to wear. If they won't give me a new one, I will have to buy one that will be about $6.00 more. They don't have those big foot lockers here and they want $6.25 for one here at the canteen. I'll ... want to have it because all I got is two sacks to keep my clothes in.
    Boy, I was surprised the other day when I got my mail and there was a letter from Ethel. I didn't even think she would write to me.

I just came back from breakfast. This is the first time I ever got a chance to write a letter this early in the morning. It is time to start cleaning up now. We didn't have to get up till 7:00 this morning.

I got a St. Patricks card from Mr. & Mrs. Laubert last week. I haven't wrote to them yet but maybe I will today or tomorrow.

We had a big parade here yesterday morning. I guess we marched 3 miles. There was a picture of it in the Detroit paper, but I didn't buy one this morning. If I get one tomorrow and it has any pictures in it, I will save them & send them home.

Elmore will not have to take my car up to Warners [garage] before the 1st of April. It would be safe to move it that far without any license.

How are they getting along with the work by this time? Have they got the manure all hauled & the corn husked yet?

I got a damn good notion to get mad at Dorothy for getting a job, because that makes another letter I have to write. But I will try and send her one letter a <u>month</u> if she sends me her address. I have got six letters to write today & tomorrow, then I will be caught up on my writing. If I do get them wrote, I can't send them because I am using my last stamp on this one and the canteen won't open till tomorrow because they are taking inventory.

I understand Warren to say that Glen was coming up to see me when he got his potatoes out, and he said that on Monday [he] was coming up the other week but he run out of money.

Well I must quit writing or it will take me all day to write this one. Hoping you are all well & happy. I will close.

Yours truly, Bob

P.S. [in print] I bet you have a hell of a time reading this letter.

[In the larger scheme of events, the attack on three battleships is a mere drop in the bucket; however, the editors frequently attempt to avoid a gloom and doom attitude. Today's headline reads: "**3 Italian Warships Hit In Battle.**" Locally, Ravenna used to be a "Saturday night" town," when folks usually came to town for fun. Now, it is considered to be a "Friday night town," since it is payday at the nearby munitions plant, the Ravenna Arsenal.]

April 13, 1941 – Bob, the reluctant warrior, writes to his sister Dorothy. There are abundant details of army life and personal opinions, which will disappear when army censorship kicks in at a

later date.
2nd Inf. Co. G
Ft. Custer Mich.
Dear Dorothy:
> Well I bet you think I forgot you. I haven't wrote you for about two weeks. Well I haven't wrote to anyone since last Sunday.
> I had to clean my rifle every nite and do my share of the house work. That's all I had time to do. The first two days I had to shoot out on the range & the other two I had to put the target up for the other fellows to shoot at. I didn't do as good shooting as I should have. I got 227 out of a possible 300. That only makes me a marksman. The classes are 198 points marksman, 249 is sharpshooter & 264 is expert. So all I can say is when I was in the army I was known as marksman Sisco.* (Ha! Ha!) Boy, that pushing up targets is a real job. We stand in a covered pit and the bullets whistle over our heads and sometimes hit the dirt and throw sand in our face, but it sure was fun. Especially the shot I took at the Sargent's dog, but I missed him. You see I was sighting at the target and this dog came past in back of the targets and when he got in back of my target, I shot and you should have seen him run.
> Boy, they finally decided to pay us the other day and I sure did need it.
> I didn't get the letter you sent for Warren until after he left today, so I will send it back to you.
> I sure was glad to see all the boys the other day. I tried to get off to go home, but I couldn't even get a decent pass to go to town.
> I wish you could have come along, but maybe you can come with someone later on.
> Ask Warren how he likes to live in Dover, Ohio.
> You asked me if I was homesick. Well here is the answer. I am not homesick, but I would like to see all of you and I would rather live back there. Well, I must close and write home. I just finished a letter to Ethel Myers. Tell Warren that I sure was glad to see them come up here.

Your loving brother, Robert Francisco
P.S. I put the return address Atwater, Ohio, so if you didn't get it up there at Clarence Pontius' place, you would get it at home.
> *Bob's army buddies called him "Frisco."
> ["**U.S. Steel Raises Pay; Strike Off.**" The steel workers

received a ten cents per hour pay raise. The leading war news is that Britain admits defeats in Greece. Locally, the manager of Ravenna's Schine Theater was robbed of $561 on his way to make the deposit at the bank.]

June 14, 1941 – From Tennessee, Bob writes to his sister.
Camp Forrest Tenn.
Dear Dorothy:
    Well I got my laundry all done now and am trying to write and get my clothes dry. It rains and I have to go out and bring them in my tent. Then the sun shines and I take them out again. The way I wash the clothes, I go down to the river and take my shoes off, then jump in, rub my clothes with soap, and when they get clean, I throw them out on the bank, then wash myself.
    I heard that I may get a chance to come home for the 4th, but don't look for me because I think it is balona [sic].
    So you got a new job now. Are you home Sat. & Sun. nites or do you have to work?
    Boy, did I get my fill on pancakes this morning. I only had 10. I would go up to the kitchen and they would give me one so I walked back through and by the time I got around to the other side, I had it ate. So I got in line and went through again. When I went through the 7th time, the cook throwed three flapjacks at me or in my pan and said, "there god damit, I hope that fills you up. So I didn't go back. I was full.
    Did you get the letter I sent you June 8th? The one I asked how old Lenora was. How old is she?
    So you think she likes me a little, eh? Well that's O.K. by me, but a little young.
    I found out that I wasn't a dead end kid the other nite when I set on a cactus. If I was, I wouldn't have got up so fast.
    These cactus plants are just like the ones they sell in the stores, but they have long prickers on and a pretty yellow and red flower. I saw a wildcat yesterday and it saw me and it must have seen me first because he run like a deer so I didn't have to.
    I just got your last letter. I have been getting one or more from you every week. I have tried to answer or send one every Monday.
    Engagements are O. K. by me in your case, but Warren is

right. So Lenora is only 15. I wish she was 18 or more. I just heard we had a pretty hard week, so I better close and go to bed. So long.

Bob xxxx

Will try to write more soon.

["**F.R. Freezes Axis Credits In U.S.**" Overseas, the British bombed Brest, where the Nazis berth their large warships.]

July 24, 1941 – Posted this date from Battle Creek, Michigan, this letter is written to his older sister Hazel Mangold. The envelope is addressed to Wilson Mangold in Randolph. It appears that Bob went home to get his car.
Ft. Custer Mich.
Dear Hazel & Family & Dorothy, etc.

Well I made it back here in time for bed check again this time. I was here at 1:30 and I stopped for a hour or more along the road. I sure was tired though.

This will probably be a short letter, but it will have to do. I haven't got much time and there isn't much news.

I may not get home this weekend because I may have to be on guard and I can't get out of it, if it is my turn. If I don't get there this week, I am pretty sure I will be home the next two weekends.

I guess I will have to take my car down to the lake and wash it tonite.

I guess I will get my Ft. Custer license all rite. I went in today and had my car inspected & registered. I went in to see a Sargent to have my car checked. He went out and walked around the car and gave me a paper that he already filled out with the words good & O.K., so that was pretty good.

Boy, we have to get up at 4:15 tomorrow morning to say so long to some Major or general. He must be a wild cuss if we have to sneak up on him after dark, or just after day lite.

Well I have to clean my rifle, wash my car, go swimming, get my mail and eat chow, so I better close now. So – So Long.

Yours Truly Pvt. Bob

P.S. If I come home, I should be there at 9:00 or sooner. I just got Dorothy and Mom's letter and it sounds like maybe Dorothy isn't up there any more, so tell her. I can't get home before 8:00 at the earliest, and maybe I won't get there at all, but I am keeping my fingers crossed.

Well So Long Again.

["**U.S. Denounces Jap Aggression**" The Japanese have begun the occupation of Indo China. Locally, Ravenna continues to become a greater boom town. The federal government selected the area as a site for 750 dwellings for defense housing at the cost of $3,300 per building.]

July 24, 1941 – The army prepares a "Progress report" to Mrs. Alice B. Francisco. It is posted on a War Dept., Official Business envelope from Battle Creek on July 30, 1941. It is a typed letter, not a form letter.

COMPANY "G" SECOND INFANTRY
Fort Custer, Michigan

24 July, 1941
Mrs. Alice Francisco
R.D. #1
Atwater, Ohio
Dear Mrs. Francisco:

    I am taking this opportunity to advise you of the progress of your son, Private Francisco, who is a member of my command. He has completed his preliminary basic training period of three months.

    Please be assured that your son is making excellen [sic] progress as a soldier, seems very interested in his work, and apparently enjoys Army life thoroughly.

Very truly yours,
[signature]
Richard H. Einfeldt
Capt., 2d Infantry
Commanding.

July 29, 1941 – Posted this date from Battle Creek, Bob writes to Miss Dorothy Francisco.
Ft. Custer Mich.
Dear Dorothy & Family.

    Well how is everybody today?

    I made the trip again O.K. and right side up. I left Massillon [Ohio] at 7:00 and was here at 1:45, so I didn't do so bad. I had a close shave just after it got dark. I started around one car and when I got up beside him, I saw a black spot on the side of the road. It was a man on a bicycle with two fish poles about 20 ft long, and no light of any kind. He was on the wrong side of the road. Well I couldn't stop because the other car had closed up in back of me and wouldn't let me in, and there was another car coming toward me. So I just stepped on it and slipped in between the car and bicycle, just missing both of them. I sure was scared because I couldn't even pass that fool on the bicycle.

Bill Leatherman [his good army buddy] came in with his finger all tied up. He said he stuck it in the electric fan. It was his trigger finger and we told him he tried to cut it off to get out of the army, and when he went to get the meat saw there wasn't set enough in it to do the job [sic].

I went over to the PX to get my pictures tonite. There was 6 good out of 8.

Well news is that, now since I just saw you all.

Boy, I am pretty tired & sleepy tonite. We went out for a 10 mi hike today and a little problem. Well Bill and I was sent out as scouts and we managed to get captured and laid in the shade for a hour or two while the others had to run and fool around in the sun. Boy, it sure is hot here today and tonite.

I heard we may have another guard this weekend, so I may not get home this weekend either. So if I ain't home, you will know I am on guard.

Yours Truly, Bob

P. S. Saving money now, you can mail my letters. [Stamps cost 3cts each.]

["U.S. On Verge Of War -- Churchill" The heat wave at Fort Custer extends to Portage County, Ohio, where the temperature is near 100 degrees.

August 30, 1941 – Posted on this date from Paducah, Kentucky, Bob writes to Dorothy. The "reluctant warrior" is exploring ways to get out of the army. Since farming is considered a vital industry and his father is not feeling well, perhaps he has a chance of being discharged like others have been.

Aug. 28, 1941
Spencer, Ind.
Dear Dorothy & Family:

I received your letter last nite and was glad to hear from you for once. I thought you had forgot me. Ha! Ha!

How many trees have you climbed with my car by now? I don't hardly think it will be any, but I just thought I would ask.

How are you and Warren, or you and the milk teats, getting along by now?

Boy, it sure is cold here nites, and the grasshoppers are thick. This time it is grasshoppers instead of ants in our soup.

Have you heard from the draft board yet? I haven't and I haven't done anything here yet, and it won't do me much good until I get back to camp. Well I hope to hear from you all soon. And hope you get a good job.

I guess I will have to close now because I haven't got any light and it is getting dark.

Yours Truly, Bob

Mom has my address.

P. S. I suppose you will tell me I might as well send you a postcard and some two cents and a envelope.

[No headline appears on today's newspaper. The top story is that Congress is expected to pass the "biggest tax bill in history." There are optimistic reports that the Americans and Japanese are reaching an accord.]

September 1, 1941 – Bob's travels continue; now he is in Arkansas. This is the start of his quest for a deferment for dependents and hardship.

Pine Bluff, Ark.

Dear Mom & Family.

We finally got down here in Arkansas and I don't blame Bob Burns for leaving the state. I thought Tenn. was a bad place but what I have seen of Ark. It is worse.

We are camping in a woods just west of Pine Bluff about 3 miles. There is pine needles about three inches deep all over the ground.

I went to Pine Bluff last evening and it is a town of about 21,500 people and about half of them are Negroes.

Have you heard anything new from the Draft Board yet? I heard that they were going to start relieving men with dependents & hardships next Wednesday. I am going to see what I can do here now, and I want you to see what they are doing, if anything, at the Draft

Board. Maybe it would help if Elmore went in to see Ray Darrow and talk to him. Tell him that he needs me worse than Uncle Sam does.

Tell Dorothy to have the oil changed in the car right away and get it greased when she gets a chance. There is no hurry to get it greased. Have No. 10 oil put in it. I guess I will send you some money to make a payment on the car, and I guess someone will have [to] lend me money to pay the Life Insurance.

Boy, I have sure seen lots of fields of Cotton and corn & Rice down here. They run any where from a patch to 200 acres or more in one field. The farms have about two cows and Fifty mules or horses. There isn't many horses though. This is the damndest [sic] place, the dust will be flying in one place and the next one it is so wet you can't hardly walk through.

Well I better close now. Hoping to hear from all of you soon.
Yours Truly, Bob
My address is.
  2nd Inf. Co. G, A.P.O. #5
  Camp Robinson, Arkansas
  Happy Birthday Mom. [in print]
P. S. No. 1
I was in to see a Lieutenant about a discharge. He said he would write a letter to someone. I don't remember who. He said he thought I had a darn good chance. I don't know if he said that to make me feel good or if he meant it. He said that it might take some time but not to get discharged. Maybe Pop will have to get a letter from a doctor and send it to the Board.

Write as soon as you hear anything and if you don't hear anything, write anyhow. I wrote a letter to Hazel and I forgot to tell her she could send me some homemade candy. The fellows thought it was pretty good. So you can tell her to send some. You can send some, but she can make it easier than you can. <u>Oh yes and better too.</u> Ha! Ha!

Well I better close again.
Yours truly, Bob
P. S. No. 2
  Here is a money order to make a payment on the car.

["Berlin Says Nazi Troops Only 16 Miles From Leningrad" Over the Labor Day weekend, civilian life in Portage County was deadly. There were 4 deaths and 19 injured in 25 auto-

automobile crashes. This brings the year's total to 40 fatalities.]

If Pvt. Bob Francisco had the *Evening Record's* September 4 issue, he could have learned that he was involved in the "Battle of Louisiana." Pvt. Mickey Dover of the 37th Ohio Infantry sent the newspaper an informed eyewitness account of the army maneuvers in Louisiana. Infantry and mechanized units were arrayed on a 100-mile front from Newton, Texas to DeRidder and Oakdale, Louisiana. "The pine woods of the Kisatchie national forest are reverberating with staccato machine gun fire as infantry troops are still merrily battling away."

Bob Francisco may not have been impressed with the maneuvers, but the smiling Pvt. Dover appeared quite satisfied that his side was winning. Mickey concluded his lengthy report: "All in all, things look bright for the fifth corps as the battle enters its final phase tonight. No substantial gains have been made by either Red or Blue forces, but the enemy mechanized attack, thanks in most instances to the heroic efforts of the Ohio division's destroyer force, has been stalled in every attempt to make substantial drives." [22]

September 23, 1941 – Still in the south, Bob writes to his mother.
Sept. 23, 1941
Dear Mom:

I received those letters and will have to send them back because they don't have a affidavit with them. I would suggest that you have Hazel type them out. Then get the people that wrote them [to] sign them before the notary public with a affidavit attached. They are no good without the affidavit. This cost me about a week or more on my discharge. They have to be signed by a notary public like Kuhn or Andy Horning. Get this done as soon as possible and send them to Custer because I will be there about the 2 or 3 of Oct. Send them special delivery so they get through quick because every day counts. I know there is a lot of bother, but it has to be done.

I may be home the first Sat. in Oct. and again I may not.

I have been pretty busy the last week. We haven't done much the last two days. Last nite I was busy swatting mosquitoes. One stung me in the eye. I swatted it and I guess I hit too hard because my eye is all swelled up. I can't hardly see out of it.

Tell Dorothy not to be too mad at Warren because he will

probably be back, because I know he isn't that bad.

Well I better close now because I think the mail is going out soon and I want this letter to go as fast as possible. Keep bothering the Red Cross and the Draft Board and hustle these letters as fast as possible.

Yours truly, Bob

Hope u get these letters back by the time I am in Custer.

Thanks for the stamps & I don't like Arkansas or Louisiana either one.

[**Sinking Spurs Navy Sub Hunt**" The U.S. Navy scours the waters off Iceland for survivors of the government owned S.S. Pink Star. Berlin warns the United States of increasing submarine warfare.]

September 25, 1941 – Bob's letter is posted to Alice Francisco from Camp Tyler. Written with a sharp pencil on a poor surface, it is difficult to read. His mailing address is Camp Robinson, Ark.

Louisiana Mud hole

Dear Folks.

Boy, have I had one heck of a time the last two days. It has been raining the most of the time and my clothes are all soaked up. The other nite I laid down on the ground and curled up with my raincoat to keep the mosquitoes off. Well, when I woke up, I was lying in about a inch of water. Here I had slept about a hour in the rain & I didn't even know it.

I guess we start back to Custer Monday on trucks. They have sent our clothes back by train, so it looks like I will be wearing some wet and dirty clothes on my trip back. What did Elmore make out up at the Draft board in Kent last week? Two more of the fellows are getting out when they get back to Custer. I sorta feel that I will make it, but I am not sure yet. I know one of the boys that work in the Office. I can find out a lot if I ever get a chance to see him. He isn't around much while we are down here. Having those letters & Affidavits back to Custer so they are there about the same time I get there.

Tell Wilson [Mangold] he should come down here to Louisiana to go fishing. They catch catfish here in their rivers that weigh from 126 pounds on down, mostly down I guess. They use big nets & traps down here.

I guess you might as well hold that Insurance paper for a while because I will be home either the 4th or 11th of Oct. I just heard that we would get 8 day furloughs but I am not putting much hopes in it.

Well I better close now and get ready to move to the next mud hole or else the same one but in a different place. There is only two hills in this state and we have forgot where they are.

Hope you all are in good health. I got the rheumatism in my hand & legs so I can hardly move when I first start out.

Yours truly, Bob

["**Revolt Spreads Against Nazi Rule**" "The uneasy rule of Nazi troops over occupied Europe was menaced today by spreading sabotage, unrest, and a flare-up of extensive guerilla war in Jugoslavia."

October 2, 1941 – Posted this date from Shreveport, La., Bob writes to his mother and family. The correspondence is on YMCA paper and envelope.

Dear Family,

Well we finally found out that we start back to Custer tomorrow by truck. We will get there the 7th or 8th. I think I will get home the 12th or 13th. So you can have my car all polished up. Have Elmore find a place I can get my driver's license on Saturday nite or Sunday some time. Maybe I will get them before I get home. If I get to Toledo early enough.

I was talking with one of the boys that is working on these discharges & he said he had wrote to the Red Cross. So I suppose they will be down to see you soon if they haven't all ready. Be sure to tell them about the mortgage and the interest, taxes, and every other thing you can think of. I suppose you have got those other letters all straight and out by now.

There isn't much news to tell you down here. Only that I saw the new Chevrolet down in some city here in Louisiana. I saw it in a hurry as I rode by in a truck. It didn't look like they changed it much.

How is the colt getting along by now? I got a idea that one of the other horses kicked him in the shoulder. Did Elmore buy that Corn Harvester or did he get someone else to cut it?

Boy the mosquitoes and flies are bad down here now. Those darn mosquitoes fly around like a big dive bomber. The buzzing around is just about as bad as their bites are.

Harris Warner sent me a carton of cigarettes yesterday. They sure come in handy. I lost my cigarette case about a week ago and the next nite I lost my knife & pencil. That is the most stuff I ever lost. I didn't mind losing the knife, but I hated to lose that case. It was the one that Hazel gave me.

Well I guess I better close now. Hope you are all right & I hope to hear from you soon.

Yours Truly, Bob

[The editors must have been avid baseball fans as the headlines proclaimed, **Dodgers Rally, Lead Yankees, 3-2"** in the World Series. Of secondary front page importance, "Germans Execute Hundreds As Resistance Grows."

November 22, 1941 – To Dorothy and the family, Bob fires off a rare angry letter.
Ft. Custer, Mich.
Dear Dorothy & Folks.

Well here it is Sat. afternoon again & I didn't get to come home. So don't try to understand what I write or read between the lines.

I had my pass all made out and a ride into Canton, Ohio. Then they said we could only have passes from 12:30 today until 12:00 tonite, then passes from 6:00 Sunday morning until 11:00 Sunday nite. The G.D. – S. of B'es didn't take our passes away but they fixed them so we couldn't go any place except Battle Creek or some little hell hole like it. This is another day like Thanksgiving Day was. About half the fellows are drunk & the other half getting drunk.

Last Thursday, Sgt. Shire, that is my squad leader, got drunk and went back to Wisconsin to go deer hunting. I can't say that I blame him though.

Well I guess I will have to go to town & see how my car is coming along.

Here it is Sunday morning and everything is covered with snow. It is sorta pretty out, but the snow is turning to rain.

I got in town last nite too late to find out anything about my car. So I guess I will have to call them up tomorrow noon.

I saw two of the best shows I have seen in a long time. They were Dead [End] Kids in Dress Parade & South of the Tahiti. Today I guess I will go in & see the Return of Jesse James.

I got your letter last nite when I came back from town. I hope you get that job, or if you don't, maybe you could go down and see the guy that Ethel works for. I haven't heard from her for over a week.

How is Elmore getting along with the world? Tell him I said he had better ketch a lot of rats. Because if I ain't out before Xmas, I am coming home for 10 days and I will get the rest of them. I mean I will get 10 days if the dirty S of B'es don't figure out some way to beat us out of them.

Has the Red Cross been down there yet? They should have. Maybe Mom & Elmore will have to go up and see them. Tell them that I was in to see the fieldman up here and he said that he would send the papers out right away. That was last Saturday. I guess I will call them up about Wednesday and see what they have to say. He said to come up any time that I wanted to and check on it.

Well I guess I have wrote enough junk to take you about a week to figure out what I said. So I better close. Hope to hear from you soon. I will write as soon as I find out any good news & probably sooner.

Yours Truly, Bob

P. S. We had our pictures taken the other day & I ordered a book like a speedometer [the Portage County Schools yearbook]. It only cost $3.75. Not bad for a rich man eh!

Continued next week. [last line printed]

[**U.S. Tanks Lead Advance In Libya"** The British were using American-made tanks in their drive from Tobruk. Across the United States labor strikes were on the rise. John L. Lewis' coal miners went on strike, which in turn caused some steel mills to shut down.]

Dec. 11, 1941 – Bob's letter is written on one sheet of military paper with the 2nd Infantry's logo and headed, "Company G, Second Infantry, Fort Custer, Michigan. He is in a playful mood with Dorothy, and he demonstrates the independence of the citizen soldier. Due to the Japanese attack on Pearl Harbor four days ago, Bob's negative attitude on army service has changed.

Ft. Custer, Mich.

Dear Dorothy & The Rest.

Well how's the little Gopher [word printed] getting along? Oh! excuse me the word is Doffer. It is funny how easy it is to get those words mixed.

Well I don't reckon that I will get my discharge now for a few months. I don't think I would take it if they offered it to me now. [A reference to the attack on Pearl Harbor.]

I heard today that we will get our furloughs yet after all. I probably won't be home for Christmas, but I think that I will get home for New Years then.

You can get that present for Elmore if you want to. I am broke now and can't send any presents or money. So you guys will either have to go without or buy them like we always did and I will send you some money next month to pay my share.

You can have my car to drive as soon as I get it home. So don't buy one of your own. It looks like I will get a chance to bring it home myself.

I signed Pop's papers but I didn't send them out. I told Mom to fill them out if she wanted to. If he does fill them out & he gets his money, he has to use it in the right way or I told her to have a guardian appointed to take care of it for him. Now I want you folks to see that this is done if it is not satisfactory to a lot of you. It sounds all right to me if it will work out like I said, doesn't it? If you don't think it will work, then just tear it up and forget that I signed it.

Boy is my left arm sore tonite? Oh! You don't know that was a foolish question to ask you wasn't it? I had no business asking you, because I know it is. Why is it sore? Oh you don't know that either. Well what the H--- else do you know. (Neither, that's what I thought.) You see I got a shot for lockjaw today. Boy did it burn? There I go asking more questions that you don't know. But I do because I was right there with it.

Boy I sure caught H--- on yesterday. You see I was wearing my black leather gloves over my army gloves to keep my hands warm and that isn't allowed. So today I fooled them. I wore my leather gloves on the inside. They were warmer that way anyway.

So you do like your job even if it is a little dirty. Well it won't be long now until you can get a better job if you want to.

Boy I finally did get this page full and was it a job. Oh you don't know that either. Boy are you dumb? You don't know, neither do I.

Hope to hear from you soon if you can figure this letter out or if you can't.

Yours Truly, P.F.C. R. E. Francisco

[**U.S. And Axis At War!**" The *Evening Record* noted; "Today it is a real World war."

PART III
Iceland
1942

P.F.C. Robert Francisco received his coveted furlough in early January. In the past eleven months he had spent time in Indiana, Michigan, Kentucky, Tennessee, Arkansas, and Louisiana. Now he is stationed in New Jersey.

January 20, 1941 - Bob is in good humor, as he posts this letter from Trenton, New Jersey. In the upper left hand corner of his stationery is an American shield with "America Forever" underneath it.

Ft. Dix, N. J.

Dear Sister:

Hi! There gopher, how's everything & everyone?

Boy you <u>auto</u> hear my dream (I dreamed that we had that double wedding you always [wd] think would be so nice.) You know (you & Warren & me and Lenora.) the best part of it was that I told it before breakfast. I guess the reason I dreamt it was because I had my fortune told, (with one of those one cent fortune telling machines) the other nite. It said my trip to foreign countries would be a success and that the one I loved would still be waiting for me when I come back. Now I don't know so much about the last part of this, but I do know there is a trip to the foreign countries some place, but I don't know where.

I heard that we was going to California from here but I have quit guessing.

If I am still here in New Jersey next week & I can get a pass, I am going to New York City or else Philadelphia and see if I can get lost. I bet I can. I guess we will get paid some time this week. I sure hope so, because I don't think I would have much luck in New York City with 75 cents.

Oh! Yeah how are you and the Jones'es [sic] getting along by now. Maybe he is some relation to the Jim Jones that used to go to school with me. And again maybe he is some relation to Bryan Jones in Ravenna, Ohio.

I ain't real sure but I think my address is Co. G. 2nd Inf. A.P.O. #1002 c/o Postmaster New York City, New York. My name Pvt. 1cl R. E. Francisco & Army Serial Number is A.S.N. 35009786, they go before the rest of the address. They change my address so often I can't keep up with it.

Well there isn't any news up here but only that there is some good looking girls up here, but I can't do anything about it without a car.

Have you got the car home yet? And what does it look like, a car or a leopard. I don't suppose a Ford garage can get real Chevrolet paint.

I hope you write soon. I haven't got but one letter since I got up here a week ago. Boy it sure is hard for me to write letters when I don't see any news to write about.

Must close and go fire up again. It is nice warm weather up here now. Just like spring.

I sure hope my dream comes true.
Your Brother, Bob.

[**"Army Bombers Sink Jap Cruiser"** It is important for the readers to know that the U.S. is fighting back; however the Japanese military victoriously rolls on. Today they are closing in on Singapore.]

Feb. 15, 1942 – Still in Trenton, N. J., Bob posts a letter to Dorothy. His letter consists of a large sheet of paper and a smaller one.
Ft. Dix N. J.
Dear Dorothy & Family:

Hi Yah! Little squirt & big ones too, how is every thing? Oh it is, that is just what I thought.

Boy is it cold up here again? Oh you don't know because you ain't here. Just don't get in a hurry & wait until I finish what I was going to say before you fly off the handle. Anyhow, it just seems that it is just like spring one day, then down around zero the next.

How does <u>my car</u> [*our* written in a rectangle above this] work now? The next time don't get Dale to fix it, take it to the garage and have it fixed or get Wilson. Anyone that even knows the first thing about a car should have known that it was the points or timing & not the carburator just by the way it acted. I either told you, in a letter or thought I did, that it needed new points. I was going to get them the next time I came home, that was before I wrecked it.

Have you got your job back yet or have you a new one? I heard you have a new job.

Did I leave my camera at home or some place else? I think I left it home. If I did, you guys can use it until I come back. This little junk camera of mine is pretty good I think, & it is handier than my good one.

Did you get the History of the 5th Division that I sent home? I guess that is what it was called. Boy am I a sorry looking cuss [his picture in the book].Oh yeah! I heard you say that, you said sure he always is.

I am all ready for that boat ride wherever it goes. I have sent one bag of junk all ready and am all set to take off any time now.

Thanks a lot for the money you sent me. I was intending to use that to come home with but now I will use it for something else. So I guess the next time I come home, it will be to stay. Remember the old saying, if you leave in a hurry and leave something accidently behind, you will be back again. I forgot my watch so I guess I will be back again after while instead of now.

Watch your step & don't do anything I wouldn't & don't make any mistakes.
With Lots of Love, Bob
P. S. I got your letter & I also got the money. Thanks a lot. [This is circled.]

[The following is part two on the smaller paper. It could have been written on the 14th.]
P. S. #1

This is probably the last letter you will get from me that won't look like a crossword puzzle because some parts of it are censored. Maybe this one will be too.

If there is anything you want to find out about or how to go about finding out something about the army, use the enclosed address

This is another early morning letter. I started it at 1:30 A.M. & it is 4:45 A.M. now. Maybe it doesn't take you that long to read it. This fireman job is about like the alarm clock. I have to call the two cooks at 4:00, two more at 5:00, two buglers at 5:30 and one other Sargent at 5:45. Then there is usually one or two others that want to get up 10 or 15 min. early.

Just think, I have been in here a year and a day & making $46 a month. That would be about equal to $80 outside, not so bad & not all good.

What did Mom find out about my watch?

You will find that Will or something like it in this letter I hope. What the Hell makes you guys think I would ever need that. Haven't you heard of Superman.

Latest rumor is that we are going to England. I hope so in a way even if we haven't any business there. I would rather go to California.

I guess I can't think of any more, but don't do what you said you might. It would be a big mistake.

So Long, Bob

[Circled insert] Dorothy you better go down and see Lenora again. I got a letter from Lenora the other day.

["**Japs Land Paratroops In Sumatra**" In the Philippines, U.S. tanks won a decisive, but small, victory over Japanese tanks on the Bataan Peninsula. Locally, the third draft registration starts today. Approximately 2,000 Ravenna area men, aged 20-45, are expected to register.]

March 12, 1942 – Of all the trouble spots in the world, Bob is surprised that he is shipped to Iceland. Iceland had been a sovereign state united with Denmark; however, when the Germans occupied Denmark on April 9, 1940, the British invaded the island. Since Iceland was a neutral country, the invasion was in violation of international law; but with the alternative being Nazi control, the Icelanders accepted British occupation. In 1941 the British feared a Nazi invasion of the home land, thus their troops were needed closer to home. Iceland's defense was then passed to the United States in July, 1941. [23]

Army censorship is beginning to be tougher, and envelopes are now stamped: Passed by U # S, Army Examiner, with the examiner's signature. The postage is now free.

P.F.C. Francisco appears to be pleased with the novelty of his situation.

Iceland
Dear Dorothy & Family:

How is everything and everyone back home? O. K. I hope. Have you went back to work yet, or did you get a better job. How is Elmore getting along with the farm work? I guess I won't get home this spring & summer to help him out on Sundays like I did last year.

If it doesn't cost too much, I would like to have you subscribe to the Farm & Dairy paper & have it sent to me. So I know a little bit about what the farmers are doing or trying to do.

Well I finally wound up in Iceland. We had a good trip up here. It was a little rough for a few days but it didn't even make me sick. It seems funny not to see a tree any place here, but I guess I will get used to it, because there isn't any here. The mountains are just like a big rock with a little moss growing on them. Some of them have a fair crop of grass on them.

I don't know how the farmers here make a living. All the animals I have seen is ponies, sheep, goats, and poultry. I haven't seen any farm tools except a mowing machine & rake.

It hasn't been very cold as I expected it to be. Maybe the name Iceland is a little misleading. I like it here even better than I did at Ft. Dix. Maybe it is because of the small chicken coops we live in or else it is because we can do things more like we want them done. There is only 10 or 12 of us fellows in a hen house, or maybe I should say Rooster house because there isn't any <u>hens</u> around.

I sure wish you could see me in my new Eskimo suit. The winter clothes they give us sure are warm

I guess I better close for now. Hope this doesn't look like a crossword puzzle when you get it. Write soon & I will get it within three weeks. Send this up to Hazel.
Yours Truly, Robert Francisco
My address is:
Pvt. 1cl R. E. Francisco ASN 35009786
Co. G 2nd Inf.
A.P.O. #810
Iceland

["**Allied Fliers Cripple 13 Jap Troop Ships Off New Guinea**" The Nazis move closer to Francisco as they establish bases in Norway to harbor their fleet, including their ace warship, the *Terpitz*.]

April 19, 1941 – Although postmarked the 28th, this letter was written on April 19th. In this and future letters Bob mentions that there isn't much about which to write. In fact, there is plenty to tell. Since landing in Iceland, "the 5th Division performed arduous and monotonous duties of manning observation posts, unloading boats, building roads and buildings, and maintaining training schedules." [24] Yet, any references to his whereabouts or duties are cut from his letters by the army censor. Hence, he makes the remark about a "jigsaw puzzle."

April 19, 1942 [Sunday]
Iceland
Dear Dorothy:

Hi! Ho! You little squirt. How does it feel to be a year older. [She turned 19 on this date.] I didn't get home on your birthday this year. So I am going to scratch you a few lines to show you that I thought of you at least.

I received some more of your letters just a little while ago and was very sorry to hear that you had been sick & had to go to the hospital. I read Mom's letter first and she was telling me about Clarence Pontius being in the hospital the same time that you was, but she didn't say why you was there. The first thing I thought was that you had got in a wreck with [circled] our [over] my car. Of course I should have known that I was the only one that could do that. I sure hope you get along fine & don't have any more trouble.

Boy, this darn letter writing is a pain in the neck. There isn't much that we can write about. I don't know if my letters look like a jigsaw puzzle or not. I try not to write anything in my letters that will be cut out. There is lots of things I could write about that I will have to tell you when I come back home some time.

What is the matter with the Pontius family? I haven't heard from any of them since I got here. I sure would like to hear from Lenora & Warren.

These mountains sure fool a person up here. They look like they are only a half mile away but they turn out to be about 2 ½ miles. Then they are so steep that you change your mind and don't climb them.

Well I guess I better start closing for I am running out of paper. Hope to hear from you soon.

Yours until the Mississippi River wears rubber pants to keep her bottom dry. Oh! no you didn't like that one. Well I know lots more.
>Bob

[The *Evening Record* did not have a Sunday edition. Monday's headline reads, **"Chinese Win Major Burma Victory."** On April 18th, Lt. Col. Jimmie Doolittle led 16 B-25 bombers on an air raid over Japan. Today's news is that the raid has caused a shake-up in the Japanese military.]

May 8, 1942 – Bob writes to Dorothy.
Iceland
Dear Dorothy:
>Hi! Ah! You little shrimp. How are you & my car getting along. I sure hope that you are both still in one piece.
>I imagine that you think I am a heck of a brother for not writing more often. It seems that I just can't get started to write. Then when I start I can't think of anything to write about.
>This rock called Iceland isn't as bad as I thought. We have had about a week of nice spring weather. The Icelanders call it summer but they just don't know any better. They have a big holiday here when summer begins. All the stores are closed in town just like Labor day at home. Boy, I found a swell place to go swimming in Reykjavik [seaport and capital]. I was surprised to find such a nice place in this country. It was nicer than the swimming pool at Summit Beach Park. There are several nice places here to swim in the ocean if it ever gets warm enough here. I imagine it does because I have seen a few diving boards along the shore. Well I guess it is about closing time because I am a little tired & sleepy. They are keeping us a little busier than we were back in the States, but I guess we can take it.
>I am sending you a little souvenir of this big rock. Hope you like it.
>Must close. Write soon & don't do anything I wouldn't.
>Your Brother, Bob.
>P. S. Mr. Censor: Enclosed please find one handkerchief.

[**"U.S. Sinks 17 Jap Ships In Great Pacific Naval Battle Still Raging"** The Battle of the Coral Sea is in progress. In a smaller article, it is noted that Mothers Day is approaching, and the war mothers are going to sell carnations on Ravenna's Main St. The proceeds are to go to disabled veterans.]

June 28, 1942 – Bob's June 26 letter is postmarked on this date to Dorothy. It is irritating enough to have someone read your mail, but to have them "nick" your letter is more so.
Dear Dorothy & Family.

Boy, was I glad to hear from you folks the other nite.

So you say my last few letters had a few little nicks in them. That doesn't surprise me any. If I wrote what I am thinking sometimes, all you would get is the date and my signature at the other end. I get pretty hot under the collar sometimes. But there is never anything so bad but what it could be worse. So you see I haven't changed a bit.

So you had a few little fancy crimps in my car. I thought that I was the only one that could do that.

Why don't you make up your mind where you are going to work. It is pretty nice to have two jobs isn't it. When one plays out you have the other one to go to.

Oh yes! while I am thinking of it. If I hear any more reports of your staying out until three or four o'clock, I am going to paddle your slacks with you in there when I get back home sometime. You know Mom has enough to worry about now.

I didn't get my smoking tobacco yet, but I don't think the mail is all in yet from this convoy.

Did you folks get the money order I sent you on May 21st? I guess that was the last letter I sent home.

No I haven't received a letter from Ethel Barwell [?] since I got up here. I guess it is my own fault though. I haven't wrote to anyone but you folks & the Pontius family. I got a letter from Vernon yesterday and now I have to answer that one. I like to get letters but I hate to answer them. I was glad that you sent me Vincent Eichler's address. I had intended to ask you for it ever since I have been up here, but I would forget it every time. So Harris Warner is going to have to come to the army. Boy, that sure does tickle me. Maybe they will make a man out of that big over-grown one. He will have to get along on a hour off for dinner instead of two or three.

Well I guess I better close now and get a little more sleep. I haven't been doing so bad the last 24 hrs. I slept about 16 hours.

This was one of my lucky days.
Your Loving Brother, Bob.
[Name etc.] A.P.O. #5
c/o Postmaster
New York, N. Y.
I am in the same old place so don't let the address fool you.

[The 28th was a Sunday, so Monday's headline reads: **"Nazis Smash British Lines In Egypt."** The FBI is looking for accomplices of 8 saboteurs who were deposited on the East coast by a German submarine.]

July 14, 1942 – Bob's letter is written on this date, but postmarked eight days later. He has just received some mail from the States that is three months late. This certainly makes it frustrating to keep up on the latest home front news, conduct business, or buy birthday and holiday gifts on time.

Dear Dorothy & Family.

Hi! You little squirt. How's every one? Just fine I hope.

I just got some of the old letters you folks sent me. Dated anywhere from the last of April to the last of May. Swell service, eh? Sure hope that my letters get home faster than that. I guess they must have sent them clear around the world.

How is your job holding out this time? I sure hope that you don't get sick and have to quit again.

How are the tires on my car holding out? They should last a long time yet if you are careful how you use them.

I went in and had my allotment raised to $40.00. That will probably go in affect August 1st. That means you will get it on about the third of September. That will do more good at home than it will do if I keep it here. Because we are making these civilians rich enough as it is. Every time I go to town I spend ten or fifteen dollars and haven't got anything to show for it. I am planning on getting a picture album and about two hundred scenery pictures of this rock. That will cost me about $8.00 in our money. I run across some of the old gang that used to be with us last summer. It was some of the fellows that were over 28 and discharged. I was talking with Leonard Walsh. He is from Akron, Ohio. His brother and him run the United Cigar Store on the corner of Main & Mill Street, or right in there some place. Pop would know where I mean, because he used to always get his tobacco there, whenever we were in Akron. He said things were about the same as ever back there. Of course, that was some time ago. He was only home for about two months, then he was called back. I guess that his little vacation done him lots of good, because he sure was looking good.

Well I guess I had better start closing now. There is lots of things that I would like to tell you but I guess we are not as good as the boys in Cleveland. They can write almost anything according to one of the letters in the Chicago paper. Perhaps they will wake up here sometime.

Oh yes about my address. Don't ever put the Division Number on my address. Write it just like I had it on the envelope.
Yours Truly, Bob.

["**Russia Warns People Of Danger**" The Red Army is reeling under the German onslaught. The Kremlin issues a victory or death statement In Jugoslavia, a German Gestapo chief was assassinated, and in retaliation the Nazis kill or wound about 700 civilians in a grenade attack.]

August 18, 1942 – Bob's three day old letter is posted on this date.
August 15, '42
Dear Dorothy & Family:
Hi! Oh! you little squirt. How's everyone?

I guess you folks are giving me a dose of my own medicine, or someone is. The last letter that I received from you was dated July 3, '42. The rest of them are either on their way or else they are in Davis [Davy] Joneses locker.

How is your job holding out this summer? How is the Monarch Rubber Co. [his former employer] running this summer? I sure hope that they get back on their feet again because I have a good chance there and it is close to home. I hear that we are going to get radio speakers in all of our huts, so we can all listen to the news reports. We only have the one radio that is any good and that is in the orderly room, & we can't all run in there to listen to it. Even if about 95% of the news is false or morale building, the other 5% is worth hearing and good to argue about.

It doesn't seem to me that it has been eight months since I was home. The time is passing faster than it did last summer when I was on maneuvers.

How is my Chevrolet running, or doesn't it run any more? Would you folks send me a pipe now to smoke the tobacco in that [sic] you sent me about two mo. ago. I can't get anything here but a cheap English pipe that isn't worth two bits. I would like a Frank Medico & a supply of filters to go with it. I also need some lighter flints. I want a pipe with a medium or small bowl, a long stem and a wide mouth piece. Maybe you think I am a little particular, but there is as much difference in a pipe as there is a car.

How is Elmore getting along with the work by now? I hope that he can get a fellow to help him through harvest, but I imagine that will be pretty hard to do.

Well I guess I had better start closing because I can't think of much more to say, & five pages is my limit.

Hope to hear from you folks soon, & I will try to make myself write more often.

Try sending my mail by airmail, it might get here quicker. It gets into N. Y. faster and catches a convoy out quicker.
Yours Truly, Bob.

["**Nazis Retreat On The Stalingrad Front**" Although the Russian counterattack appears to be successful, the Germans will still press on to Stalingrad. On the Western Front, the Americans and British commence around the clock air raids.]

September 21, 1942 – Postmarked Sept. 27th, Bob's letter is allowed to ask about home events and to render an opinion on them, but anything about the 5th Division is forbidden.
Dear Dorothy & Family:

Hi! You little squirt. How's everyone back at Randolph? I was glad to hear that you are still working good. I hate to see you have to work, but that is the only way to succeed. Boy, if I hear of you going on a strike like some of the shops are doing, I won't even own you as a sister. But I know that you know better than that. They should take the strikers & put them in the army. That would teach them a lesson.

So you think <u>my car</u> is running good. Have you had the valves ground in it yet? If you haven't, then I would suggest that you take it to some good Chevrolet garage and have the motor checked, because I don't know when we can ever get another car, so we have to take care of this one.

What kind of job does this Carl Ervin have? Or doesn't he have to work?

I was sorry to hear that Harley was in the hospital. What was wrong with him? Have you got his address for me yet? I haven't heard from him or Warren for about two months. I don't know if I said something that made them sore, or if they are too busy to write.

Did you send me Ethel Myers' address yet? If you did, I haven't received it, but it may get here with the next batch of mail. I can't even find her old address. That is the one she had when she lived in Canton.

I think that it would be safe for you to send me travel pictures I believe that I get most of the mail, but it is sometimes a month before I get it.

Boy, this darned letter writing is a pain in the neck. I heard a rumor that they were going to loosen up a little and let us write letters like the soldiers do in the other places. If that is true, it will give us something to write about.

Well I see by our detail list that I will have a night off again. So I guess I can catch up on my letter writing. I am only one letter behind schedule now & that is Hazel's. So I guess if the wind doesn't blow the hut away, I will get it wrote.

I must close now, hoping to hear from you soon. Hope you are all feeling fine.

Your Loving Brother, Bob.

["**Stalingrad Bombarded; Nazis Gain**" Locally, a farm almost two miles from the Francisco farm is struck by a tornado which causes damage to buildings and the corn fields. It is announced that married men with children will be subject to the draft in October 1943.]

October 31, 1942 – Posted this date to Dorothy, part of this letter is cut out.
Oct. 29, 1942
Dear Dorothy & Family:

Hi! You little squirt. How's the world treating you? Say, what's wrong, did you break your arm or forget how to write. I haven't heard from you in a coon's age. Oh! So you think the same about me. I will try to do better than I have been. The last letter I received from you was dated Sept. 10, '42.

I am keeping a record on the letters I send you folks. So let me know if you get them. [Some Civil War soldiers used the same system.] Send me the date of the last one I wrote you, [it] was dated Oct. 14th.

How is your job holding out? I sure hope that you can keep working all winter. How is our car running or doesn't it run any more? Oh! no I am not hinting that you could have wrecked it, for I am the only one that can do that. I just thought maybe you forgot to turn on the switch. Ha! Ha! Boy, that sure was a joke on the car.

Did you ever find out what was wrong with Harley? When [was] he was in the hospital, about two months ago? I haven't heard from him since he was in Maine.

Did Warren have to go to the army yet or did his job keep him out for a while longer? The last I heard of him he expected to go about the first of Sept., & he hasn't wrote since.

The last I knew of Harris Warner he was in California. He hasn't wrote since he left home.

There is about four people that I would like to have you send me their addresses if you can get them, they are: Ethel Myers, Harley & Warren Pontius & Harris Warner. Perhaps you have sent them all ready but they didn't get here yet.

Boy, it sure seems funny to try to read & write with one of these old kerosene lamps.

Well I guess there isn't much left to say [about one line cut out here] & tell you about the weather.

I must close now. Hoping to hear from you soon.
Your Loving Brother, Bob.

[**MacArthur's Planes Hit 4 Jap Warships"** Due to the importance of the war, the Ohio gubernatorial race is described as "a dull affair." Another article reads: "New War Taxes Raise Cost of Smoking, Drinking, 'Phoning."]

November 23, 1942 – No doubt hearing that v-mail service was faster, Bob decides to send a v-mail letter to his family. What may have taken six weeks by boat could now be reduced to twelve days or less by air. So, Bob acquired a packet of the special v-mail forms and wrote his message in the appropriate space. His letter was then microfilmed, and the roll of film weighing about seven ounces and containing over 1,500 letters was flown to the destination closest to the Francisco home. The film was then developed, and the resulting letter was one-fourth the original size. When Bob's family received the letter, it was on one side of a 3 ¾ inch square, and they may have needed a magnifying glass to read it. Nevertheless, v-mail was not only faster, but it also saved weight and space for other military supplies on cargo planes. [25]

Dear Mom & Family: How are all you folks feeling this nice weather? O. K. I hope. How did the fellows make out the first day of the hunting season, or couldn't they get the ammunition this year? Was [name?] out or couldn't he get off? What is his address? I thought that I had it but I couldn't find it, so I couldn't send him a Christmas card.

Tell Elmore [his brother] to keep up the good work. I sure am glad to hear that he is doing so good.

I guess that when I get back I will have to let him take care of the business end & I will stay home and do the work. You better not tell him that because he may remember it and I am not much of a worker. I haven't received the package you folks sent me yet, but it will probably get here in the next mail call we have. I got the fruit cakes that Hazel sent me and they sure were good. You can tell the mail carrier that he had better find out what he is talking about, because there is no such order out that you can't send food through the mail. If there is, a lot of people are violating it.

Boy, this is just like ---p here at this camp. We have no electric lights, so we use candles & lanterns. We bought a gas lamp for about $12.00 and used it two nights & days and it is on the [word?] all ready.

I guess you folks will have to get your Christmas presents out of the money I send home. They don't have anything worth buying up here. I must close now and wish you a Merry Christmas.
Your Loving Son, Robert

["**Soviet Trap Perils 375,000 Nazis**" The Red Army and the Russian winter were closing in on the German invaders. On the home front, married men could expect to be called up in December.]

December 17, 1942 – In this letter to his mother, Bob reverts to regular mail because he attaches a money order.
Dear Mom & Family:
How are all you folks this nice wintery day? I hope you are

all feeling fine.
    I think I have a pretty good record for the past nine months. I have only been on the sick list once & that was only for a little cold. Then I had a few teeth fixed too, but that is to be expected with a old man like me. [He is now 27 years old.]
    I received the v-mail letter you sent me on Nov. 30th. It was about two weeks old when it got here, but that isn't bad. When I think of how it used to take your letters either a week or more to catch up with me when we was on maneuvers.
    I didn't realize that it had been so long since I wrote you a letter. The last one I wrote was on Nov. 28th. I wouldn't blame you if you would give me a good paddling when I come home.
    Hazel was telling me in a letter that you have been having a little snow & ice lately, especially on the day that Wilson left for Pa. to go deer hunting. We had our first snow on Howard's birthday, but there wasn't very much.
    If Elmore keeps on having as good luck trapping, he can quit farming. I imagine that furs are a very good price this year.
    I am sending you the money order to spend in any way you like. I had intended to send it home for a Christmas present but I couldn't get in to town when I wanted to, so I just waited until they were making them out here in this camp. So it is a little late.
    I just can't seem to think of any more to write about. So I must close. Will send a V-mail letter in a few days, perhaps.
Your Loving Son, Bob.
[In print] Censor notice
Money Order Enclosed.
    ["**Half Of Rommel's Forces Trapped**" Gen. Montgomery's British forces are pushing "the Desert Fox" back in Libya. In Ravenna the Civil Defense is preparing to inaugurate blackouts in January. Air raid wardens have been on the alert and there has been a medical mobilization. The nearby arsenal could be a prime target for an enemy air attack.]

December 24, 1942 – On Christmas Eve, Bob writes to Dorothy.
Dear Dorothy & Family:
    Hi! You little squirt. How's everything going with you?
    I received the letter that you wrote Nov. 15. It was just a little over a mo. old but that's O. K. so long as they get here. The V-mail

does come through a little faster than the other. The V-mail letter that you sent me on Nov. 23 got here in about two weeks. Did you folks finally find time to have a card party? I imagine that you are planning another one for New Years eve. Sure wish I was there but I guess I will have to wait until next year.

It doesn't seem like it has been almost a year since I have been home. I hope the years don't all go as fast as this one did, after the war is over.

What do you mean that you may have some news for me that will sweep me off my feet? Hope you haven't any foolish ideas. Ha! Ha! Have you and Ervin [Lashley] moved to Alliance yet? What kind of a place can you get down there? I never thought that I would care much about living in that town unless I could live over on the southwest side.

Here it is the night before Christmas but it doesn't seem much like it. Xmas isn't Xmas without a tree and your own family. I believe that we will have part of the decoration though, even if we can't have them all. I always did like a white Christmas.

What do you mean our car is running O. K., did you buy a half interest in it that I know nothing about? I am glad to hear that you are taking such good care of it. I was pretty sure that you would or I would never let you have it.

We are all looking forward to a good Christmas dinner tomorrow. They just opened a new mess hall this morning. Boy, it is pretty nice & just around the corner from the hut that I live in.

I got a letter from two of my old buddies that got discharged just before the war. They are both back in the Army and up here somewhere. I will have to try to pay them a visit, if I get time & can find them. They were John Yarian and Earl Leach. I don't know if I ever told you much about them or not.

There isn't much news that I can write about, so I must close. Hoping to hear from you soon. The last letter I wrote you was Dec. 6th so I can't blame you if I get a bawling out for not writing more often. Your Loving Brother, Bob

P. S. Did you ever send the pictures of you and Ervin that I asked for?

["**Reds Take Another Important Town**" Another front page story discusses the role of God in the war. Eddie Rickenbacker, who had miraculously recovered from his injuries in the Atlanta plane crash two years ago, was lost in the Pacific Ocean. After 24 days in a raft on the open sea, he and the other survivors were rescued on November 13, 1942. On the eighth day of the ordeal, seemingly out of nowhere a sea gull swooped down and landed on Rickenbacker's head. Rickenbacker slowly raised his hands until he could grab the bird by its legs. This gift from heaven provided food, and they used the intestines for bait to catch mackerels. [26] An officer familiar with the Philippine campaign remarked, "There were no infidels in the foxholes of Bataan."]

1943

January 30, 1943 – Bob would like to know more about his sister's new beau, Ervin Lashley. He also envisions coming home after the war and telling of his experiences.

Dear Dorothy:

Hi! There you little squirt. How is everything with you now days. I sure hope that you are feeling fine & are happy.

I hope you will forgive me for not writing for so long. I just couldn't think of anything to say & didn't have much time to say it in.

How is Ervin making it in the Army? I sure hope he likes it better than I do. But he probably doesn't, that is if he is as much like me as you say he is. It may be okey for him to be like me in civilian life, but it sure isn't a paying proposition for him to be like me in the Army. Because that's where I am just no good.

I received a letter from Dale the other day. He talks like he had it pretty nice in the Air Force. He will probably get to see lots of country. Harley seems to be traveling around lots & he went to the same school.

How many times do I have to ask you for a picture of Ervin? You sure can't be so <u>homely</u> that you break the camera every time. Ha! Ha! I guess that should get me a picture or a slap in the puss when you see me again.

How is <u>our</u> car running now? I'll bet it isn't getting many miles on it now that you only get 4 gal. of gas per week. [rationing] Did you go back to work again now that Ervin is in the Army, or are you staying at home again now?

I am on a 5 day furlough or rest period or whatever you want to call it. There isn't much to do but rest. I will say that I am having the best time that I have since I left the States. And we all consider it a good break. Because it gives a chance to catch up on our letter writing and sleep. I get about 12 hours sleep a day. The only bad part about it is that there is only one day left. Then I start to work again.

Boy, I sure hope this war ends soon, because I have got so much to tell you folks the first time I see you that I probably won't give you a chance to get a word in edge ways. I must close now & write Hazel & Mom a few lines.

Your Loving Brother, Bob.

[**"Bomb Berlin On Anniversary"** It has been ten years since the Nazis came to power. For an anniversary gift, the allies bombed the German capital.]

February 14, 1943 – Bob is unaware of the sad event at home.
Dear Dorothy & Family:

Hi! There you little squirt. How are you feeling these nice wintery days. O. K. I hope.

Tell Pop I said happy birthday. I sure missed the chicken dinner but this is the third time, and they say three times & out. So I guess that means that I am to be there for his next birthday dinner. [Bob's father died on February 1st, thirteen days before his 67th birthday.]

Boy, my letters sure do take long enough to get home. Don't they? Perhaps they will come through faster again now. I am going to try to send more V-mail letters, if I can get the forms. I was glad to hear that Ervin didn't have to come in the Army quite as soon as he had expected.

Where does Ervin's brother live in Marlboro? Does he live out toward Myerses [sic]? That is where I have an idea it is.

What do you mean by that crack about the rough carpenter? Because I can do pretty good. (Ahem!) Oh, I almost broke my arm that time, patting myself on the back.

So you don't get to very many shows. You probably wouldn't like them if you could go. About all they know how to make now is some war or fifth column pictures.

How much gas do you get a week now? Can you get any more if you need it? [Rationing is in effect.]

Boy, it sure is hard for me to write up here, where there isn't anything we dare write about. I should think it would be easy for you to write back there where there is lots of news. But you do write about two letters to my one.

Well I will have to close now and get at least five hours sleep, because there's a big day's work ahead tomorrow. I just don't seem to know enough to go to sleep when I have a chance.

Hope to hear from you again soon. I will try to write a letter next time.

Your Loving Brother, Bob.

Bob sent two newspaper articles from his stay in Iceland. One is a picture of Cpl. John N. Finnerty in front of his hut with deep snow and ice. Bob printed on it: "One of our barracks, very little snow where I am." The other article is titled: "Icelandic Lesson, Lesson Twenty Four." The topic was swimming. The left column is Icelandic, and the adjacent column is the English translation. Bob printed at the bottom, "I will talk like this when I come home."

[**Battleship Richelieu, 3 Other French Warships In U.S. To Join Allied Fleet**" In North Africa, American forces are engaged at the Faid Pass in Tunisia.]

March 15, 1943 – V-mail letter to **Mrs. Ervin Lashley** (Dorothy) in Atlanta, Georgia.

Dear Dorothy & Ervin: Hi there you little squirts. How is the world treating you all down in Georgia? O. K. I hope. I imagine you both will be hillbillies when you come back home. Thanks a lot for the picture that you sent me. It sure is a good one. When I look at it, it looks just like you were standing right in front of me. – What camp is Ervin stationed at? Or is he staying in town while he is going to school? – I am glad that you & Hazel took that trip down in Ga. It will make both of you appreciate home a little more. As for the long ride down there, that just shows you a little of what the Army boys have to put up with. That ride on a train isn't anything after one ride a few days on a boat. Now it closes the end of my paper again, and I haven't said anything, so I must close. Hoping to hear from you soon. Your Loving Brother, Bob.

[There is no glaring headline on today's *Evening Record*, but the lead story assesses how much longer the war will continue. The United Press executives state: "Allied War Triumph Certain But It May Take Longer Than Most People Think."]

April 10, 1943 – This V-mail is postmarked April 10, but the letter is probably written on April 1. The right margin is very dark, making it difficult to read. It is addressed to Dorothy Lashley in Atwater, Ohio. Dear Dorothy & Family: -- How are all of you folks back in Randolph? Feeling fine I hope. – There isn't much [news] up here that I can write about. So this letter will probably be pretty dry just like the most of them that I write. I ran across another one of my old friends the other day. John Yarian from New Waterford, Ohio that is up near Youngstown. He was one of the fellows that I used to haul back from Ft. Custer. He doesn't have any love for the place either. – It would be nice if Ervin would get to stay in Ft. Hayes. Wouldn't it? Then he might have a chance to get home once in a while. That would be too nice to ask. Think of it though. – Boy, I hope I never see another phonograph again. We have one of the darned things in our hut & it runs all the time. Just spoils a good song. – How are they coming with my car? It should be fixed by now. But parts are probably pretty hard to get. – Well I guess I have to close now and drop Ethel a few lines before she thinks I forgot her.
Your Loving Brother, Bob.

[**"Axis' Tunisia Defenses Crumbling"** Locally, the Ravenna leaders are gearing up for a War Bond drive.]

May 1, 1943 – Bob's V-mail to Dorothy is postmarked on this date. Dorothy turned twenty years old on the 19th.
April 19 [1943]
Dear Dorothy & Family: -- happy Birthday you little squirt. I bet you thought that I had forgot all about you. I had one of the fellows that was lucky to get into town [to] try to get [you] a birthday or Easter cards. But he said all he could find weren't fit to send to his worst enemy. So you will have to be satisfied with a V-mail. If I ever get to write. – How are all of you folks and how are they getting along with the spring work? What is Elmore doing about the farm? Is he going to try to run the whole thing or is he going to leave about half of it idle this year? I wish that I was back in the States, then I could get a furlough & help him out with any work. – How does Ervin like the Army by this time? I sure hope that he is in a good outfit & not one like I am in. Must close now.
Your Loving Brother, Bob.

[On this May Day, the big news is John L. Lewis' striking

coal miners: **U.S. Takes Over Mines.**" At this critical time, President Roosevelt orders Secretary of the Interior Harold Ickes to take possession of the mines. Locally, 148 pints of blood were donated in the Kent blood drive.]

May 24, 1943 – Bob's affection for Ethel Meyers is becoming more apparent.
Dear Dorothy & Family:
Hi! There you little squirt. How are you all? I guess that's the way you hillbillies say it.
I hope that you are all O. K. and as happy as can be expected or a little happier. I just received your letter of May 4th and I have a few minutes to myself tonite. So I will answer it and have it off my mind.
Now it is my time to bawl you out for not writing Ethel. The way I understand it, you haven't been writing her very often, especially since you went to Georgia. And you know that she likes to hear from you as well as she does me.
What camp is Ervin stationed at in Ga., or is he just going to school there?
Who did Ray Siffert marry? The last that I knew of him he was going with Alma Eichler & a few others. And what about Lee, is he still home or has he been called in the Army?
You folks don't keep me very well posted on my neighbors. Of course, I understand that they will probably all be moved away before I get back home, (1950) but I would like to know where they went, etc.
I am sending you a picture of myself. So you won't forget what I look like. The picture itself isn't so bad but the wrinkles in my clothes are awful. I guess I need a WAAC for a tailor to keep me dressed neat. I will try to do better next time, if I ever get back to town again.
Must close now. Hope to hear from you soon.
Your Loving Brother, Bob.
[**"Nearly 1,000 RAF Planes Smash At Ruhr In Heaviest Raid Of War"** On the home front, the big news is the United Rubber Workers' strike in Akron, the Rubber Capital of the World, where 38,000 workers walk out.]

June 2, 1943 – This letter leaves no doubt how Bob feels about Ethel.

Dear Dorothy & Family:

Just received your long letter of May 26th today. That one sure made good time. I wish that they would all come through like that. I also got your letters of May 19th & 21st. I got them two days ago.

I hope that you enjoy your train ride back from Ga. better than you did the ride down there.

Yes, I remember quite well the nite of Feb. 12th 1941 and every nite & day before that. The memories of the past are greater in our minds than the present memories are. I guess it is because they were so much pleasanter.

What do you mean that you are glad that I am still being true to Ethel? How else could I be to someone that I think so much of as I do her? You know how you feel about Ervin. That's the way it is with me. I got a letter from her that she sent May 23rd. She sent me one of her pictures. Boy, she is more beautiful than I had remembered her. This time I am going to do all that I can to keep from losing her. As you remember, I almost lost her once. You probably can't imagine how I felt. But it was no one's fault but my own. Then when I found out that I still had a chance, I sure felt better.

Did you folks get the pictures that I sent you? I sent yours out on May 24th. So you should soon get them & see what I look like again.

I wish we had some of the extra heat that you folks have back there. We are having a much warmer & drier summer than we had last year tho. So we can't complain.

Well I guess I will have to close now. Because I haven't any more to say. I was going to write you eight pages like you did, but they made this paper too big. So I settled for four pages.

Hope you are all feeling fine. And I am hoping to hear from you again soon.

Your Loving brother, Bob.

[**"WLB Refers Coal Strike To F.D.R."** Leslie Howard, the 50-year old British film star, and 12 others are killed when the Germans shoot down their plane over the Bay of Biscay. Four years ago, Howard played Ashley Wilkes in "Gone With The Wind."]

June 8, 1943 – Bob addresses this V-mail to Mrs. Erwin Lashley (Dorothy).

Dear Dorothy & Family: How is the world treating you by now? I sure hope that you are feeling fine and are happy as can be expected. Haven't heard from you for about a week and I guess it has been that long since I wrote. – There isn't much of any news to write about, but I will try to fill up this page. – Just received a letter from Helen. She says everything is O. K. out around Akron. And she also said that she hadn't heard from you since you went to Georgia. She said that she figured that you were too busy. I don't know what she thought you were doing, because you didn't go down there to work. – Well, I guess I will have to start closing and write Ethel & Helen a few lines, while I have time. Hope that I get a letter from you next mail.

Your Loving Brother, Bob.

["**British Commandos Raid Italian Island As Churchill Reports Massive Allied Undertakings Are Impending**" Allied bombers and British naval units are blasting the harbors and coastal batteries of Pantelleria.]

June 17, 1943 – It is the same old thing for the 5th Division in Iceland - construction and physical training. For a different look, Bob cultivates a pencil-thin mustache.

Dear Dorothy & Family:

Hi! There you little squirt. How is the world treating you? Ok, I hope. I imagine that you are glad to get back home again. I know I would be.

I was sorry to hear about Ervin's brother. But I guess that is the way things have to be sometimes.

It must be that you don't rate with Ethel like I do. For she always answers my letters just as quick as she gets them.

Why don't you go down and pay her a visit now that you are back home? She is working days now, and is home most every evening.

I guess about all she goes out is on Saturday evening when her & Maxine go to the show.

Yes, I can imagine Boyd Siffert working hard. He is one fellow that I would like to see in the Army. He use to always talk about joining the Army. But that was before it even looked like we would get into the war. He never wants to say very much to me when

I get back or there will be at least one strange face in Hell.

Yes, I guess I was just speaking of that 1950 stuff. Or at least I hope I was.

The mustache that I have is OK over here where there isn't any fussy girls. But I guess I will have to shave when I come home to visit some of the girls back there. I don't think Ethel would like it.

I wonder if you would find out for me when Ethel's birthday is. I hope that it isn't over yet. Because I would like to send her something or have you get her something for me.

Well there isn't much news to write about, except that you probably won't hear from me quite so often now for a while, because it looks like I would be pretty busy for a month or so.

Well I must close now and write Ethel a few <u>lines</u>. Hope to hear from you again very soon.

Your Loving Brother, Bob

[**"Bag 77 Jap Planes In Big Battle"** The big battle was over Guadalcanal. In the European theater, the British bombers are hammering Cologne, Germany.]

July 8, 1943 - At the cost of six cents, Bob airmails a letter to his mother. For quite a while, he has been walking away from mail call with no news from home.

Dear Mom & Family:

How are all of you folks back home? O.K. and feeling fine I hope. What is wrong that you haven't been writing me lately? This is the fourth letter that I have wrote since I heard from you. If I said something or done something that you didn't like, I would sure like to know about it. Of course, I know that you are awful busy, but it doesn't take long to write a V-mail.

How is Elmore getting along with the work by now? I imagine that he is making hay and harvesting potatoes. I walked past a field of new mown hay last evening and the smell of the fresh hay sure made me feel a little homesick. But I guess I will get over it, for I did last year.

I don't believe that the crops here are as good this year as they were last year. Even if we did have a drier & warmer summer.

Hazel says that they have an awful nice batch of potatoes this year. I hope that ours are just as good.

Did you get to talk with Ethel when she was down there a

few weeks ago? If you did, what do you think of her?

Well, there isn't much that I can write about any more. So I guess I will have to close for now & write Hazel a few lines. Hope to hear from you real soon, for I am beginning to worry a little about you.

Your Loving Son, Robert

P.S. Did you ever get that picture that I sent you?

["**Nazis Inch Ahead In Russia**" It is reported that 30,000 Germans have died in the latest battle. From allied headquarters in North Africa, a United Press correspondent states: "The gigantic challenge confronting the allies in assaulting Hitler's European fortress slaps you in the face when you enter this war theater and become aware of the tremendous preparations underway."

July 10, 1943 – Bob is relieved and delighted to hear from Dorothy and his mother. Their letters took a little over two weeks to reach him.

Dear Dorothy & Family:

Hi! There you little squirt. How are all of you folks back home today? Okay I hope.

Just received your letter of June 21st along with Mom's letter of June 24th. So I decided to answer yours tonite and Mom's & Ethel's tomorrow. So tell Mom that I will try to write her a better letter than the one I wrote on the eighth.

What did you mean by the remark that you answer your letters before they get gray hair? Perhaps I have a guilty conscience.

What makes you think I would learn to dance? There isn't anything here fit to dance with except my buddies. And they would know that I was crazy if I started dancing with another fellow.

What makes you think that I would almost die laughing if I seen you? I have seen a pumpkin seed before.

How is Ervin getting along now since he made Cpl? I imagine you have heard from him by now.

Well, I just got back from the drill factory. Now I have all my teeth fixed. That is, what I have left. I guess this guy is a pretty good dentist, but he is a little rough. He can take a root and build a pretty good tooth on it. But I don't know how long they will stay. If they do, I think I will get him to build a foundation for my house (after the war). He should be good at that too.

Well there isn't much news that we can write about. So I guess I will have to close for now. Besides, this is the last sheet of paper I have & I can't get any until tomorrow.
Hope to hear from you all soon.
Your Loving Brother, Bob
["**Report Allied Invasion Forces Establish Bridgeheads In Sicily And Drive Inland**" In regard to the Sicilian Campaign, President Roosevelt declares that this is "the beginning of the end" for Hitler and Mussolini.]

August 9, 1943 – Bob V-mails to his sister at the Atwater mailing address.
Dear Dorothy & Family:
Hi! There you little squirt. How is the world treating everyone back home? Okay I hope. Just received your letter of July 27th, so I guess it is my turn to write now. [I] Should have wrote sooner, but I just can't get started. I haven't even wrote Ethel a letter since Aug. 1st. [I] sure am slipping. I sure was glad to hear that you went down to pay her a visit. You don't know how much I wish that I was where I could go and see her & you folks once in a while. That is about the only thing that I can say for the army, and especially this trip over here, has done for me. [That] Is to appreciate my home & folks. I guess I have run out of paper, so I will have to close now. Hope to hear from you soon.
Your Loving Brother Bob.
["**Report Coup To Oust Hitler Near**" At this point in time, this is an optimistic report based on rumors. It would be closer to the truth if it were Mussolini, whose government has surrendered to the allies. Locally, two juveniles are arrested for stealing gas rationing coupon books from the OPA board offices for war price and rationing. The thieves operated their own black market.]

September 15, 1943 – In August, the 5th Division moved to Tidworth Barracks, England. Bob's small-sized stationery is postmarked the 18th and mailed to Dorothy in care of Alice Francisco.
England.
Dear Dorothy & Family:
Well I finally did get started to write again. I have been too busy working and enjoying myself to write many letters. Don't get

me wrong and think that I enjoy my work for I haven't changed that much. But we do get a little more frills down here than we did in our last station.

How are all of you folks back home? O. K. and keeping busy and happy I hope. I know you [are] busy enough. Have you heard from Ervin lately? I hope they don't send him overseas yet, or never have to.

There isn't much of any news that I can write about. But I will try to finish out this page. I bought small paper so my letters would have more pages in them, but now I have less to buy.

Tell Mom that I will write her the next time I write some. I wouldn't blame her if she gave me a real bawling out like I did here one time. I know I have got it coming. Tell her that I said happy birthday, even if it is a little late. [Alice Francisco's birthday was on Sept. 6.]

I have been to Bristol and Bournemouth. Both very nice cities. They are about like Cleveland & Akron. Easy to get lost in, especially during a blackout.

I think I will go to London in a week or two. They say that is a wonderful place.

Well I have to write Ethel & Dale a few lines yet. So I guess I will have to close for now. Hope to hear from you soon.
Your Loving Brother, Bob.
P. S. I knew I was forgetting something. My current address is:
PFC R. E. Francisco 35009786
Co. G 2nd Inf.
APO # New York City

Subject to change without notice. For it is almost too short and handy for us to keep.
So Long. Bob.

["**Allies Stem Nazi Drive At Salerno**" Up against the German army and rugged terrain, the allies are finding that the Italian Campaign will be more difficult that the Sicilian action. The Americans are throwing more troops into the 24-mile wide beachhead, and with the aid of massive naval and air shelling, the German counterattack is being repulsed. Locally, the 3rd War Bond Drive has reached over $445,000 in Portage County, The goal is $3,100,000.]

October 10, 1943 – With the change of scenery and the prospects of a pass and furlough, the Yanks of the 5th Division are in good spirits.
England
Dear Dorothy & Family.

Hi! There you little squirt. How are you and the rest of the family getting along? All feeling fine and working hard I hope.

I hope you folks have heard from me by now. I have been writing to you or Mom at least once a week ever since I have been over here. So you will get a stack of them one of these days soon I hope.

We haven't had a mail call for over a week now. So I am looking for some mail too. The last letter I got from you was the V-mail of Sept. 23rd. I got it on Oct. 1st. Our mail has been coming in real good up until now.

Tuesday Oct. 12th I guess I will start on my eight day furlough if nothing happens to stop me. I finally decided to go to Bath instead of London. I will see London on a 48 hr. pass. It's too big of a city for me. I like a city about the size of Canton or Akron. That's why I like Bournemouth, Bristol & Bath. My money goes fast enough there and London is a little more expensive. About like New York. There isn't much to do in any of the towns but eat, go to the shows, and walk around and look at the scenery.

Last Thursday & Friday I was in Bournmouth again and we went out sightseeing in a taxi cab. It was a little expensive. We only had the cab two hours and it cost us four Dollars. But I guess it was worth it. For I saw some of the prettiest homes & country that I ever saw.

Has Ethel been up to see you folks lately, or has she been too busy? She really does have a lot of work to do, and I know she isn't afraid to do it.

You have the same opinion of her as I do. And if there is anyone that is any nicer I never have met her, and I never want to.

Well I guess that I will have to close for now and get ready for supper. Then go to a show this evening.

Hope to hear from you real soon. And I hope that my mail starts coming through faster.
Your Loving Brother, Bob.

[This is a Sunday, so the *Evening Record's* Monday's headline reads: "**U.S. Troops Flank Volturno Line.**" Any good news from the blood bath in Italy is eagerly sought. In the Pacific Theater, it is reported that the Americans massively bombed and shelled Wake Island on October 5 and 6.]

October 27, 1943 – The 5th Division has moved to Northern Ireland, where it begins advanced training for the invasion of France.
Ireland
Dear Dorothy & Family:
  How are all of you folks back home? I hope that you haven't all broke your arms. But it is beginning to look that way to me. For I haven't heard from any of you for almost a month now.
  How is my little niece getting along? If it wasn't for Ethel, I wouldn't even know about her.
  Now that I bawled you out for not writing, I will probably get a whole hand full of letters from you tonight when we have mail call after supper. I know that you folks are awful busy so I guess I will have to cool off a bit and forgive you this time.
  I have been moving again, this time not quite so far. I am in North Ireland and I don't like it very well. It is not near as nice as the place that we just came from.
  I still say there is no place like home & I won't be satisfied until I get there. And I hope that it won't be long until I get there, not over a year any way.
  It won't be long now until Xmas and I haven't done anything about it. I guess that you will have to do just like you did last year and have Elmore or someone get my presents for you folks.
  I want you to get Ethel something nice. Like a dressing table, cedar chest or anything that she can use and wants.
  There isn't much that I can write about, so I guess that I will have to close for now. Hope you are all well, and I hope to hear from you soon.
Your Loving Brother, Bob
  [Dorothy honored Bob's request to buy Ethel's Christmas present, which was a cedar chest.
  On this day the headline reads: **"Russians Trap Big German Forces."** The condition in Italy is aptly described with: "Allies Slog 5 Miles In Italy." In Washington, President Roosevelt proposes a one billion dollar postwar program offering a one-year vocational or academic training to ex-service men or women.]

November 18, 1943 – Postmarked this date, a blue eagle is at the top of Bob's stationery.

Nov. 14, 1943
North Ireland
Dear Mom & Family:

How are all of you folks back home? All feeling fine I hope. I am sorry that I bawled you & Dorothy out for nor writing. But I hadn't heard from either of you for so long. And I knew that if you were sick, Ethel would tell me so.

How much stuff did Elmore buy at Emmitt's sale? I hope that he bought some of his tools. I imagine things sold pretty high though.

I guess I should write Elmore a letter again one of these days. The last one I wrote him was May 27th and the last one I got from him was April 8th. So that makes us even. But I guess it's my fault for I guess I have more time to write than he has.

No, you won't need to send all of the things that I sent for. Just the watch is all I need now. Things aren't so hard to buy over here. So I have bought everything but a watch. They cost too much and they are hard to find.

Boy, I wish that I could be home to help Elmore husk corn. But that won't be this year. I sure would like to see Dorothy's baby too. That 50 dollars that I sent for is for my furlough again. I have spent the other fifty on passes and chow in town. I am going to try to make this last because I think the money is needed more at home.

Well, I guess I will have to sign off for today, because I owe Ethel, Hazel and Glen letters. So I will have to step on it if I get them wrote today.

Hope this letter finds you all in the best of health. And I hope to hear from you soon.
Your Loving Son, Robert

[Nov. 18 - **"Allied Planes Raid Norway, Reich; Soviet Army Junction Traps Nazis"** On the Italian front, the "British Gain 2 Miles In Italy." Locally, the OPA orders a Ravenna gas station to suspend service for two weeks for an infraction of the rationing rules.]

December 6, 1943 – From Northern Ireland, Bob writes to Dorothy.
Dear Dorothy & Family:

Hi! There you little squirt. How is everything going with

you? Okay I hope.

I was glad to hear that you were down to pay Ethel a visit the other night. You two should get together just as often as you possibly can. Ethel tells me that you are a real pal and I believe her. She sure thinks a lot of Jean [Dorothy's daughter] too. Yes, I think that she pulled a pretty good trick on Mrs. Weisel by switching those letters around.

You asked me if I wanted that picture of you and Jean. You should know better than to ask such foolish questions. For you know that I always like pictures from home.

Speaking of pictures. Did you get the pictures that I sent you on Nov. 21st? While I think of it, did you get that Christmas present that I told you to get for Ethel? Anything that costs from ($5.00 to $26.00) that she could use. Let me know what you got her.

I got a letter from Vincent the other day, but I haven't got around to answer it yet. I got it just after I came back from London, so I guess I won't get to see him for a while yet. If I could have got it before I took my vacation, I would have tried harder to find him. For I wasn't sure that he was still there.

Hope that you can read this scratching. I can't. I am trying to write fast to keep warm. We have burned our ration of coal and there isn't much heat in the building. It isn't so awful cold here, but it is damp and the cold goes right through. It hardly ever freezes here.

Well there isn't much to say. So I guess I will have to sign off for tonight.

Here is a little souvenir of Ireland.

Hope this letter finds you all in the best of health and hope to hear from you real soon.

Your Loving Brother, Bob.

["**3 Front Offensive Set By Big 3; Nazi Troops Mass At Turk Border**" It is stated that the allies are mapping a peace that will last "for generations."]

December 25, 1943 – On this Christmas Day in Northern Ireland, Bob's thoughts are of home. On his blue eagle stationery, he writes to his sister.

Dear Dorothy & Family:

Merry Christmas folks. How are all of you folks this morning? I hope that you are all over your colds and are feeling fine again.

Hope that you have a nicer Christmas day than it looks like we would have. It has already rained once this morning and it looks like it would be a rainy day, like most of the rest of them are up here. Christmas isn't Christmas without snow.

We were pretty lucky this year and got the day off. Last year, most of us either worked or was on guard. And I sure hope that my next Christmas isn't in any way connected with the Army. This makes the third one that the Army has spoiled for me.

Yes, I got the Christmas box that you sent. It got here sometime in the first of Nov. I wrote you and thanked you for it on Nov. 11th according to my records. But if you didn't get the letter yet, you probably will in a few days. Thanks a lot for the things that you sent, if you don't get my other letter.

Did you ever get the letters I asked you to get the presents for Ethel and the rest of you folks? I sent that out on Oct. 27th and Nov. 14th.

I sure hope that you got Ethel something. For I would hate to not give her anything after all the things that she sent me. Let me know about it as soon as you can, because I am a little worried that you didn't get the letters. And that would sort of mess things up a lot.

I hope that you will excuse me for a few minutes, for I have to go to chow now. And I sure don't want to miss that.

We sure had a good Christmas Dinner. One of the best that the Army ever put out. But it's nothing like a meal at home. We had Turkey, Dressing, Mashed potatoes, sweet corn, coleslaw, mixed pickles, cranberry sauce, cake, bread, butter, coffee, and a pack of cigarettes. Not bad, eh? Probably better than lots of people had back home.

The Red Cross gave us candy and sweaters. I was lucky enough to get both. The way they give the sweaters out, they asked for fellows with the first names of Robert James and George. That's as far as they got. All we had to do was show our dog tags to prove our names. Boy, there was lots of Roberts. Even Bill changed his name for a few minutes with someone's dog tags.

I don't blame Ervin for wanting to trade a coconut for a snow ball. But he will have to trade with you. For all I could give him would be a mud pie. For there isn't any snow here. And I am sure he wouldn't want any mud.

Believe it or not, I went to church last night and the roof didn't fall in either. And I plan on going again tomorrow.

Have you been down to see Ethel lately? If you haven't, then you had better get on the ball. For she thinks lots of you and the kid.

Well I guess I will have to sign off for now and write Ethel a few lines yet today. Tell Mom that I'll drop her a line in a day or so.

Hope this letter finds you folks in the best of health and happiness.

Your Loving Brother, Bob.

[The *Evening Record* employees did not put out a newspaper on Christmas, a Saturday. As usual, there was no Sunday edition. Monday's headline reads: **"Yanks Invade Tip Of New Britain."** The Yanks also capture two more ridges in Italy. Gen. Eisenhower confidently predicts winning the war in Europe in the coming year.]

1944

January 9, 1944 – Bob writes to Dorothy in care of .his mother.
Dear Dorothy & Family:

Hi! There squirt. How is everything back home? Just received the letter & card that you sent Dec. 24th and have a little time of my own, so I guess I'll try to answer it.

I guess I owe you a letter for it has been two weeks now since I wrote you. I guess time is passing faster than I thought.

Thanks for doing my Christmas shopping for me again this year. I hope that this is the last Christmas that I will have to have someone do my shopping for me. But you're doing a grand job & I just may let you keep it up even after I do get back there.

No, I haven't heard from Ervin yet. So I guess that will be another letter that I will have to keep looking for. I am sorry that I haven't ever wrote him a letter yet. I just can't get started. It seems that I never get caught up with the people that write me. I usually write from seven to ten letters every week. It doesn't sound like much but it's hard for me to do Boy, this sure has been a swell day for ducks. It was raining this morning when I got up, and it's rained all day. But that's not unusual for this place. I can honestly say that I haven't seen thirty days of good sunshine in the past two years. Boy, I guess us fellows got hooked again. We rented a radio from a little shop here in town. We have to pay $2.00 or 10 shillings a week for it. That's more than the thing is worth. But it makes a noise and we do

get the news, time, & a few American programs on it. Perhaps I should buy the thing. Then I could take it out and smash it when it gets one of its squawking spells.
  Well I guess I'll have to close for tonight and write Ethel a few lines. Hope this letter finds you all well & happy.
  Write again just as soon as you can.
 Your Loving Brother, Bob.
  [This is a Sunday, so there is no local newspaper. Monday's headline reads: **"Germany's Peril Grows In Russia."** The U.S. marines are slugging it out on New Guinea. The allies are still fighting near Cassino, Italy.]

January 23, 1944 – Bob sends a jovial letter to Dorothy. Maybe the good mood was due to the Jack Benny Show.
North Ireland
Dear Dorothy & Family:
  Just a few lines today to let you know that I haven't forgot your address yet.
  I've got about four of your letters here. So I guess I'll play a dirty trick on you and answer them all in one. Hope you don't mind too much.
  I just wrote Mom a V-mail night before last and Elmore a letter yesterday, so you folks will get all three letters on the same day, or I suppose that's the way it will be.
  So you think I should call *Jean* [Dorothy's daughter] by her right name, eh! Well I don't know what you have got to squawk about for she is my niece, not yours. So I guess I'll call her whatever I want to.
  I haven't got that letter from Ervin yet, but I have been looking for it every mail call. I haven't wrote to him yet either. I can't find his address again. I have his old address in my book, but it wouldn't do much good to send it there, because the war would probably be all over before it caught up with him.
  There is one thing I would like to know about. Why do you always refer to my car as my car every time it needs repairs, and your car when everything is going O.K.? Go ahead and drive it all you want to, but don't smash it up too bad. Be sure and don't break the steering wheel, for if I have that much left when I get back, I may be able to have a new car built around it. Oh! Oh! don't get mad, I was

just joking. Boy, you sure made me laugh when you told me that Boyd Siffert is a farmer. I consider that as a insult to us farmers.
    We just heard one of Jack Benny's late programs. It was the one he broadcasted [sic] last July 23rd. Not bad, eh? But it was good even if it was old. It's better than listening to these English Programs.
    Well I must sign off for now and write Ethel again. Hope to hear from you again soon.
    Your Loving Brother, Bob
    [Another Sunday. For a change, this Monday's rare headline has nothing to do with the war: "**Kent U. Trustees Name President.**" George A. Bowman, the new college president, came from the Youngstown public school system. In Italy, there are high hopes for the new beachhead at Anzio. Locally, the 4th War Loan Drive in Portage County thus far has netted only $276,455.]

February 6, 1944 – While American soldiers are dying and suffering in many places around the world, the Washington politicians are worried about their absentee vote. In a 44-42 vote, the Senate allows the soldier absentee federal ballot. Pvt. Francisco has other matters to think about.
North Ireland
Dear Dorothy & Family.
    Hi! There squirt. How is the world treating you? Oh, it is. That's what I thought.
    I just noticed that I haven't wrote you since Jan. 23rd. That's only two weeks. (So don't blow your top.) It just happens that I don't owe any one a letter now. (Are you mad yet?) Well, if you ain't, I guess I will have to wait until I get home again (1980) to pick on you. Then I'll make up for the years that I have lost.
    You know what? Oh, you don't. I didn't think that you did. I got one of my ambitious spells and wrote Ervin a letter the other day. I'll bet he will be surprised. I got the letter he wrote Dec. 7th on Jan. 25th. So I guess that wasn't so bad. Only seven weeks old when it got here.
    Boy, Uncle Sam sure gave us Privates in the Infantry a dirty deal. They gave the infantry men a raise in pay because their job was so tough. But the men that do the dirty work didn't get the raise. It was mostly the noncoms that got the raise. And there was already too much difference in their pay and a Pvt's [pay]. Of course, that is my

idea and most of the other privates.

No, your letters haven't been censored lately. But if you know anything that you think would be cut out, don't write it, for that is one thing that is important.

I don't know when I will be back home, and I couldn't tell you if I did know. The same goes for when I think the war will end.

Well I guess I will have to close for now.

Hope this letter finds you all in the best of health and happiness. Write whenever you can.

Your Loving Brother, Bob.

[**"Russians Annihilating 175,000 German Troops In Ukraine"** Another article states that " U.S. Warships Bombard Jap Home Island In Surprise Raid."]

Feb. 13, 1944 - Bob notes the third anniversary of his induction.
Dear Dorothy & Family:

Hi! There squirt! How is every little thing at home? All going along fine I hope. Just received your letter of Feb. 1st. That one sure did get here quick. Only ten days old.

Thanks for the nice bawling out that you gave me. I guess that I had it coming. For I didn't write every week like I should have. I was trying to write you one week and to Mom the next week. But I guess that didn't work out so hot, did it?

I got another snapshot of Ethel the other day. She looks more beautiful in every picture that I get of her. Sure hope that it won't be long any more until I can look at her and won't have to be satisfied with pictures any more.

I am glad that you found time to take Jeanie down to see Ethel. I guess she thinks as much of the baby as you do. For she is always writing about her.

Yes, I can sew that darned Hash mark [sleeve stripe] on now. Sure hope that I don't get another one before I get out of the Army. Three years ago today was my first real sad day in my life. If I have to stay much longer, I know I'll never amount to a darn for anything again. For I only know about half of much now as I did three years ago.

I guess I'll go on another furlough the 6th of Mar. or about then. We are going to Scotland this time. Then I'll be ready to leave this part of the country. Because after I see Scotland, I have seen all

of Great Britain that I care to see.
   Well I guess I will have to close for now and call it a day. Hope to hear from you again real soon.
   Tell Mom I'll write her in a day or so. So long,
Your Loving Brother, Bob
   [The 13th was a Sunday, so the *Evening Record's* Monday headline reads: **Finland Negotiating For Peace With Russians."** Deferments for 18-22 year-olds in vital industries will soon be discontinued.]

Feb. 21, 1944 – From Northern Ireland, Bob writes to Dorothy.
Dear Dorothy & Family.
   Hi! Squirt. Surprised to get a letter from me so quick? It's only been a week since I wrote you the last time. I've wrote once a week now for the last four weeks. So you can see that I haven't broke my arm.
   I can't help it if you didn't get them. It's not my fault that you live so far out in the sticks that the mailman has to swing in on a grapevine, and they are big now.
   Boy, I sure wish that I could buy some of those bananas that Erwin has too many. I haven't seen a banana for two years now. What do they look like?
   I imagine I will be getting a letter from him again one of these days. He wrote me on Dec. 7th and it got here Jan. 26th. Then I answered it on Jan. 30th. So at that rate I should get a letter in about a month.
   I can easily understand your trying to get our car to run on water, but I can't understand how the bolts & nuts and the rest of the junk got in there. Have you been driving it around without a gas cap on the tank?
   You're lucky to get off by just paying $2.50. You know they might have fined you for hoarding a junk pile. Or isn't it that bad back there?
   I got a letter from Vincent the other day. He was saying that Gib was going to get a new tractor this spring. Has he got it yet?
   Do you get to see very many shows any more? Or don't you have any one to go with? I imagine Ethel would go with you, if she isn't too busy.
   Would you get Ethel something for Easter, for me? Some-

thing like a dress, hat or whatever you can find. Take the price of it out of the money I send home. Get something for the rest of you folks too.

Well I guess I will have to sign off for today and go out and get some supper. The chow at the mess hall wasn't so hot tonight. I guess the cooks thought they had a day off too.

Write whenever you can. I'll try to do a little better than I have been.

Your Loving Brother, Bob.

["**2,000 More U.S. Planes Blasting Germany Today**" In Italy, the Americans beat back the German counterattack at the Anzio beachhead.]

March 20, 1944 – Following his furlough, Bob is back at the old routine in Northern Ireland.

Dear Mom,

How is everyone back home today? All busy and feeling fine I guess. I was going to write to you yesterday, but I just couldn't get it done. I guess I just wasn't in the mood.

What is this that I hear about Elmore buying another team of horses? Who is he going to have drive them? Or did he sell the other team? Boy, they sure will put Elmore in a jam if they take Gilbert in the Army, won't they? Or does he know of someone else that he can get to help him with the work once in a while?

It seems funny that I haven't run across some of the fellows from back home. For I have seen several Yanks in the first two years, but no one that I was to know. Well, it wasn't so bad to get back to work again as I had thought it would be. I guess they were breaking us back in sort of easy. Or maybe it's just the calm before the storm. But we did have a pretty easy day's work. I did get pretty soft those twelve days that I was riding around. I wish that I could have found some souvenirs to send you folks. But I couldn't find any. They either sold out or never made such things.

Well I guess this isn't much of a letter, but it is the best that I can do tonight. Because there is too many fellows in the hut. And about the time that I get started to write, someone either walks between me and the light or starts asking questions and talking about different things. So I'll sign off for tonite. Hope to hear from you again real soon.

Your Loving Son, Robert

[Today's headline is another rare non-war topic, **"Bus Plunges In River; Scores Die."** In a freezing snowstorm, the bus plunged into the river at Passaic, New Jersey. In Ohio the first day of spring is also greeted with snow and freezing temperatures. In Italy, the allies are still trying to take Cassino.

Mar. 25, 1944 – Judging by Bob's second sentence, rumors are afloat as to a move.
North Ireland
Dear Dorothy & Family:
Hi! Folks! How's everyone back home tonight? All feeling fine I hope.

I don't know what's going to happen, but somehow I got around to write you a letter this week before I get one from you.

We just got through putting a radio back together. We rented a different one a few days ago and it didn't work so hot. So one of my buddies and I tore it apart this afternoon. We had pieces all over the table and one bed. And the fellows was betting that we couldn't get it all back together again so it would work. Well when we got done, all we had left was two little screws that we couldn't find places for. But it works better now. We can [wd?] get the states now. Just heard some of that good hill billy [sic] music. That's something that we don't hear much over here.

I was going to catch up on my writing this afternoon. But I guess that I won't get much done for it's almost 11:30 now. But that's the way it always works out when I plan my work for Sat. afternoon. So I'll have about five letters to write tomorrow if nothing happens.

How is Elmore getting along with his plowing work or is it still too cold to do much there yet?

We have been having some nice weather here lately. About like the middle of April back home.

And I guess I've caught my usual spring cold for I can feel it sneaking up on me tonight.

Well I guess I have to close for tonight and get some sleep. Hope to hear from you soon.
Your Loving Brother, Bob.

[**"Soviets Drive Germans To Border"** All previously deferred men under the age of 26 are ordered to get the pre-induction test. Bandleader Tommy Dorsey has an engagement in Akron. He will pick Kent State University's "Chestnut Burr" queen.]

April 2, 1944 –
Dear Dorothy & Family:
    Hi! Squirt and the rest of the folks. How's everyone and everything back home?
    Just received three more of your letters last Friday night when I got back to camp. I guess you must be getting most of my letters now. If you have got enough to answer, [write] two of them in one. But I can't kick for I'm going to answer all three of yours with one.
    So the gear shift finally went to the dogs. I was a little afraid of that when I bought the car. But I guess we can't kick much for it did stand up to some pretty hard treatment. I know I was pretty hard on it, and I don't think you was much easier. For I never seen a woman driver that was easy on a car in any way.
    Yes, I guess your opinion about the Waves and Wac's [sic] is about the same as mine. And perhaps the two of us can convince Ethel that it's no place for a decent young lady like her.
    That buddy of mine from Canton, that I was telling you about, was Nick Votolato. I don't think that Ethel knows him. For she don't know anyone that I do back there.
    Yes, I finally got that picture of you and Jean. Thanks a lot for it. Jean sure is a cute little rascal. And I hope she is just as onery [sic] as you were, or are.
    No, I haven't heard from Dale or Ervin for quite some time now. But some of the mail is a little slow getting here, so I'll probably hear from both of them soon.
    Well I guess I'll have to start closing now for I still have to write Ethel yet today. This will be one letter that I hate to write her, for I know I'll hurt her feelings, when I tell her what I think about her joining the Waves or any other like it. I didn't want to say anything about it, but she wants my honest opinion about it. So that's the way it is. Well I must sign off now. Hope this letter finds you folks all in the best of health.
    Write whenever you can. And tell Mom to take a little time off some day and write me a few lines.

Your Loving Brother, Bob.

[The 2nd was a Sunday. The previous day's headline read: **"Planes Continue Smashing Against Jap Bases; Fifth Army Smashes Ahead One Mile In Surprise Attack."** The allied drive in Italy is intended to outflank Cassino. The other lead article stated: "Truk, Other Nip Islands Hit In Raids." The income tax deadline is approaching and no one will escape the IRS man. In the new rules for servicemen, "the first $1,500 of military pay should be excluded... Husbands and wives who are temporarily apart, such as couples separated by the husband's leaving for the service, should be considered as living together."

April 19, 1944 –With the chance of combat in the near future, Bob sends Ethel's precious letters home.
Dear Dorothy & Family:

Hi! Squirt. Happy Birthday. How do you feel now that you are a year older. And old enough to know something now. Or doesn't one year more make any difference? (Ha! Ha!)

I received two more of your letters today. They were April 1st & 4th. Not bad, eh? I am sorry that I didn't get around to write you a few lines Sunday, but I was too busy puttering around with some old watches. Some of the fellows are beginning to wonder if I was a farmer or a junk dealer when I was a happy civilian.

No, I don't think that any of you folks need to worry about me running off with any of these girls over here, because the best of them can't even begin to compare with Ethel.

No, I don't know when I will be home, because I don't know when the war will end. Your guess is as good as mine. But I don't figure I'll have to stay over here much more than a year yet & maybe not that long. Who knows? If I had my way, I would catch the next boat headed that direction.

Oh Yes. Before I forget it. I sent a bunch of Ethel's letters home the other day. You can store them away in my clothes dresser with the rest of them. I don't know why I kept them, but I didn't have the heart to burn them up.

Well we are having some more of this nice Irish weather. It has rained all day. It's a very common thing over here to meet one of the civilians on the street, and he will say, "Good afternoon, tis a nice day." Then after he has put his umbrella up, or stepped in a doorway to keep dry, he says, "if you have your raincoat with you."

I did see the dust fly once since I've been here though. I guess it was just a accident. Well I have about run down again. So I guess I'll have to close again.

Hope to hear from you again real soon. Tell Mom I'll write her one of these days soon. (Happy Birthday)

Your Loving Brother, Bob.

["**5,000 Planes Rock Reich In Pre-Invasion Raids.**" The German troops on the Atlantic Wall are in "the highest state of alarm." At Anzio, the Americans beat back another German attack.]

May 18, 1944 – The intimation that he and his buddies are doing nothing, while others are fighting, strikes a raw nerve with Bob.

North Ireland

Dear Dorothy & Family.

Here is a few lines your way again tonight. Hope it doesn't make you mad to get two letters in one from me. I received three letters from you so far this week. The one I got tonight was the one with Donna Jean's picture in it. Thanks a lot for the picture. I guess I'll put it in the little folder with Ethel's picture. Then every time I look [at] Ethel I'll look at Jean too, which will be quite often.

I thought all the time that food was rationed back there. Oh it is. Then how the devil did Donna Jean get so fat in such a short time?

So the Pontius Family think that Harley and Warren are just about winning this war by their selves, and I am just setting over here on my fanny having a good time. If I had my way I would be glad to change places with either one of them at any time. They are at least working at something they like a little bit. That's more than what I can say for what I am doing. And if we are getting a break now, it's nowhere near what we have got coming. Because anyone that has put well over a year in Iceland like we did, deserves more than a few passes and eight day furloughs, and spend the rest of our time trying to find the top of the highest hill in North Ireland, and we will probably see as much action as either Harley or Warren, if we haven't already. Boy, I sure would like to have went along with Elmore to the State sale this spring. I haven't been to a sale since I was home on my furlough in 41. These people have a kind of a community sale here once a month, but I never managed to have any time off when they [rest of letter missing]

[At last, **"British Troops Capture Cassino."** In France, it is reported that Gen. Rommel has called an emergency council of war.]

May 25, 1944 – Although he has time to attend a "show" and to engage in some friendly chatting with the civilians, P.F.C. Francisco has been preparing for the landing in France.
North Ireland
Dear Dorothy & Family:
Hi! Squirt. How's the world treating you now? Hope you are feeling fine and not too disgusted with me for not writing sooner. No, I haven't broke my arm. I guess I have just been too cozy to do very much writing.

I received your letter of May 18th last night, but I still haven't got the one from Mom yet. It will probably get here in a day or so. Please excuse the mistakes for I only have a few minutes to write tonight before bedtime. And I can't write very good if I am in a hurry. It probably looks to you as if I am always in a hurry then, because I am far from being a good hand at writing.

Oh, I see now you've got to admit that you are a big stiff. I guess you will just have to put your day's work a little closer together. Then a day's work won't get you down.

Boy, this darn weather sure gets under my skin. I have done a little washing this afternoon, and I hung it outside today. But about the time it was almost ready to bring in, it started to rain and I was out to a show. So now I'll dry them inside if it takes a week. But that is common weather for this place. I always did think it was just like Iceland, only someone got ambitious and planted a few trees and bushes here & there. And it doesn't get quite as cold there than it does here. The civilians say that they start swimming the last of this month, but I don't see how they can stand it.

Well there seems that there isn't much more to write about, and I have already run past time for the light to go out. So I guess I'll have to sign off for now. Hope to hear from you again real soon. And I'll try to write again in a day or so.
Your Loving Brother, Bob.

[**"Two Allied Armies Join In Italy."** The Anzio breakout and the allied push through the Gustav Line has finally been achieved. The cost of the allied successes appear every day on the front pages. Pictures of local men, who have been killed, wounded, or

MIA, are a frequent occurrence.]

June 4, 1944 – Bob's letter is postmarked June 6 (D-Day).
North Ireland
Dear Dorothy & Family:

Hi Squirt. How's everything back home? I hope you are all feeling as good as I am now.

No, I haven't broke my arm yet, and I haven't forgot that I have got a very nice little sister either. I just didn't get around to write as often as I should have. Guess I spend too much time writing to Ethel, but you can't blame me for that, can you?

I sure was glad to find out that Harley found time to go up and pay you folks a visit. Did he tell you much about Italy and what things look like there?

This time I'm going to fool you and not give you the devil about my car. I guess you would call it my car if it's in the garage for repairs. How does Ervin like it down there in New Caledonia by now? I hope he likes it better than I do this place over here.

Did you get to go down to see Ethel on her birthday this year? I sure hope that you did. But I don't know how you would manage it without a car. What did you get her for me this time? She sure thinks a lot of you, and she's just crazy about Jeanie. She says that she don't know what she would do if it wasn't for you and Maxine to help keep her cheered up. So just keep up the good work.

How hard is it to get airmail stamps back there? We can't seem to get them over here any more. So how about sending me some with your next letter? You won't need a request for that.

Well I guess I'll have to sign off for now, because there isn't much to write about and I'm not in a writing mood tonight. Write whenever you can and I'll try to do the same.
Your Loving Brother, Bob.

[As usual, the *Evening Record* does not have a Sunday edition. The headline for Monday the 5th reads: **"Allies Occupy Rome, Pursue Nazis."** Another article states, "Waves Of Allied Planes Pound Atlantic Wall."]

June 18, 1944 – It has been twelve days since the allies landed in France, and Bob and the 5th Division are still training in Northern Ireland. On this Sunday, Bob writes to his sister.

Dear Dorothy & Family:

Here is your weekly letter. It may be a little short and not too sweet, but it will have to do for a letter.

I received your very welcome letter of June 3rd the other night, but I was too tired or lazy to answer it then.

So you think that Donna Jean is a little ornery. That's good, now you see what you used to be like. I wish that I was there so I could teach her more devilment to get into. Boy, would I get even with you.

Now that you have got the car running again, I hope that you can manage to go down to see Ethel a few times before your gas is all gone. You sure have a time keeping that car running. First, you are out of gas, then when you get gas the car is broke down. Now you see why I always wanted to trade cars every year or so. Let someone else worry about the repairs.

I think I'll first buy a jeep when I get back home again. Then I'll paint it a nice bright red with yellow wheels. That should look pretty good. Oh, you don't think so either. One thing I know, I'll never have another green or olive drab car or piece of machinery of any kind, because it would remind me of the Army.

I hope Ervin is right about when he will be home again. And things are beginning to look as if he may be right. But that's something that none of us know very much about.

How is Ervin getting along with his work by now? I hope that he isn't as disgusted with everything as he was the last letter I got from him, but I don't blame him in some ways.

Well I guess I'll have to close for tonight and get some sleep, for we have got a lot of <u>fooling around</u> to do tomorrow.

Hope to hear from you again real soon. Tell Mom I'll write to her in a day or so.

Your Loving Brother, Bob.

[At home, many a doorstep will be visited by a serviceman bearing bad news. The previous day's headline reads: **"3,283 Yanks Killed In Invasion."** Since the landing in France, 12,600 Americans have been wounded. In the Pacific Theater, the Yanks are in a "do-or-die" battle on Saipan.]

July 17, 1944 – The 5th Division landed in France on July 9th at Utah Sugar Red Beach in the St. Mere Eglise area. Now assigned to the V

Corps, First Army, the division moved up to relieve the battle-worn 1st Division. [27]

France

Dear Dorothy & Family:

Thanks a lot for the pictures that you sent me, and the letters. They sure come in handy. Well I finally got to see part of France, and it's the nicest place I've been since I left home.

They say that it looks like Ohio, but I can't quite agree with them. I do think that it was real pretty country before the war though. But I'm quite sure that things have changed a good bit over here in the past month or so.

Well I guess maybe I'll get a chance to finish this letter today. We had another mail call today, so I guess we will get our mail now for a while. I guess maybe they will be delivering our mail in Berlin before long. But that won't be so bad for we all know that is our only way home. I got four letters from Ethel and one from Hazel today, but I don't think that I'll get around to answer them for a few days. So if you see either of them, just tell them I haven't forgot them and I'll get around to write them a few letters while I am still over here.

Ethel tells me that you are getting a nice tan this summer. So I know that you are getting plenty of fresh air, sunshine and exercise.

Well there isn't much that I can write about now, but I guess I'll have lots to tell you when I get home again. Must close for now and get some sleep while I can. Tell Harley that we aren't just putting in time any more like he thinks we are.

Write soon and I'll write again sometime.

Your Loving Brother, Bob.

[**"U.S. Patrols Smash Into St. Lo."** Locally, Portage County is very close to meeting the $747,000 goal of the 5th War Loan Drive.]

Bob Francisco's command structure now reads: Company G, 2nd Infantry Regiment (Col. A. W. Roffe), 5th Infantry Division (Maj. Gen. S. Leroy Irwin), XXth Corps (Maj. Gen. Walton H. Walker), and Third Army (Lt. Gen. George S. Patton, Jr.).

The 5th Division went into combat at Vidouville on July 26th. On August 3rd, the division was assigned to Gen. Patton's Third Army. After the breakout at St. Lo, 22 miles south of St. Mere Eglise, the 5th Division was ordered to proceed 100 miles south to the Vivre River, seize the bridges over the Maine and Loire Rivers, and to capture the city of Angeres. This move was intended to cut off the Germans retreating from the Brest Peninsula.

The Fifth then swung to the northeast to St. Calais, a distance of 65 miles. Another 50 miles toward Paris brought them to Chartres, "The City of Cathedrals," which came under the division's control on August 19th. The Americans decided not to become bogged down in Paris, so the 5th Division swung to the south to bypass the "City of Light." Thirty miles from Chartres was the targeted city of Etamps, which fell on August 22nd.

AUGUST 25, 1944 - With a lull in the action, Bob writes to the folks at home to let them know that he is still all right.
France
Dear Dorothy & Family:

Hi! Squirt and the rest of you folks. How's everything back home? All O.K. and kicking I hope.

I received your v-mail of Aug. 8th the other day, so I decided that I had better get on the ball and drop you a few lines. We had a drenching rain ... the other day [Pencil on a paper crease difficult to read.] and I guess we all got pretty well soaked. I know I did, and I don't think it rained any harder where I was than it did where the rest of the fellows were. But the sun is out again now and we were lucky enough to have time to dry our stuff out again. So everything is O.K. now.

I'm going to have to ask you to do another favor for me, I guess. I want you to get Mom and Howard something for their birthday for me again this year. I guess I'm a little late for Howard, but it's better late than never, I guess.

Just heard part of the news, and it sure did sound good. I didn't get there in time to find out what was happening in France and Italy, but those Russians are doing O.K. They are the ones I'm pretty interested in anyhow. For the sooner they get in Germany, the sooner I'll come home. But I don't expect to get home before next spring sometime. So I guess you will still have to take care of our car this winter.

Well, there isn't much more to write about, so I guess I'll have to sign off for now. Hope you will excuse the short letter this time.

    Write whenever you can and I'll try to do the same.
Your Loving brother, Bob.

    ["**Germans Flee Robot Coast; Americans Fight In Paris.**" The headline referred to the area where the "robot bombs" were manufactured. The outlook for the end of the war appears to be rosy, as Gen. Eisenhower predicts that the war could be over by Christmas. In Washington, the outlook for the boys coming home also appears to be bright. The benefits of the G.I. Bill are being touted on the front page. "Veterans returning from World War II will have a far better chance of fitting themselves back into civilian life than those that have returned from any previous war."

    The Marne River was crossed, and Reims fell on August 29. The next target was Verdun, where the French stopped the Germans in World War I. (That eleven month battle cost the French 540,000 casualties to the Germans' 430,000.) Verdun was attacked and captured on September 1. In 27 days the 5th Division had traveled and fought over a 700 mile course. [28]

    The Germans were on the run, but the Third Army's advance ground to a halt for lack of fuel. The supply line to the English Channel was hard-pressed to haul the precious gasoline to Patton's fast-moving army. In addition, much of the supplies were funneled to Operation Market Garden, the massive airborne attack on the bridges in Holland. The paratrooper drops and glider landings began on Sunday September 17; and the operation ended on the 25th with the Germans still in control of the bridges.

    At Verdun, Walker's XXth Corps had to wait five crucial days for supplies and gasoline. Meanwhile the German expertise in military organization took advantage of the U. S. Third Army's delay. On the east side of the Moselle River, retreating elements were reorganized and reinforcements brought up. The German 88 artillery pieces, the best in the opposing armies, were waiting to smash the advance of the U. S. tanks and armored vehicles. Also waiting were the Wehrmach's mortar squads, which were noted for their pinpoint accuracy. Nebelwerfers were carriage-mounted 6-barreled rocket launchers that fired their screaming missiles in 10 seconds. Their explosions sent chunks of shrapnel that could slice a body in half. The MG 42 machine guns were strategically in place, ready to fire

1200-1800 rounds per minute.

On the morning of September 7, 1944, the 5th Division was refueled and ready to renew the advance on Metz. "...The 5th Infantry Division was somewhat dispersed on the morning of 7 September. General Irwin had expected to put its weight in an attack to the south of the 7th Armored elements and now found his division caught off balance. The 2nd Infantry (Col. A. W. Roffe) had been brought forward behind the right wing of CCA with the mission of containing Metz by direct attack from the west... At 0830 the 2nd Infantry jumped off in a frontal attack with two battalions and moved past the Franco-Prussian War tombs and monuments. Three hours later, quite unaware of the enemy works ahead, the 2nd slammed hard into a well-organized German defense line on the spur between Amanvillers and Verneville held by the tough troops of the *Fahnenjunkerschule* regiment. Losses were heavy, with fire from cleverly concealed machine guns and artillery sweeping across the front and flanks of the regiment. Here the 2nd Infantry finally was checked in the first of a series of fruitless assaults on the western outworks of the Metz position. [29]

On September 7, Bob Francisco is only four days away from his 29th birthday. Heading into battle, his only personal possessions- the things which he values or holds dear - are a lighter, fountain pen, billfold, a picture frame (certainly photos of his niece and sweetheart which he received on May 19, 1944), one Canadian dollar, an English souvenir of some sort, 52 francs, and one U. S. dollar. [30]

Most likely, Bob experienced the same conditions as Herman Force, a fellow Metz combatant who fought with the 10th Armored Division. There was "fatigue from lack of sleep because it was almost impossible to find a comfortable place to sleep. Add to this the enemy harassment and interdiction fire... Only three or four hours of sleep a night eventually drained one's stamina. For me, it also caused severe headaches... Then there was frustration. Imagine that everything that you do is stymied by mud, snow, fog, wind, rain, freezing cold, or intense heat. Then add the lack of sleep plus very few hot meals... We all agonized over the possibility of death and of being badly wounded. From the very first action, this fear was exacerbated as all around us: men had legs and arms blown off, received grievous cuts and puncture wounds and lost their sight or hearing. Those killed instantly were the "lucky" ones. Fear shadowed us constantly. We were told never to stop to give aid to a fallen soldier; to do so would make one a stationary target." [31]

To Bob Francisco, being "lucky" would be to survive this hellhole of deafening noise, cordite fumes, shaking earth, shrieking missiles of death, and excruciating cries for medical attention. Being "lucky" would mean returning to the serenity of the farm, marrying Ethel, and raising a family. However, Bob's luck ran out this September morning when amidst the violent chaos a piece of shrapnel fractured his jaw and skull.

Alice Francisco was standing outside her farm house talking to the coal deliveryman. She noticed every car that drove over her dusty country road, and this one coming up the road slowed down as it approached her house. It was a somber-faced Western Union man, who was bringing her a telegram from the War Department. She took the telegram into the house and began to sob.

The front page of the *Evening Record* carried the photographs of Robert Francisco and Sgt. Laverne Keevert of Kent, Ohio. "Lefty" Keevert died from chest wounds received when he bailed out of a Liberator bomber over Romania. Personal information on Bob was also printed.

October 23, 1944 – A letter of consolation to a grieving mother. Postmarked Oct. 23, 1944 at New Philadelphia, Ohio. To Dorothy Lashley from Mrs. Wm. R. Leatherman, R.F.D. 1 New Philadelphia, Ohio. Handwriting on the front of the envelope: "Letter from Robert's buddy's Mother in service when Robert got killed & their son was wounded."

Roswell, Ohio
Oct. 23, 1944
Dear Mrs. Lashley,

This is Bill's mother writing this letter. My daughter-in-law wrote the other one for me. I wanted your letter answered right away and I was too nervous, for you see we had become great friends with Robert, but we always had called him Frisco for we did not know his first name. You see, there is another buddy. There was the three of them. I don't know if Robert ever told you folks about Stanley Gibb, and they was all three together on the 3rd of September yet, for Bill wrote me and Stanley wrote his mother, and they would always tell us about him. They was sure to say he was O.K. and they both said in their last letter that he was O.K. on the 3rd of September, but I was up to see Mrs. Gibb yesterday and Stanley is O.K. but she got five letters from him last week, but he did not say one word about Bill or Robert. She knew Bill was wounded, but she could not understand why he did [not] say anything about Frisco, and she wondered why he wrote five letters home in one week, when we have been getting one every four weeks. They were just as shocked as I was to hear about Robert. Did he ever send any pictures of himself home? I have one of him and Bill together about my family. There is just me and the Mr. at home. I have two sons married. They each have two children. The oldest has two girls, the other one has a boy and a girl. Bill is my baby, and he was 27 the 28th of August, and we live on a little farm of 40 acres, but we don't farm, not since Bill has been away. We did keep cows up till this spring. My health is too poor. My husband works at the la-del [sic] in town. He is away from home from 5:30 till 5:30 in the evening. I have the bronchial asthma. I can't walk no place and the neighbors are not close, and with everybody working, no one comes much, but I am trying to keep my chin up for I am only one in a million or two. Mrs. Gibb took your address. She said she was going to write you. They are a very nice family to know. If you folks would like to come down, come any time you want to. Just come to New Philadelphia and take route 39. That will bring you to Roswell. Come up past the schoolhouse, and on your right will be a big white hall, and on it will say Miner's hall. Right past that a few feet is a road at your left. But anyone in Roswell can tell you where Bill L. lives. I am going to write on the next page all I have heard about Bill. It says: "Dear Mrs. Leatherman, I am pleased to inform you that the latest report from the theater of operations states that on 24 September your son was making normal improvement. You have my assurance that when additional information is received concerning his condition, you will be notified immediately." And that is all I know about him. There was another paper saying I would not receive any mail from him, and on that paper they told me to put five words and send it back, and it said that would be all the kind of a letter he would receive from me till I get another word from them. It is hard, but I just will have to wait. If I only knew how he was wounded. I don't know if you can read this or not. I was so glad to hear of your family. I pray God to bless and be with you all in your sorrow, but only a Mother knows the real sorrow and I sure am thinking of her. Hoping to hear from you again. Love to all. Mrs. Leatherman.

Alice Francisco wanted her son's body returned home and buried in the family plot. On June 18, 1946 she began a lengthy correspondence with the Adjutant General's Department and the Memorial Division of the Quartermaster General. With a somewhat shaky hand, the 63 year old widow wrote as follows:

Adjutant General.
Washington D. C.

Dear Sir
I am writting to find out when my son's body will be brought back to the U. S. and what I have to do. His name was P.F.C. <u>Robert Edwin Francisco</u> 35009786 Co. G. 2nd Inf. 5th D. He was drafted form the Kent service station Feb. 13th 1941 and left the U. S. from New York. I dont know for sure what Army he was with in France but I think it was the 9th.

Yours Cincerly
Mrs. Alice B Francisco

Over two months later, the Memorial Division responded to Alice's letter and apologized for the delay in answering. In fairness, the delayed response was due to more than military red tape and the correct office forms. Now that the fighting was over, the next of kin for 292,131 combat dead and 115, 185 non-combat dead were now faced with the decision as to the final resting place for their loved ones. In part, the Memorial Division informed Alice of the following:

29 August 1946
...The Official Report of Burial discloses that the remains of your son were interred in Plot B, Row 9, Grave 222, in the United States Military Cemetery, Campigneul, France, located twenty miles southeast of Reims. France.

The War Department has now been authorized to remove the remains of our honored dead, at Government expense, to the final

resting place which next of kin may designate....
[The information pamphlet and proper forms will be mailed to her.]
[However,] As you probably know, the supply of steel for the manufacture of caskets is at present uncertain. Without this essential item, the projected movement of remains cannot properly be initiated. This fact and the necessity for complete coordination of movement in many parts of the world make it impossible, at this time, to estimate when the mentioned forms will be mailed.Every effort, however, will be made to shorten the time between now and the date of mailing and your desires will be acted upon with a minimum of delay...

In June of 1947, Alice Francisco and others who had soldier relatives buried overseas received letters extolling the scenic cemeteries where their loved ones rested. Perhaps the Army was attempting to ease the minds of the next of kin and to spare them and the Army the gruesome task of digging up bodies which were not embalmed and thus putrid. Perhaps they were badly deformed or even incomplete.

Dear Mrs. Francisco:
Inclosed herewith is a picture of the United States Military Cemetery Champgneul, France, in which your son , the late Private First Class Robert E. Francisco, is buried. It is my sincere hope that you may gain some solace from this view of the surroundings in which your loved one rests. As you can see, this is a place of simple dignity, neat and well cared for. Here, assured of continuous care, now rest the remains of a few of those heroic dead who fell together in the service of our country.
This cemetery will be maintained as a temporary resting place until, in accordance with the wishes of the next of kin, all remains are either placed in permanent American cemeteries overseas or returned to the Homeland for final burial...

Alice Francisco persisted and completed the necessary forms, and one year later on August 16, 1948 the body of Bob Francisco was disinterred and shipped home. Arrangements were made for the Wood Funeral Home in Ravenna to handle the funeral. On November 5th the Columbus General Depot wired the funeral director: "Remains of the late PFC Robert E. Francisco ASN 35009786 being shipped to you accompanied by military escort on Train No. 8 Erie Railroad. Leaving Columbus Ohio 1:45 A.M. Ten November. Request you make arrangements to accept remains at station upon arrival and that you immediately pass this information on to next of kin."

At 7:35 A.M. on November 9, the remains of Robert Francisco arrived at the depot in Ravenna, one day ahead of schedule. Sgt. Jesse T. Trost, the military escort, reported: "Met by funeral director at train station. None of family there to meet the train. Funeral director said next of kin would not be in to view the body till Saturday. Next of kin lived 15 miles away. No way for me to see her."

On November 10, the funeral arrangements were announced on the front page and in the Death Notices of the *Evening Record*.

November 11 was Armistice Day. Today, in a tribute to the men of Randolph who lost their lives in World War II, a memorial monument was dedicated in front of the town hall. The featured speaker was Fred Espenchied, the former Randolph High School principal, who knew most of the young men being honored. Money for the memorial was raised by private contributions and an appropriation by the township trustees. On the 3ft. X 6ft. face of the gray granite marker were the names of the eight men who were killed. One of those was Robert E. Francisco, who would have been 33 years old on this date.

At 1:00 Saturday, November 13, private services were conducted by Rev. D. L. Springer at the Wood Funeral Home in Ravenna. Burial was at Hillside Cemetery in Randolph. At the grave side a small band of about twelve grieving people heard the last words and the military shots fired.

If there was any consolation at all, the grave site was under a tree and faced farm fields which Bob would have loved to work.

P.F.C. ROBERT E. FRANCISCO

KILLED IN FRANCE

Another infantryman killed on Sept. 7, in France, is Private Francisco, son of Mrs. Alice Francisco. The Randolph soldier had seen service in Iceland, England and Ireland before going into France shortly after the invasion. Francisco attended Randolph high school and left to help his father on the family farm. At the time of his induction he was employed at the Monarch Rubber Co.

Francisco went overseas early in February, 1942. He is survived by a brother, Elmore, and two sisters, Mrs. Wilson Mangold and Mrs. Ervin Lashley.

Robert Francisco

Delbert Hazel Robert Howard

CHAPTER NOTES
"YOUR LOVING SON, ROBERT"

1. Original letter of William Jackson Francisco to his brother Charles. Courtesy of Howard Mangold in Randolph, Ohio.
2. *The Evening Record*, (Ravenna, Ohio), February 11, 1941.
3. *The Evening Record*, February 13, 1941, page 1 photo.
4. *Ravenna Republican*, (Ravenna, Ohio), "Randolph," Sept. 16, 1915.
5. *The Akron Beacon Journal*, (Akron, Ohio), "War And Baby Killing," September 11, 1915.
6. "Lusitania," www.greatships.net/lusitania.html
7. *Ravenna Republican*, "Pursued By German Zeppelin," Sept. 23, 1915.
8. Scott Derks, *The Value of a Dollar 1860*-2004. (Millerton, N.Y.: Grey House Publishing, 2004); *Ravenna Republican*, Reo advertisement.
9. *The Akron Beacon Journal*, page one photograph and story of Battery D's 50th reunion, September 11, 1915; *Ravenna Republican*, "Struck By Alliance Car," September 9, 1915.
10. *Beacon Journal*, September 11, 1915.
11. *Beacon Journal*, September 11, 1915.
12. *Ravenna Republican*, "Randolph," September 12, 1921.
13. *Beacon Journal*, several front page stories including, "Screen Star Now In Cell," September 12, 1921.
14. *Beacon Journal*, "Photoplays," September 12, 1921.
15. *Ravenna Republican*, "First Woman Summoned For Portage County Juries," p. 1, September 12, 1921.
16. *The Evening Record*, (Ravenna, Ohio), "Bulletins," p. 1, September 11, 1928.
17. *Ibid.*
18. "Life and works of E.M.R.," germanculture.com.ua/library.
19. *Evening Record*, entertainment section, September 11, 1928.
20. *Evening Record*, "Randolph," September 11, 1928.
21. *The Evening Record*, (Ravenna, Ohio). Source for all of the headlines following the Francisco letters.
22. Mickey Dover, "With the Army on Maneuvers," *Evening Record*, September 4, 1941.
23. Wikipedia, the free encyclopedia at wikipedia.org/wikihistory… The history of Iceland.
24. "5th Division WWII History," at 5thdivisiondiamonddust.com…

25. "What is V-Mail?" at merkki.com/dson5.htm.
26. Edward V. Rickenbacker, *Rickenbacker, An Autobiography*, (Englewood Cliffs, New Jersey: Prentice-Hall, Inc., 1967), p 296-339.
27. "5th Division WWII History," at 5thdivisiondiamonddust.com...
28. Ibid. p2.
29. 5th Division WWII History and *The XX Corps Crossing of the Moselle*, www.army.mil...
30. Department of the Army, U. S. Human Resources Command, Individual Personnel File for Robert E. Francisco.
31. Maj. Herman Force, *FDU magazine*, www.fdu.edu/newspubs.... p 1

CHAPTER THREE

HENRY BERNARD WISE
CLASS of '36

Part I
To Europe -- The Hard Way

Stateside rehearsals were over as Barney Wise and the 101st Infantry Regiment walked up the gang-plank on August 27, 1944. At last, they were headed for the big show in Europe. The convoy carried the 26th Infantry Division, nicknamed the "Yankee Division," which was comprised of the 101st Infantry Regiment, the 104th Infantry, and the 328th Infantry. Amid the approximate 15,000 troops, the convoy ships and their personnel, mounds of equipment, machinery, and materiel, the individual soldier seemed but a speck in the panorama.

Although actual combat could not be duplicated, for the most part the men of the 101st Infantry thought they were as prepared as they possibly could be. One soldier remarked that "his training with the 101st Infantry of the 26th Division was pretty good and they did things which prepared them well." Later on, he would say that "nothing can prepare anyone for combat!" [1]

Concerning his nearly six months' training at Fort McClelland, Alabama, a disgruntled 104th man believed his outfit to be primarily a spit-and-polish one. "All that time I learned how to shoot a rifle, how to do a bayonet charge, how to parade, how to clean up the Mess Hall, how to do KP, how to peel potatoes and onions, how to wash dishes, how to salute and address an officer, how to pack my field pack, how to wait on an officer, how to march, how to do guard duty, how to make my bed, how to sweep a floor, how to sanitize body wastes in the field, how to dig a fox hole or a slit trench, how to crawl through the mud, how to crawl under machine gun fire and how to clean my plate.

I did not learn anything at all about how to survive in combat, how and when to shoot at an enemy, how to find my way in the dark, how to read a map (except in the most basic way), how to take care of my body in the snow, rain, and frost, how to take care of my feet when they were wet for weeks on end, how to bandage a serious wound, how to ferret out the enemy, how to respond to enemy fire, how to call in artillery support, how to work with the Tank corp [sic], how to identify the enemy, how to deal with captured enemy, or how to SURVIVE UNDER ARTILLERY AND MACHINE GUN FIRE!" Furthermore, "Most of the Officers were as green as were those they were training and most of the non-coms knew even less than the officers... We were over-exercised and treated, at times, brutally..."[2]

Although Barney Wise was also a green soldier, he was not a fresh-faced kid just out of high school or college. He had put in years of hard work on his father's farm in Randolph, Ohio; and at the time of his induction - September 4, 1942- he was driving for a Ravenna oil truck company. The responsible 28 year old soldier had plans for a bright future. He carried a picture of his pretty fiancee, Marjorie May.

From Fort Jackson, South Carolina, Barney wrote to his sister on February 16, 1943.

Hello. Haven't heard from you for sometime or didn't you get the card I sent from down here? How is Hubert [his brother-in-law] by this time? Also the rest of the family?

How's the weather been? It has been pretty good here up till about 3 days ago, it rained and got colder. I think the coldest was about 15 degrees which is pretty cold for S.C.

We are back to training again, I guess they thought we plaid [played] around long enough. I thought basic training was tough but that was easy compared to this, have a full hour of exercise every morning & then drill for the next hour & they want to hike at the rate of 5 miles an hour. Just trying to make us tough I guess.

Was on guard duty today and last nite but am all finished now. Started last nite at 7:00 & was on 2 hours & off 4 hrs.

We are now a part of the 2nd Army. The commanding General I think is General Ben Leon. [Barney may be referring to Lt. Col. Bernard A. Lyons, 2nd Battalion of the regiment.]

I don't know how long we will be here, I guess nobody does. Was to town Sat. afternoon & evening. Had a good meal for a change & went to a show & then back to camp.

Can't get a weekend pass any more, boy! They are sure getting strict around here since we joined the 2nd Army.

We live in wooden huts now, a little better than those tents up at Ft. Meade. There are about 12 besides me in this hut including the first Sgt.

Just finished a letter to Gustie [another sister], guess they are glad that Ray didn't pass. Wonder if Paul will pass, probably won't be long till he is called. [Ray and Paul are Barney's nephews.]

That is all the news I know, so will sign off.

Your Brother
Barney

In November, Barney mailed a postcard from Camp Campbell, Kentucky. He was in the HQ Co., 2nd Bn. The card has a colorized picture of the Motor Pool at Camp Campbell. "An infantry battalion headquarters & headquarters company (authorized strength - 126) contained the battalion's headquarters cell, a communications platoon, an ammunition and pioneer platoon, and an antitank platoon. Elements of this company operated all over the battle area in support of the battalion's forward and rear command posts and the letter companies." [3] Barney did not say what his particular role was in the battalion headquarters company.

Hello,

Just a card to let you know I am back on the job again. Got back to camp 5:30 AM Monday morning, train was late. Thought I would have time to write more letters this week, but didn't. Had [Mission?] from Sun. to Wed. Am ok. Hope you are all the same.

Barney

[Of all the correspondence that Barney surely wrote, these are the only known surviving pieces.]

Barney was not the kind of person to feel sorry for himself; and when the 101st landed at Cherbourg, France on September 7, 1944, he could tell that the American GI's, the German enemy, and the French citizens had a much worse time of it. The battle-scarred city finally fell to the Americans on June 29, when the Germans surrendered their last strongholds in the harbor area.

Other units of the 26th Division were landing further down the peninsula at Utah Beach, where at a bloody cost the 4th Division and paratroopers secured a foothold on the continent on D-Day. Another ten miles across the Carentan Estuary lay Pointe Du Hoc and Omaha Beach, where it was a near thing for the 29th and 1st Divisions on June 6-7. There were over 3,000 casualties. Signs of destruction and death were all over the French coastline.

Thousands upon thousands of others obviously were in the same fix as Barney Wise. In Barney's graduation class there were 24 teenagers -- fifteen boys and nine girls. Nine of the 15 boys were now in the service, and some of the girls had relatives serving Uncle Sam. The mid-30's were hard times, but they seemed simpler and certainly less dangerous compared to this.

Part II
From Whence We Came

The 1935-36 school year opened on September 3, and as usual the first day had an ambience of its own. As the students entered the brick building, they were greeted with smells of fresh paint, varnish, floor wax and soap, and the mustiness of non-use over the summer months. The excited chatter and hellos to friends filled the air as the teachers and principal shepherded them toward their assigned rooms. Anticipation mixed with a bit of trepidation heightened the excitement.

The year book, *The Speedometer*," stated: "September 3 found so many new students pouring into Randolph High School this year that principal, F. C. Gilmore, started looking for the "Pied Piper." However, these newcomers gave us no reason to be sorry for their numbers, and we are looking forward to the time when they will emerge as leaders of the school. It seems certain that they will be able to bring honors in scholarship and in sports." [4]

For Barney Wise and the seniors, this was the culmination of their twelve years in school and a mile stone in their young lives.

From seventeen to eighteen years ago, the Class of '36 was brought into a violent world. At the time of Barney's birth (January

23, 1916), the Great War in Europe had been raging for seventeen months. In another thirty-four months, the combatants' grand total of estimated casualties would amount to 27,624,109 of whom about seven million were dead. The peace only planted the seeds for an even greater catastrophic war. In the end the slogans, "war to end all wars" and "making the world safe for democracy," were merely empty words. The eleventh hour of the eleventh day of the eleventh month -- Armistice Day 1918-- temporarily ended the slaughter. As one Great War historian remarked: "Only the dead have seen the end of war." [5] In Barney Wise's future, Armistice Day would become the equivalent of Caesar's Ides of March.

Life in the America of 1916 was no guarantee against "lead poisoning." In 1911, an Akron man had moved to Texas, married a Texas gal, and become a rancher. Now in January 1916 the new rancher and a companion goaded their horses across the Rio Grande in search of stolen cattle. They discovered their cattle in a corral next to a Mexican house. Their enquiries were greeted with a hail of bullets, and as they spurred their horses back to the border, the Akron man fell dead from his horse. His companion escaped to tell the tale.

Mexican justice was swift and harsh. The *Akron Beacon Journal* gave the lurid details on January 24th's front page: "Bound together with a rope and standing shoulder to shoulder against the adobe walls of the Juarez cemetery while dawn was breaking Sunday morning, and the church bells were pealing matins, Bernardo and Frederic Duran faced a firing squad of Caranza soldiers for the murder Friday afternoon of Bert Akers [the Akron man]... The last words of the two brothers as the grim Mexican troopers in their colored blankets leveled their guns and prepared to fire, were: "Watch and see how Mexicans die, you Americans."

"Oh, for a carbine now. I'd show you Americans something. Our death will not go unavenged," one of the brothers cried just before he was shot.

Both crumpled at the first volley, but the elder [brother] was not dead. Capt. Ortiz advanced and with his revolver fired a bullet into the brain of each -- the mercy shot." [6]

On a lighter note, the entertainment scene in Akron was thriving. At the Grand Opera House the comedienne May Robson was starring in the play, "The Rejuvenation of Aunt Mary." Over at the Colonial Theater "one of the costliest" vaudeville presentations graced the stage. The Strand Theater offered a silent film, which indicated that the anti-German propaganda had not yet swept the nation: " 'The Battles of a Nation,' a German war picture, will be shown at the Strand Monday, Tuesday and Wednesday in place of the regular program. They were taken on the eastern front during the successful campaign which resulted in the fall of Warsaw." Elsewhere, the Winter Garden, the East Market Street roller rink, scheduled a grand masquerade. "Prizes will be awarded for best costumes, most comical and most original costumes." later in the week, roller skating would be postponed for a boxing match on Tuesday and the McKinley Day banquet on Friday. [7]

In Randolph Township, the home of the Wise family, the lengthy local news report indicated the writer's quest to fill the homebound winter hours. Some of the items follow.

"Randolph is still waiting patiently for a resident doctor; unless the situation be as it was said by a man in the store the other day; people now have a chance to die a natural death."

The advent of the automobile was bringing better roads and more traffic to the farm community. "The brick pavement must be different from the Broad road mentioned in the Scriptures, now that the sidewalks are very muddy it is quite convenient for pedestrians to take the pavement. Old and young are warned of danger, but if one is careful to walk near the edge of the right hand side, keeping ears and eyes open for meets and passes, there is but little risk. The greatest danger is, either driving or walking, is getting rattled, and turning the wrong way, or turning either way when the right thing to do is to keep going straight ahead.

What would the fathers have thought if they had been told that in the next generation funeral processions in country towns would go at the rate of 30 miles , as was the case the other day in Randolph."

The aforementioned funeral may have been that of Gary McRice, the son of an escaped slave and Civil War battle hero. "Gary's brother, Ed McRice agreed to pay expenses. [K]nowing that he could not meet the expense without great inconvenience to himself and knowing too that he was industrious and economical, Vin Proehl and Perry Winchell volunteered to help him. In a few hours $90 was raised in Randolph and taken to Alliance [where Gary McRice died]. Bills paid and everybody pleased. Another instance as evidence that

Above - Barney on the left and his brother Sylvan

Left - "My mother, me, Gustie, Syl, Barney, and Vic."

Above - Barney appears to be entertaining the family with a harmonica. Behind him, his sister Madelyn is enjoying the moment.
Right - Marjorie May, Barney, his sister Madelyn Wise, and Marjorie's brother Raymond.

people generally are ready to help the worthy poor." [8]

When Barney turned six years old in 1922, Warren G. Harding was in the White House. The newspaper editor from Marion, Ohio had campaigned with the slogan of getting the country back to "normalcy"; but was it normal for his Secretary of the Interior, Albert B. Fall, to be convicted of bribery and sent to prison? In the world of sports, a young phenomenon with the New York Yankees began hitting home runs at an abnormal rate. Even a normal activity like dancing was pushed to the limits, when a couple won a contest by dancing for twenty-seven continuous hours. [9]

Then, the age of prohibition was anything but "normalcy." Eight miles north of the Henry Wise farm, the county seat of Ravenna saw the arrest and conviction of two men who had challenged the 18th Amendment. One night, two of Ravenna's "finest" staked out the Etna House, the large stone hotel on Main Street, where there had been some suspicious activity. One of the culprits "drove up to the hotel late at night and ran into the hotel with a suitcase. When he came out, the officers made for him, whereupon he attempted to destroy the liquor, breaking one bottle and pouring out the contents of another. However, a large container of corn whiskey was seized by the officers as evidence." One of the whiskey runners was fined $1,000 and costs; and the other was assessed $500 plus having his automobile confiscated and later sold by the authorities. The Etna proprietor was on parole for a violation the previous summer, when he was fined $1,000 and costs. Now, he had to serve out his former sentence. Considering that the average income in 1922 was $1,201, the fines were pretty stiff. [10]

In Akron, the silent movies, known as "Photoplays," were striking the death knell for vaudeville. Only one theater boasted vaudeville entertainment, another offered a play called "Mother and Son," but seven theaters offered "Photoplays." Tom Mix, the western star, received the most acclaim. In language that would have a different meaning in years to come, the *Beacon* reported that Tom Mix "amazed them with a new show of power as a gay adventurer playing on their feelings and performing daredevil stunts that should give him the title of a modern D'Artagnan." [11]

On Barney's sixth birthday, profound grief gripped eighteen

million Catholic subjects in the United States. "First reports of the death of Pope Benedict XV bowed the heads of all catholicity in solemnity and sorrow... Benedict XV worked for peace and during the early part of the world conflict sought to prevent the war from extending so as to draw in other countries. He endeavored to emphasize that there is a moral as well as legal aspect to neutrality as did no other man during that period." [12] This event affected the Wise family who attended St. Joseph's Catholic church in the western part of Randolph township. In another year, Barney would begin his eight years of elementary education at the parish school.

However, in some quarters, the Catholic church members received no sympathy. The 1920's saw the KKK expand to four million, "most of whom were dedicated to the hatred of Jews, Catholics, Negroes, immigrants, the League of Nations, and pacifism." [13] In the St. Joseph's parish, a cross was reportedly burned on the church's front yard; and on another occasion a flaming cross graced a school board member's yard because he suggested that the local buses also transport the Catholic students to their school, since the buses drove past the school. Perhaps some citizens might have wondered if this was actually the age of "abnormalcy."

On Barney's thirteenth birthday (January 23, 1929), the weatherman in Ravenna did not appreciate the frigid weather. Said he: "There is nothing more changeable than the weather. For that reason, says a columnist, we should speak of the 'weather woman' instead of the 'weather man' " Whether man or woman, the residents were tired of the ice cutting the motorists' tires, slush spattering the pedestrians, walkers falling down at every icy corner, and cars skidding all over the streets. There was not much about which to cheer since clouds and snow were in the forecast.

Awaiting his March inauguration, President-elect Hoover and his wife Lou apparently had few worries, especially the weather. In Miami Beach, "Herbert Hoover went into seclusion today…He plans to do a lot of fishing, but not even this activity could entice him today away from the luxurious lodge that is to be his home for the next four weeks." Surrounded by secret service men and Florida state police, "Callers identify themselves and disclose their business, if any, before being admitted to the grounds. All around him are the blue waters of the bay." [14] This aloofness from the common man, the crash

of the stock market later in the year, and the ensuing economic depression spelled stormy times for Hoover.
 Amidst the reports of the usual tragic accidents, criminal activity, and killings were other interesting items. The Fraternal Order of Eagles was sponsoring an Ohio bill providing for old age pensions under certain conditions for persons over 70 years of age. The pensioner would receive $25 per month as long as his total income did not exceed $300. Taxes were to be levied to create the fund. Of course, this legislation had as much chance of passing as the local snowballs surviving in the netherworld.
 From Des Moines, Iowa the director of school attendance, Miss May Goodrell, states, "The small boy of today likes to go to school, thinks a lot of his teacher, enjoys his books, and gets a 'kick' out of the games at recess.... There's little 'playing hookey' nowadays, Miss Goodrell tells you with a smile... Irregular school attendance, Miss Goodrell discloses, can be blamed more upon the parents than upon the children. 'We find that boys and girls are kept out of schools to help at home,' she relates, 'to go on errands, to visit relatives -- in fact for any reason at all." [15] Perhaps, Miss Goodrell's comments could have been submitted to the popular newspaper cartoon panel, "Ripley's Believe It or Not."

After school on September 3, 1935 clusters of girls with books clutched in their arms excitedly gossiped about their new classes, the latest crazes, boys, other girls, and their teachers. Some of the boys scurried off to football practice. If Barney had any interest in football or any other sport, it had to take a back seat to helping out at home. In the spring he plodded behind two horses and a one-row corn planter, a task that required strength, stamina, a steady hand, determination, and patience. In these Great Depression times Barney's father needed to supplement his meager farm income with an outside job, so he applied for a foreman's position with the WPA (Works Progress Administration), which was enacted by Congress on April 8, 1935. The WPA was a government project for unemployed Americans. In return, the government acquired new roads, bridges, parks, airports, and artistic works. So, with the farm chores and harvest, Barney had no time for extracurricular activities. Nevertheless, he had an interest in his under-sized and under-manned classmates, who possessed a keen competitive spirit and believed that they could win against the odds.

The Orange and Black

The leader of coach Lester Campbell's 22-man squad was senior captain, Vernon "Vernie" Neal. The Brockett boys also were formidable football players. Wayne was a 145-pound junior, who anchored one of the guard positions, while the handsome, six-foot senior Scott played tackle or provided bruising blocking and ball-carrying from the fullback spot in Coach Campbell's single wing attack. Young Ned Brockett was one of the substitutes.

Another substitute was freshman Lamar Jenior, who graduated from St. Joseph's elementary school. Lamar claimed that he didn't know much about football, but he was flattered that Scott Brocket personally asked him to come out for the team. Lamar's cousin Bernie was quite a player; the 175-pound junior starred at his guard position. Perhaps Scott figured that Lamar had good bloodlines.

Although Coach Campbell would experiment with personnel in different positions, Vernie Neal was expected to move from fullback to his old position of quarterback. Dale Neal, a 165-pound freshman, earned the guard slot opposite Bernie Jenior.

Casimer Zukowski, a six-foot junior, possessed a football name and the center position. Jack Baughman, a "lanky 145-pounder," manned one tackle spot, and senior Paul Merzweiler the other tackle. Joe Nuspl, another senior, was in the backfield along with fellow classmate Clarence Guthier. Freshman Lamar Jenior thought that senior Roy Knapp was also a "tough egg."

The boys would get their first test on September 20 when neighboring Atwater High School came to visit. Kickoff time for the Friday contest was at 3:30 on the worn down field behind the school. The two football officials were ready. (Just this fall, the referee's pay per game rose from $4 to $5. The head linesman received only a dollar for his efforts.)

The boys pulled on their leather helmets, which were only good for preventing cuts and cauliflower ears as well as smooshing down one's hair. An exception was the rugged Scott Brockett, who disdained playing with a helmet. So, amidst the cheers and encouragement from their friends, the boys trotted out to the hot and dusty field for the season opener.

After a scoreless first half, the Randolph Tigers came to life. Sportswriter Oliver Wolcott summed up the game: "Randolph turned in the biggest surprise by trimming Atwater by a score of 14-0... Randolph's dark-horse football team cracked the lid of the new season with a second-half 14-0 victory over a lighter and inexperienced Atwater eleven on the Randolph field."

"Most of the first half of the game was played in Randolph's territory with Atwater doing practically all the ball carrying. Neither team looked good on the offense as both squads threw orthodox football to the winds in an attempt to score.

A change of tactics in the second half brought a rapid change in the game as Randolph resorted to orthodox football. Scott Brockett, who had played the first as an end, was shifted to fullback, and it was his consistent line plunging and end running which scored the first touchdown. The Atwater eleven was helpless before the onslaught of the Randolph line. [Vernon Neal ran for the extra point. There was no two-point conversion rule.]

V. Neal, Randolph quarterback, executed some brilliant open field running in the final stanza and finally scored. [Paul Clark ran for the extra point.] The second half of the game was all Randolph, with Atwater scarcely seeing the ball."[16]

The BIG GAME was next on tap. Last year the Tigers visited their neighbors to the west, the Suffield "Red Devils," and were soundly thrashed 25-0 by the eventual champions. Enthusiasm, confidence, and expectations were riding high in Tiger land. Tom Wolfe, writing for *The Evening Record and Daily Courier-Tribune*, visited Randolph High during the week.

"They're stirred up over at Randolph about the game next Saturday with Suffield. Yes sir!

Ever since they tasted blood last week against Atwater, the Tigers have been itching to sink their claws into the Big red team. They still have vivid memories of the 25-0 shellacking tacked on them by the Red Devils last year...."

Wolfe had brought the newspaper's loving cup, which would be donated to this year's county football champion. Upon seeing the cup, one member of the Tigers remarked, "You might just as well leave that here for good and save yourself the trouble of bringing it back,' and the rest of the squad echoed him to a man."

"Confidence like that goes a long way toward building a good ball club, but unless there's something to back it up, it may melt away like [heavyweight boxer] Max Baer's bankroll when the cleats start flying....

Not at all certain to be favorites in the county race until they can get by the Suffield hurdle, the attitude of the team is aptly summed up in these words of their coach -- 'We will meet our opponents with eleven men on the field, and hope to give a good account of ourselves.' " [17]

The BIG GAME had a special time and venue -- Saturday afternoon (September 28th) on the fair grounds in front of the Randolph Fair crowd. The Tigers were sent reeling from the onset, but after one quarter of play, the score was 0-0. In the second quarter the Big Red resorted to a bit of trickery, a flea-flicker play from Saxe to Roudebush to Butler for a touchdown. "The try-for-point was an attempted drop kick blocked by the whole Randolph line." The Tigers simply could not stop the big and talented Big Red backfield. Saxe plunged for the second touchdown. "A moment later he bucked through the center for the ace point."

Trailing 13-0 at the half, the Tigers grimly hung on in a scoreless second half. The sportswriter summed it up:

"Coach Harlan Fry's 1935 edition of the Suffield steam roller football [team] humbled an optimistic Randolph aggregation by a score of 13-0 at the Randolph fair last Saturday.

Outclassing their Tiger hosts in every department of the game, the Suffield huskies scored first downs at will, though a stubborn Randolph defense held its opponents scoreless for three quarters....

Lateral passes, line bucks, and end runs were displayed by the Big Red, varied with cannon-ball thrusts off-tackle. Only the sterling tackling by Scott Brockett, V. Neal and Clark kept the game from being entirely one-sided....

Randolph's team displayed lack of polish on the offensive, with the line playing very mediocre ball. Coach L. L. Campbell's protegees showed plenty of spirit but will need many nights of practice before they can assume the role of giant-killers to Aurora, Garrettsville, Ravenna and other teams still remaining on their schedule." [17]

The Tigers licked their wounds and came back fighting the following week against an out-manned Freedom squad.

"Scoring its first touchdown in the first period when John Zupan, the referee, ruled interference with Guthier, Randolph went on to defeat Freedom by a score of 20-0. V. Neal plunged through the center of the line for the extra point.

V. Neal paved the way for Randolph's second score when he intercepted a Freedom pass deep in Freedom territory and raced to the eight-yard line before he was tossed to the ground. Two line plays carried the ball to the two where W. Brockett [probably Scott] plunged over for the score. Neal again hit the center of the line for the extra point.

Freedom resorted to a passing game in the final quarter but Randolph intercepted several to halt drives toward the goal. Taking one intercepted pass, Randolph reeled off three consecutive first downs to place the oval on the one-yard line. Here V. Neal was again pressed into service and plowed through the right side of the line for a score." [18]

Next on the schedule was a team from the northern part of the county, which came to Randolph on October 12; and the result was the "Year's Biggest Upset." Oliver Wolcott reported the results.

"Little Randolph stepped into the Portage county football picture long enough Friday afternoon to erase Aurora from the title chase by a score of 6-0 in the biggest upset of the year.

With V. Neal breaking away in the first period for a number of long runs Randolph swept Aurora off its feet and finished the opening period in possession of the ball on the one-yard line. However, Aurora's line held and [they] kicked out of danger.

Again in the third period Randolph started a march goalward for a distance of 60 yards but this time the team was not to be denied and S. Brockett went over with the winning score.

On the kickoff Aurora opened up. Kamer took the kick and lateralled to T. Truce who raced 60 yards before going down. Aurora plunged to the five where Randolph held and took the ball when T. Truce passed over the goal line to Kamer, the ball sliding off the latter's finger tips. Aurora [was] kept on the defensive most of the game by V. Neal's off-tackle and end sweeps and Brockett's line plunging." [19]

With a three and one record, the Tigers then traveled to their northern neighbor, Rootstown, on October 18. This autumn day was a grand one for Vernon Neal and the Tiger offense. Vernie racked up five touchdowns. Paul Clark and Scott Brockett each garnered an extra point.

"Randolph scored a 32-6 victory over Rootstown to maintain its record as the upset team of Portage county. Scoring 14 points in the first period as compared to Rootstown's six, the Randolph eleven had little trouble scoring its second straight victory. Forty and 50 yard runs by Victor [sic] Neal, Randolph halfback who scored all of Randolph's touchdowns, was the feature of the victory." [20]

The Orange and Black went on the road to Windham on October 25th. It was Scott Brockett's time to shine. "Randolph, the county's surprise team, once again tallied a victory by defeating Windham 13-6 in a ragged but rough encounter. Scott Brockett, bruising Randolph fullback, scored both touchdowns for Randolph while Steigerwald tallied for Windham. The teams entered the fourth period with Randolph leading by a single point when Scott Brockett punched the Windham line for the second marker." Vernie Neal plunged for the extra point. [21]

The next contest was with the league's co-favorite, Garrettsville on November 1. The "G-men" were just too tough for the visiting Tigers. They opened a 21-0 halftime lead and cruised the rest of the way. "Garrettsville resorted to nothing more than line smashes to score a 28-0 victory over Randolph's surprise team. The defeat was the second of the year for the Randolph eleven." [22]

The never-say-die Tigers hosted the Mantua "Hilltop Outfit" on November 8th. "Little Randolph snapped back into the county winning group Friday afternoon by beating Mantua Village high school by a score of 20-0 after taking a shellacking last week at the unbeaten Garrettsville eleven.

Coach Lester Campbell's boys scored their first marker in the second period when [Paul] Merzweiler planted the pigskin between the uprights. Scoring again in the third and fourth periods with V. Neal capturing the honors, Randolph continued its surprise tactics for the year. V. Neal added two points to the Randolph total when he snagged McLaughlin behind his own goal for a safety." [23]

The Ides (15th) of November proved a bad omen for the Randolph Tigers. Ravenna Township scored a touchdown in the first and last quarters to shutout Randolph 12-0. The Orange and Black finished with a 6-3 record, far better than anyone expected except the boys themselves. [24]

Nothing was written about the Tigers' last game, because the focus was on Suffield's 62-0 rout of Windham. One week later, the Big Red claimed the county championship. "Sifting through a swirl of snow flakes and Garrettsville's crippled line with equal ease, swivel-hipped Bob Roudebush led Suffield's Red Wave to a decisive 14-0 victory and the 1935 Portage county football championship." [25]

As 1935 wound down, everyone in town could agree that the depression was "really tough;" but the times certainly weren't dull. When the notorious Ma Barker and her gang of bank robbers and killers were gunned down by the FBI in January, the populace and the news media didn't shed a tear. In March, Adolph Hitler announced the rearmament of Germany. Although this violated the Versailles Treaty, the Fuhrer was given a free pass. Huge dust storms swept the Midwest causing many to flee the "Dust Bowl" of the United States. In June, James J. Braddock (later dubbed the 'Cinderella Man') defeated the flamboyant Max Baer at Madison Square Garden for the heavyweight championship. The new champion was beloved by all dark horses everywhere. Will Rogers, humorist extraordinaire, could make people laugh during painful times; so in August it was a national tragedy when he was killed in an airplane crash off Point Barrow, Alaska. In September, Sen. Huey Long, the "Kingfish," was assassinated in Louisiana. Whoever missed the demagogue wouldn't miss him long. On September 30, President Roosevelt dedicated Hoover Dam, truly a manmade marvel. Locally, strike violence made the biggest news. One strike occurred in Barberton at the Ohio Insulator Company. Two company guards, two bystanders, two children, and one picket were seriously injured and scores of others received minor injuries in the 24-hour riot which saw beatings, tear gas canisters, and brick throwing. Later in the week, the sheriffs had to close the plant to stop the battle.[26] In December, the United States Supreme Court denied Bruno Hauptman's plea to escape the electric chair. In February, he was found guilty of the Lindbergh baby's death. He would be electrocuted on April 3, 1936.

The sports page of the local paper reported that 46 men and boys were killed this past football season, 26 of them on the high school level. "The greater portion of high school injuries resulted from head on tackling or inadequate equipment. [See the picture of

Vernie Neal's helmet.] The figure, however, is not as startling as it may seem because there were approximately 616,000 youths playing high school football this season against 65,000 on college teams."[27] Nevertheless, Randolph High School was proud of their football team and probably relieved that the boys all survived. Said the *Speedometer*: The athletic program of the year has aroused a great deal of enthusiasm and has been extraordinarily successful. The football team brought home a number of victories over both old and new rivals. The invulnerable Vernon Neal and Bernie Jenior, both were selected as all-county stars. Brockett, Guthier, and Zukowski were also outstanding players." [28]

  The athletic young man's fancy now turned to basketball. Scott Brocket would often have the boys come over to the farm to practice in the large barn. After sweeping the hay off the dusty floor and moving any farm machinery off to the side, the lads would fire away at the bushel basket nailed to one of the end walls. With Scott's driving competitiveness and quick temper, the skirmishing on the barn floor could become rough and heated.

  It was a time when the "cracker box" gymnasiums were packed to the rafters with screaming, sometimes obnoxious, basketball fans. Both teams and the scorer's table were often on an elevated stage at one end of the floor. (At Randolph, the stage was on one sideline and flanked by the locker rooms. On the other sideline there were folding doors which opened to the hallway. Above that was the small balcony.) Boundaries ran close to the stage, the outside and end walls, and near the bleachers. The foul lane, or "keyhole," actually looked like the end of a skeleton key; and due to the shortened floor, the back court line was frequently the opponent's foul line. In 1935-36 there was a center jump after each basket, which when added to the close quarters, made for tight, low-scoring contests. With the close confines came pandemonium and dripping sweat for all. However, compared to the Brockett barn, the Randolph gymnasium with its brick walls and varnished hardwood floors seemed modern and spacious.

  The Randolph Tigers opened the basketball season on December 7th with a 32-14 romp over Palmyra. Clarence Guthier led the way with 14 points. [29] That victory was followed by another on December 13th. This thriller produced more print in the local newspaper.

"Randolph high school gained the distinction of scoring the first upset in the Portage county high school league basketball league [sic] by blasting Paris' powerful quintet by a 35 to 33 score in a scorching battle.

The victory marked Randolph's second of the season and definitely established Coach Campbell's [actually Coach Moyer's] hoopsters as powerful contenders for the 1935-36 county championship....

Randolph gained an early lead and then withstood a gallant Paris rally to emerge victorious. Behind 22 to 16 at halftime, Paris pecked away at Randolph's lead in the final half and threw fear into the hearts of Randolph rooters as it almost drew up even in the final minutes of play.

Guthier was the big gun in the Randolph victory, firing in seven field goals for a total of 14 points...." [30]

Tom Wolfe visited Randolph within the week to assess the Black and Orange for his readers.. His remarks follow.

"They're not nicknamed the Tigers for nothing at Randolph high school. Like the dangerous jungle beast of that name, Tiger athletic teams have been making it a habit the past season to lurk in wait for more powerful but careless foes, settling the issue then with a sudden leap on the unsuspecting victims.

During the past football scramble, the Randolph team earned the moniker of dark-horse simply by virtue of its tendency to bump off more favored opponents

And now with the cage season only two weeks underway, the Orange and Black have already achieved notoriety for recording the first major upset, a thrilling 35-33 victory over Paris, powerful contender for the league crown....

Greeted by four lettermen at the beginning of the season, Coach Vernon Moyer, starting his first season as pilot at Randolph, refused to be optimistic. He took one look over the rest of the field and said, "No sir, we haven't got a chance. The competition is too tough. We shall be lucky to win half our games." (Was Coach Moyer just blowing smoke, or was he really such a pessimist?)

If the start made by the Tigers can be taken as a criterion of the rest of their progress through opposition ranks, Moyer will look like a better coach than a prophet.

The four veterans who form the nucleus of Moyer's team this season are Wayne and Scott Brockett, Clarence Guthier, and John Herchek.. Scott, a lanky six foot, two inch lad, jumps center.

Brother Wayne, a junior, holds down the right guard post, while Paul Clark, a first-year man, keeps him company at the other guard. Guthier and Herchek cavort at the forward berths.

Guthier, a star end in football, transfers his ability to the hardwood, and is probably the outstanding offensive threat on the Orange and Black club. In the Paris upset, the speedy senior pitched in 14 points to lead his mates in scoring.

Twelve other boys of promising ability round out the squad. Only two of them are seniors, the rest being mostly sophomores and juniors, a fact which bodes no ill future for future Tiger teams.

The aforementioned dozen lads are: Alex Homery and Roy Knapp, senior forwards; Bill Bettes, junior guard; Glen Hartman, soph center; Chuck Franks, soph forward; and Ned Brockett, Andy Neidert, Paul Clark, Walter Eichler, Glen May, Glen Gougler, George Kissel, and Charles Anderson, all freshmen."[31] [Practice for the boys often took place in the evenings due to the farm boys having to go home after school to help with the chores.]

The Tiger's last game before the Christmas break was with their old nemesis, the Suffield Big Red. Suffield and Garrettsville were expected to lead the way in basketball as they had done in the football season.

"Suffield and Garrettsville, logical contenders for the county basketball crown, now held by Suffield, continued their winning streaks Friday as county league teams halted their league conquests [sic] until after the holidays.

Suffield overcame a stubborn opponent in Randolph while Garrettsville upset Aurora by a top heavy score. It was Bob Butler, Suffield forward, who spurred the Big Red quint to its victory over Randolph's Blue and White [obviously a reporter's gaff] by a score of 30-20, with a 10-point attack.

The Suffield cagers held an 18-12 lead at halftime and continued to hold the advantage although Randolph fought every inch of the way against insurmountable odds. Herchek, Randolph center, scored seven points to lead the Randolph five. [Guthier, the Tiger's high-scoring forward, was held to four points.] The Suffield seconds scored a 10-point victory by defeating Randolph reserves 26-16 in the preliminary game." ³²

The Orange and Black could only hope to continue winning and get a second chance at the talented Suffield five.

During January 1936, basketball news took a backseat to the bitter cold weather. Ohioans were counseled to "dig in" as temperatures plunged to 5-10 degrees below zero. For a 68 year old Dayton man, January 22nd just wasn't his day. "He apparently had been locked out and fell back, striking his head, while trying to climb in a window. He froze to death while lying unconscious [on his front porch]. Another unlucky weather victim was a Randolph boy who had recently been treated at Ravenna Memorial Hospital for a broken arm. The lad was carrying a pail of water with his good arm, when he slipped on the ice and broke the same injured arm at the elbow. However the news out of Michigan on January 23rd was absolutely the worst: "Hell Frozen Over At Last." "All Hell's frozen over. Snow today blankets the deserted village of Hell, known as Reeves Mill Pond, or Highland, and there is at least six inches of ice in the creek, known to some residents of southern Livingston county as the 'River Styx.' " ³³

In spite of the cold weather, progress flourished in Randolph. "The new sidewalk has been completed from the school house to the square, and a traffic light has been installed at the intersection of roads 224 [old Waterloo Road] and 44. The work was done by the WPA." ³⁴

In the middle of February, Michael Guthier, the last of Randolph Township's Civil War veterans, passed away at the age of 91. Guthier was a member of the 6th Ohio Cavalry. ³⁵

The junior class was rehearsing for the annual class play, which would be presented on February 24th. The production was "Oh, Susan!", a farce comedy in three acts. Among the cast were two standout football players, Bernie Jenior and Casimir Zukowsky. ³⁶

On the basketball courts across the county, the league remained tight since the Christmas break. Randolph won six in a row to raise their record to 8-1; but the Big Red remained undefeated at 9-0. The county tournament at Kent State University would decide the championship.

In the opening round of the tournament The Tigers cruised to a win over Aurora.

"Coach Lowell Van Deusen's Green and White five, led by

Tony Truce with 10 points, tossed the biggest scare of the evening into a well balanced Randolph five but was unable to stand the pace after the intermission and dropped the tilt 34-22.

It was Scott Brockett, tall Randolph center and Guthier, diminutive forward, who paced the Tigers to a well earned victory. Coach Vernon Moyer's boys were unable to locate the basket in the first half missing easy shots under the basket on almost every attempt but during the closing half the Tigers left little doubt as to their superiority over the Aurora five." [37]

In the second round of the tournament, the Black and Orange squeaked by in overtime. Tension was terrific in the overtime period, because the contest went to whoever scored first.

"In another Saturday night thriller, Coach Vernon Moyer's Randolph Tigers won their way into the semi-finals with an overtime win over Atwater.

Marked by closeness of guarding by both teams, the game wound up in a 19-19 stalemate, after Scott Brockett had tied it up in the last moment for Randolph. John Herchek, brother of Kent State coach Mike Herchek, had passed to Brockett when he might have taken the shot himself.

In the last second of the overtime, with the tie unbroken, Guthier heaved a long one from mid-court that swished neatly through for victory, 21-19." (Meanwhile, the Suffield Big Red, kept pace with the Tigers by eking by Garrettsville 29-28." [38]

As the tournament was rising to an exciting crescendo, the newspaper hype also increased.

"Favorites for the tourney trophy appear to be Coach Harlin Fry's Red Devils, following their comeback 29-28 victory over Garrettsville last week...

Cage fans, still a little dizzy following the whirl of games all day last Saturday, will focus their attention on the big center court at 9 o'clock when Freedom and Suffield come to grips...

Randolph Darkhorse

No less crucial than the Freedom-Suffield game will be the Randolph-Paris clash on the same court at 10 o'clock. Vernon Moyer's Tigers, regarded as the dark horse team of the tourney, will shoot the works against the Nightriders...." Paris was hoping to get another chance at Suffield which snatched the tournament trophy out of their hands the previous year.) [39] [It is interesting to note that many coaches went by nicknames -- Dutch, Swede, Mac, etc. -- and even the players addressed them as such. However, the prize coach's nickname in Portage County may have belonged to Gomer "Mutt" Lewis of the "clever Edinburgh combine."]

The sports page headline for February 28 read: "Randolph Trips Paris; Suffield Whips Freedom."

"Shackling Cass Richards and Wayne Griffith, the latter the leading scorer in regular county play, Randolph's Tigers clawed their way to a decisive 32-22 victory over the Paris Nighthawks [called the Nightriders in the mid-week article] in the finale in the second week of the county tournament at Wills gym in Kent Thursday night.

So carefully were Richards and Griffiths covered they were only able to score seven points between them in the first half of the game. Richards tallied a free throw in the early part of the first period but did not get a basket until the closing minutes of the third quarter while his teammate Griffith found the ring for a two-pointer near the middle of the third period and registered again shortly before the game ended.

It was the diminutive Guthier that started Randolph on its climb to block the path of the Big Red Suffield team which barely beat Freedom's fighting squad last night.

At the close of the third period Randolph had piled up a 23-9 margin, which even a final spurt which netted Paris 13 points, failed to overcome. However, it was Glen Hartman who paced the winners with 11 points." In the earlier contest of the evening, Suffield easily handled the Freedom team 24-12. [40]

On leap year day, there was plenty speculation but no conclusions about the upcoming county championship game. In these dire depression times, it seemed as if everyone loved the underdog -- or "darkhorse." The February 29 sports headline proclaimed: "Randolph, Suffield Clash For Tourney Trophy," which was followed by "Randolph, Darkhorse Team, Slated To Play, "David Role."

"You probably couldn't have found one guy in ten a week or so ago who'd have bet an old straw hat on Randolph's chances of copping the county trophy.

But today -- any time up to 3 o'clock -- you'll have no difficulty locating backers for Coach Vernon Moyer's Tiger crew.

Their workmanlike progress through the tournament field has

stamped them as likely possibilities to puncture Suffield's dream of empire.

When the two southern loop quints come together on the big center court in Wills gym at 3 o'clock this afternoon, fans will witness a reenactment of that old favorite, "David and Goliath"-- or -- "The Little guy who Punched the Big Mug on the Nose and Got Away With It."

Will Furnish Fireworks

Everyone is not quite certain that Randolph will get away with taking a figurative poke at Suffield, but all are quite sure the Tigers will make a real try -- which is a cinch to provide some fireworks...." [41] With such high expectations, one could only wonder if the Orange and Black would have their hopes dashed again as in the 13-0 Suffield victory during the football season and the Big Red's easy 30-20 basketball victory on December 20th.

The Tigers and Big Red knew each other well, and their defenses were tenacious. Suffield took the early lead but not for long as Glen Hartman "counted a goal from under the basket then John Herchek dropped two free tosses into the basket." Suffield's Virgil Butler "also connected with a charity toss as the period ended with Randolph leading 4-2." Butler knotted the count at 4-4 and then the Big Red took the lead, but Herchek pivoted and scored to knot the score at 8-8. Then the Suffield five reeled off five unanswered points to take a 13-8 halftime lead.

"After Memmer was loose under the basket to score a sleeper shot, Suffield was not headed until Scott Brockett scored two consecutive baskets to tie the score 16-16. Roudebush slipped one in for Suffield with slightly more than four minutes remaining in the game. Here the score remained until Brockett counted the tying basket on a pass from Herchek with little more than a minute remaining to be played.

The former county champions had a fine opportunity to shoot ahead in the final minute when Hartman fouled Memmer but the Suffield boy failed to connect on either shot."

Tied at 18-18, the game went into a sudden death overtime period.

Under fire, the Suffield team could have grabbed the championship from the upstart Tigers, but the team missed five shots under the basket in the overtime period. "Randolph had dogged the

Suffield team during the entire game but it was Scott Brockett who drove under the basket to take a pass from Glen Hartman and in the same motion sent the sphere spinning through the ring with 37 seconds remaining in the period and snag the game and title. The basket, according to the sudden death ruling of the state athletic commission for tournaments, gave Randolph a richly deserved victory.... The new champions have waited a long time to get a shot at the title and so confident were the boys that there never was any doubt in their minds as to the eventual outcome. A wild crowd rushed out onto the floor following the game to completely surround the new conqueror of a team that had held sway in the county for the past two years. It was also a hostile crowd which booed every Suffield effort in the greedy quest for the champions' downfall...."

For the new champions, Oliver Wolcott's March 2nd game report kept the victory glow burning. "**Randolph Tops Suffield; Wins 1st Cage Title.**"

"Scott Brockett and his Randolph team mates were the toast of Randolph high school today after the Randolph 'Wonder team' gave the dope bucket a healthy kick to upset Suffield Saturday to win its first Portage county basketball title in the history of the school.... Saturday's win was Randolph's 10th straight victory and its twelfth of the season against one defeat..." [42]

"The official tournament all-star boys' team picked by the officials following Saturday's game gave the new champions, Randolph, three places on the team of 10 players.

Scott Brockett, Alex Homery, and John Herchek were selected to represent the Randolph school..." [43]

Could the Tigers maintain their momentum into the state basketball tournament? They would be competing in Class B with the other smaller schools. The big city schools competed in the Class A tournament.

In the first round, "Randolph continued its majestic swing through tournament play in the first game of the sectional meet by defeating Paris, one of the most stubborn foes, by a score of 23-21.

The Tigers took the lead in the opening period and breasted the quarter mark with a 6-0 lead. During the second period, Paris located the basket and pushed the county champions to the limit as the period ended 14-10.

Coming back after the intermission Randolph once again displayed a burst of speed to check the Paris attack at three points while adding six more, making the third period score 20-13.

Paris again spurted in the final period with Griffiths and Richards showing the way, but were unable to overcome the advantage built up by the Tigers in the early periods. [Paris'] Griffith paced the scorers in the game with10 points, while Herchek and Scott Brockett, hero of the county championship game, tied for high honors with six points each." (Suffield lost to Beach City from Stark County.) [44]

The fear of all tournament contenders is the sudden acquisition of a cold shooting hand. Unfortunately for the spectators, both Randolph and Canton Township couldn't find the range in a low-scoring tilt. The action, or lack of it, led the Portage County scribe to exhibit a little sarcasm.

"It was stormy weather for Portage county teams last night as the double-barreled sectional tourney drew near its close...

Randolph's Tigers, county Class B champs and winners of their first tourney round against Paris, were the first victims of the evening, bowing to Canton township 23-11.

Both teams fired at the basket for over three minutes before McNeal, Canton guard, finally broke the ice with a free throw. During the first two periods, the Tigers kept Coach Herb Eichenberg's boys well covered, although neither team seemed able to locate the hoop when an opening appeared.

At halftime the count was 6-4. Canton and the scorekeepers were becoming drowsy when McNeal began to find the range. The fast-stepping ace romped out to sink 14 points and Randolph's hopes for a place in the finals..." [45]

The Orange and Black "dark horses' finished their season with a 13-2 record and the school's first county championship. In these dreary depression days, their exploits and spirit certainly enlightened the hearts of the locals and other interested sports fans. However, with the calamitous events of the coming days and the passage of time, the echoes of their fame would gradually fade away.

In the middle of May, the school year was on the wane. A spirit of "Auld Lang Syne" and a touch of melancholy ran through the group of 24 seniors, as old friendships with cherished memories

Randolph Tigers 1935-1936 Champs: 1st Row - Clarence Guthier, John Herchek, Wayne Brockett, Scott Brockett, Alex Homery, Glen Hartman. 2nd Row - Coach Vernon Moyer, Vernon Neal, Charles Franks, Roy Knapp, Dale Neal, Paul Eichler, Principal Gilmore.

Some of the 1935 All-County Stars. Vernie Neal is third from the left.

were soon to part. On one hand there was a proud sense of achievement and an eagerness to get on with life; yet, there was some trepidation for the troubled and uncertain future.

The junior-senior banquet was held Saturday evening, May 16, at the Robin Hood in Kent. Baccalaureate services for the graduating class occurred on Sunday evening in the school auditorium. Class night was held on Tuesday the 19th. Graduation was on May 21st with Alva I. Cox of Cleveland delivering the commencement address and Rev. William Joel conducting the services.

"A class of 24 graduated Thursday night from Randolph high school, being one of the largest senior classes in the history of the school. Carl Lang was valedictorian and Mildred Wearstler salutatorian..." [46]

The Class of '36 faced an uncertain and turbulent world. Der Fuhrer was rapidly rearming the German nation and bullying the European countries into concessions. Il Duce had designs for a new Roman Empire in Africa, and the Japanese were ruthlessly steamrolling over the weak opposition in the Far East. However, on a practical and personal basis, the biggest challenge for the young Americans was how to support themselves with even the basic necessities of life in this Great Depression.

Some of the graduates desired a college education, but finances were the main obstacle. Scott Brockett studied animal husbandry at Ohio State for one year and attended a school in Milwaukee, Wisconsin for two more years.

Vernie Neal decided to attend the University of Akron in the fall of 1936, but after one month, he decided that the college life was not for him; so he enlisted in the United States Marine Corps. The military life appealed to the rugged Randolph Tiger, and he even played some football for the Quantico Marines. (It is quite unlikely that Vernie was permitted to carve a skull and crossbones on his leather helmet as he had done in high school.) Five years after graduating high school, Neal was stationed at Pearl Harbor when the Japanese attacked. On that peaceful Sunday morning, the only thought of combat for Vernie and his buddies was in the current pillow fight in the barracks. Then all hell broke loose for real. [47]

In early December 1942, Sgt. Vernon Neal was on furlough

in Randolph, Ohio. Loris Troyer of the *Evening Record* interviewed the veteran of the fighting on Guadalcanal, and the article made page one on December 11. The article provided a glimpse of combat on the tropical island and exhibited the Marine's fighting spirit.

"United States marines, living up to the leatherneck tradition, have the 'situation well in hand' on Guadalcanal, stemming all Japanese attacks.

So says Master Technical Sgt. Vernon H. Neal, son of Roy Neal, Randolph, who is home on furlough after spending 60 days on the Guadalcanal front.

U. S. leathernecks on Guadalcanal live through practically the same routine every day. They leave their fox-holes at daybreak, work till 8 a.m., eat and then work some more. Between 10 and 12 every day there is a Jap air attack. Men on Henderson airfield head for the beaches to get out of the target area and marine planes take to the skies to chase the attackers. After the attack, marines return to Henderson field and continue their work on fighter planes, Later in the afternoon they eat again, work till dark and climb into their fox-holes to spend the night.

SOME ROUTINE!

If the marines call this routine, we wonder what they call action.

Sgt. Neal , who recently started his seventh year in the marines, doesn't believe the Japs will retake the American position. Although out-numbered, marines are taking a terrific toll of Japs with every attack, both on land and in the air.

Sgt. Neal, with an aviation engineering force, landed on Guadalcanal after the raiding party of marines had captured Henderson field. He landed in a Higgins boat launched from a destroyer.

At Henderson field, the marine aviation crew took over the supply of gasoline and food left by the Japs in their haste to escape the raiding party's fury. The marines ate the food and are using the Jap gasoline in their trucks. The octane content of the gas makes it unsuitable for use in marine planes.

Sgt. Neal, relieved after spending more than 60 days on Guadalcanal, spent his time repairing planes to meet new Nipponese attacks, which came daily 'just as night and day.'....

He recalled one attack in which marine fighters downed 23 of

25 attacking planes while the Yanks lost only three.

The air is not the only place the marines are taking a heavy toll of Japs. In one day's fighting the ground forces killed 1100 Japs and lost only 28 marines. Front lines of the ground battle were at one time only 500 yards from Henderson field, according to Sgt. Neal.

Speaking of the morale of the soldiers on Guadalcanal, Sgt. Neal, only 24, said 'there isn't a man on the island who would like to be some where else.

Both American and Japanese forces on Guadalcanal are being relieved periodically. Neal arrived on the island in August and left there by plane on Oct. 30. He left on a plane loaded with injured marines.

ALL WORK, LITTLE PLAY

Life on Guadalcanal, he said, is dull except for the fighting. There is no time for recreation and there wouldn't be any recreation if there was time. The tropical heat is oppressing.

Main dishes of marines are corned beef and Spam, although upon several occasions the food supply ran low because of sea battles around the island.

Neal, while appreciating the fighting ability of the Japs, claims they are stupid.

'For instance,' he said, 'a crazy Jap will take a hand grenade in each hand and race for a machine gun nest, knowing that it is certain suicide.'

Jap bombers have never done considerable damage on the island, he said. When marine planes take to the air, the Nipponese drop their bomb loads where ever they happen to be....

Before seeing service in Guadalcanal, Neal was in New Caledonia, New Hebrides and Pearl Harbor...

Neal's 30 day furlough will expire Dec. 22 and he is applying for an additional 15 days.

When he reports for duty after his furlough, he will be stationed on the west coast. Marine physicians ordered that marines seeing service on Guadalcanal be assigned to duty in the United States for at least six months....

[Neal] joined the marines to see some action and 'he's seen it.' [48]

On the other side of the world, Roy Knapp, that "tough egg" from the Randolph Tigers, maintained his reputation. Roy was in-

ducted on March 11, 1942. In the bitter European winter of 1944-45, Knapp was with the G.I.'s who were fighting in Germany. The *Evening Record* published his picture and the following information: "Staff Sgt. Roy Knapp, son of Mr. and Mrs. O. J. Knapp, of Randolph, was recently awarded the bronze star for heroic action in the European theater.
Overseas since last January, Sgt. Knapp landed on the Normandy beachhead on D-Day. The last letter that was received by his parents was written from Germany.
Sgt. Knapp has been in the army since Nov. 13, 1942. A brother, Pvt. Paul Knapp, is attending school at Camp Lee, Va. "[49]

Paul Nau, Class of '36, was inducted into the service on March 20, 1941; and over the war years he received considerable newspaper print from the local correspondents to the *Evening Record*. It was reported that Sgt. Paul S. Nau was "boss of the first platoon, Co. A, 9th Battalion at the Medical Replacement Training Center, Camp Pickett, Va.... His job at the MRTC is to teach new recruit's the elements of the difficult and dangerous task of the medical soldier, who serves on every fighting front, wherever there are American troops." After serving three years, Nau had received his commission as a second lieutenant at Camp Davis, S.C., and he was later promoted to Captain and was stationed in the anti-aircraft artillery at Camp Rosecrans, Cal. [50]

As for other members of the Class of '36 who saw service time: Valedictorian Carl Lang became a corporal, Uncle Sam got Glen Breden on February 11, 1941, Paul Eichler was inducted on June 29, 1942, and Bogdan Odadzin was snapped up on September 28, 1942. By mid-1943, Uncle Sam needed more men, even those married with children. One news item noted the visit of Mrs. Clarence Guthier and her 19 month old daughter to Camp Carson, Colorado, where T4 Clarence Guthier was stationed with Co. A 171st Engineer Battalion. [51]

Mildred "Ruth" Hilliard became Mrs. Malon Spangler. Ruth's brother Bob (Class of '32) was killed in Italy on January 12, 1944.

Then there was Barney Wise who was inducted on September 4, 1942.

THE WRIGHTS
RAVENNA, OHIO

My brother
Uncle Barney Wise
Killed in France in 1944 and buried there W.W.2

The sun shines on the snow-covered ground at the Wise family Farm. Barney poses with his parents, Henry A. and Mary O. Wise.

Barney's military standing:
Third Army, Gen. Geo. Patton
XII Corps
26th Division, "The Yankee Division"
101st Infantry Regiment
2nd Battalion
Headquarters Company

PART III
FROM CHERBOURG TO ST. AVOLD

After landing in France on September 1944, the Yankee Division moved east in a somewhat piecemeal fashion. On September 20th, the 101st Engineer Combat Battalion was ordered to remove extensive minefields from Carteret, where they cleared approximately seven thousand mines.

Supplying the vast, fast-moving American armies, which were pushing toward the German border, was approaching the crisis stage. Thus, a series of "Red Ball" express highways were created from the beaches of Normandy and the quays of Cherbourg to the fighting fronts hundreds of miles to the east. During September, 3,000 men of the Yankee Division were assigned to nineteen provisional truck companies for the "Red Ball" run. When the 26th Division was alerted for combat duty, these men returned to their former duties. [52]

On October 22nd, the 104th Infantry attacked enemy positions in the Montcourt Woods. In the dense forest a profusion of mines and booby traps awaited the 104th; German pillboxes were advantageously placed; and the enemy dug shelters up to twelve feet deep. Perhaps it was here that the 104th's Pierre A. Winfret learned his cardinal rules for surviving combat.

* Never but never expose yourself to the enemy.
* Never walk along or stand on a skyline.
* Never get out of your foxhole.
* Change firing positions as often as possible.
* Never run standing up, run in a crouch.
* Throw hand grenades from the prone, if possible.
* Do not follow trails, if possible.
* Always make sure there is a round in the rifle chamber.
* Never, but never, group up.
* Camouflage everything and anything.
* Move in the utmost silence possible.
* Get rid of all noisy gear.
* Never issue verbal commands, if possible.
* Use tracer ammunition only if absolutely necessary.
* Avoid any and all contact with enemy material.

* Never approach a fallen enemy, do not take your eyes off him, be ready to kill him.
* Stay hidden as long as possible and as much as possible.
* Bury everything you don't want.
* Don't display command insignia.
* If you take prisoners, strip them to the buff.
* If you get lost in the dark, freeze where you are until dawn breaks.
* Lay down as much fire power as you can; fire, fire, and fire some more. [53]

By early November the Yankee Division was reassembled in the XII Corps sector of Gen. George Patton's Third Army. Posted 15 miles to the east of Nancy along a 13-mile stretch, from left to right the XII Corps was composed of the 80th Division, the 35th Division, and the 26th Division. The 104th Infantry assembled on the left of the Yankee Division's sector and opposite Salonnes and Vic-sur-Seille. The 101st Infantry was in the middle on highway 414, which led to Moyenvic. On the right of the division, the 328th Infantry faced Moncourt and Bezange-la-Petite.

Barney Wise's 101st Infantry faced Cote St. Jean (Hill 310) just north of Moyenvic and about 15 miles east of Nancy. According to James Haare, the area is a rolling, agricultural country with many small villages, most of which are no more than 250 inhabitants in size. Barney's prospects for going unscathed in the upcoming action were slim indeed, since "casualties in the infantry ran about 90%, so one's chances of surviving were rather limited." Awaiting the 101st on Hill 310 were the soldiers of the 361st Volksgrenadier Division and a regiment of the 559th Volksgrenadier Division. With their backs to the Fatherland and Der Fuhrer's ruthless goading, these German troops would not be content to hole up on the defensive; they would be more than willing to counter-attack in an attempt to annihilate the advancing Americans.[54]

"Beginning on 5 November, the first date possible for the attack according to Third Army plans, rain fell with only brief intermissions. On 7 November a downpour began that lasted without a break for twenty-four hours." Many army and armored officers believed that the campaign was beginning a month too late. In this weather air support was out of the question; and there were serious concerns as to whether the tanks and other vehicles could negotiate the deep November mud. It was assumed that G.I.'s like Barney Wise could slog through the mud and the cold, rainy November weather. Nevertheless, Patton could wait no longer for good air support weather, and he issued the code words, "Play ball." At nightfall on the 7th, the infantry slowly plodded through the rivers of mud to their jump-off positions. [55]

November 8 at 0500 hours, the "ballgame" began as the 26th Division Artillery and XII Corps Artillery began the hour barrage. "The XII Corps artillery plan again was elaborate and detailed. Tactical surprise would be sacrificed in order to bring the greatest weight of metal against the forward positions, on which the Germans had worked and sweated for a month... The seventeen battalions of corps artillery would fire a preparation for three and a half hours (H minus 60 minutes to H plus 150), with 20 battalions of division artillery strengthening the fire during the first thirty minutes... To this terrific fire the 90 mm guns of the anti-aircraft artillery battalions, the 3-inch guns of the tank destroyers, and the 105-mm howitzers of the regimental cannon companies were pushed forward close behind the infantry's line of departure... [56]

For many men of the 101st, "the deafening, ceaseless, foreboding roar of artillery on this morning marked a standard by which future mornings could and would be judged." [57] For others, it would be the last artillery barrage that they would ever hear.

In the wet, early morning darkness, Lt. Col. Bernard A. Lyons inched his men to the jump-off position, and at 0600 the infantry moved out. Their first objective was to take Moyenvic and the bridge over the Seille River.

The German elements in Moyenvic were taken by complete surprise with the loss of 542 prisoners taken. Stealing from house to house, the men of Company E captured the bridge before the German demolition crew could destroy it. Moyenvic was in American hands by 0645, and troops were crossing the Seille River. [58]

The next target was Hill 310. "The forward slopes extended for some fifteen hundred yards, mostly open but dotted here and there with lone trees and small clumps of woods. Company E moved up the slope to assault, but about five hundred yards from the top of the hill was stopped by murderous fire delivered from the German entrenchments on the crest and field guns firing from the village of

Marsal. This fusillade cost E Company its commander and several men. Company F, following on the left, lost all of its officers. The two companies crowded together, seeking shelter where they could, and tactical organization was lost... About 1100 G Company was committed, but its commander was hit while crossing the Moyenvic bridge and the company remained on the slope below E and F. An hour later two companies of the 3d Battalion arrived on the slope in accordance with the time table earlier arranged for an attack by column of battalions, but the assault could not be started forward again. Here the infantry huddled through the afternoon, the clumps of trees where they sought cover continually swept by cross fire and by German guns on the crest. As dusk came on the enemy guns blasted the slope with a 20-minute concentration, causing heavy casualties and further disorganizing the American assault force." After undergoing a day of miserable, muddy weather conditions, a rain of shrapnel from mortars and artillery shells, sniper fire, and machine gun bullets, the Americans' initial attack on Hill 310 was a failure. [59]

On the 101st Infantry's right, the 328th Infantry was advancing on Bezange-la-Petite and receiving the German backlash with the corresponding casualties. Amidst the carnage was Cpl. Alfred L. Wilson of the Medical Detachment. "He volunteered to assist as an aid man [in] a company other than his own, which was suffering casualties from constant artillery fire. He administered to the wounded and returned to his own company when a shell burst injured a number of his men. While treating his comrades he was seriously wounded, but refused to be evacuated by litter bearers sent to relieve him. In spite of great pain and loss of blood, he continued to administer first aid until he was too weak to stand. Crawling from one patient to another, he continued his work until excessive loss of blood prevented him from moving. He then verbally directed unskilled enlisted men in continuing the first aid for the wounded. Still refusing assistance for himself, he remained to instruct others in dressing the wounds of his comrades until he was unable to speak above a whisper and finally lapsed into unconsciousness. The effects of his injury later caused his death. By steadfastly remaining at the scene without regard for his own safety, Cpl. Wilson through distinguished devotion to duty and personal sacrifice helped to save the lives of at least ten wounded men." Alfred Wilson, a native of Fairchance, Pennsylvania, would be awarded the Medal of Honor. [60]

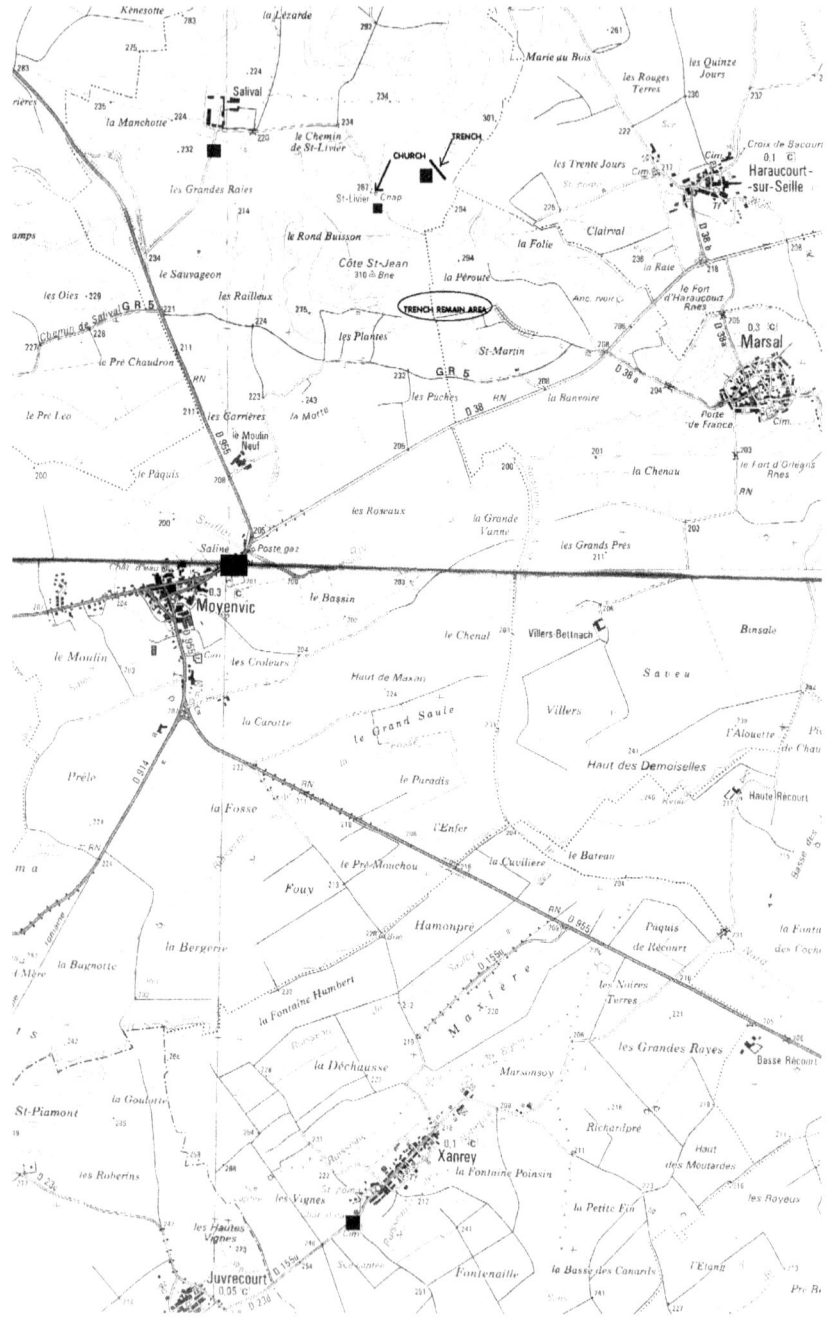

During the night, German artillery plastered the slopes of Hill 310 where the Americans were dug in. The casualty list increased. Meanwhile, at 2:30 A.M. the plan to take Hill 310 was revised. Company G was to move out of Moyenvic and to rejoin 2nd Battalion which was pinned down on the slopes. One company from 1st Battalion was to move to the right of the hill, while another was to move to the left of 2nd Battalion. 3rd Battalion was ordered to attack to the left of the hill abreast of 1st Battalion. With the muddy terrain little support could be expected from the tanks; and with severely limited visibility, the artillery would also be of little help to the G.I.'s. [61]

The gray, gloomy dawn of November 9th greeted the sleep-deprived soldiers with intense anxiety, more physical discomfort, and the smells of cordite, damp farm land, and death. The weather had suddenly turned colder and there was a rain and snow mix. Some of the men, who had shed even their field jackets the previous day, shivered from the exposure. "We lived like animals in our own holes in the ground in the mud, cold, wet, and rain under artillery barrages and sniper fire. Men were killed every day. Then came the Third Army offensive of November 8. It was Hell all over again, but there was no lull. We were still covered with mud and we were wet, cold, hungry, and miserable. After attacking one day, we had to get out of our holes and do it all over again the next morning against an enemy that contested every few yards of ground." [62]

Climbing out onto the contested ground near Moyenvic was Thomas J. Haugh with the 101st Infantry. "...a friendly rifle company and its supporting machine gun platoon of Company D, 101st Infantry, were subjected to a heavy barrage of enemy artillery and mortar fire. Although exposed to the hostile fire, ... the Technician Fifth Grade and an aid man attached to Company D, courageously proceeded through the impact area and gave effective first-aid treatment to the wounded of his own platoon and, in addition, rendered medical aid to the casualties of the supported rifle company. For six consecutive hours under the continuous hostile shellfire, he moved among the wounded, organized litter bearer groups and directed the speedy evacuation of the casualties to an aid station. His unusual courage under fire, strong initiative and commendable solicitude for the wounded reflect the highest credit upon Technician Fourth Grade Haugh and the armed forces of the United States." The

Andover, Massachusetts native would later receive the Silver Star citation for his "gallantry in action in the vicinity of Moyenvic, France on Nov. 9, 1944." He would also receive the Bronze Star and three Purple Hearts, although he accepted only one of the latter awards.[63]

At the end of this long horrific day, 1st Battalion was unable to advance, therefore 2nd Battalion was still pinned down on the slopes. 3rd Battalion was successful in taking Salival and continued to the northeast.[64]

In the murky weather of November 10, the 3rd Battalion was trying to blast the Germans out of the woods northeast of Salival. The 2nd battalion was still pinned down. At 1610 C Company was ordered to assault the right flank of the hill, and it succeeded in taking the ridge. The enemy counter-attacked, but C Company still held. Then the Germans tried to shell the Americans off the ridge; but in spite of heavy casualties, the company held its ground.

The bitter irony of Armistice Day - November 11 - saw the enemy finally driven off Hill 310. The 101st Infantry's fight for Hill 310 had cost the regiment 478 officers and men killed or wounded. One of the casualties removed from the hill was Barney Wise, who had been severely wounded the previous day. Suffering from severe abdominal wounds and a fractured pelvis, Barney died from his horrible wounds on Armistice Day.[65]

Mary O. Wise, Barney's mother, would receive his last worldly possessions. The good Catholic man had his rosary beads, a prayer book, and a religious medal when he died. In addition, Barney carried a steel mirror, a fountain pen, a mechanical pencil, two keys, a rifle medal, and a pen knife. His watch was missing the band and crystal. His two gold-colored rings were also damaged - the stone was missing in one ring and the other was broken and badly bent.[66]

The announcement of Barney's death appeared in the hometown newspaper. A service photograph showed a smiling citizen soldier. The article read:

"Pfc. Henry B. "Barney" Wise, was reported dead on Armistice day in France, according to word received by his parents, Mr. and Mrs. Henry A. Wise of Randolph.

Two telegrams were received by the parents late Friday afternoon. The first announced that the infantryman had been seriously wounded in action on Nov. 10, while the second one reported that he had died on Nov. 11 after being hospitalized for one day.

First member of the St. Joseph's parish to give his life in service for his country, memorial mass will be said for private First Class Wise at 8:30 o'clock Wednesday morning. Rev. F. J. Bertram, pastor of St. Joseph's church, will conduct the mass.

First mail in more than a month was received by the family last week. A letter received by his brother, Sylvan, on Friday was written Oct. 24, which said, "No one should ever have to work again after going through what we are here. We are dodging shells and bombs practically all of the time."

Born in Randolph, the infantryman had lived there all his life. He was a graduate of St. Joseph's [parochial] school and of Randolph high school in 1936. Assisting his father on the farm, Private First Class Wise worked for the Ravenna Oil company as a truck driver for about two years before entering the army 26 months ago. He had been overseas just about two months after receiving infantry training in Georgia, Tennessee, and South Carolina.

In addition to his parents, he is survived by three brothers, Stanley and Sylvan of Randolph, and Victor of Ravenna; three sisters, Mrs. Clarence Kemmery of Suffield, Mrs. Hubert Knapp of Ravenna, and Madelyn at home; and his fiancee Miss Marjorie May of Kent. [67]

Barney Wise's body was temporarily interred at the U.S. Military Cemetery at Limey, France, 18 miles northwest of Nancy. After his parents complied with all of the standard military forms, the Quartermaster General wrote them on April 5, 1949 that the remains had been permanently interred at the U.S. Military Cemetery at St. Avold.[68]

PART IV
EPILOG

Over the years, Barney's aged parents surely missed their boy, and his siblings lamented the loss of a loving and loved brother. Twenty years after Barney's death, his brother Stanley requested the government to put a flat granite marker in St. Joseph's Cemetery in memory of his brother. In what probably created some resentment, the Chief Memorial Division wrote that Barney was permanently interred at St. Avold; and he curtly concluded, "In view thereof, a memorial marker may not be furnished." [69]

In 1946, Barney's fiancee decided to get on with her life. She married a local fellow, probably someone that Barney knew and of whom he would have approved.

Sixty-three years after the tragedy on Hill 310, few of Barney's contemporaries and close relatives remain. Of those, memories have faded in some cases. They deeply appreciate the sacrifices of the WWII dead; but they just cannot remember much about the nice fellow who lived on the farm down the road.

However, the old crowd remembers Vernie Neal, who was an all-county football player, a Marine veteran, and a "real character." Furthermore, Vernie's untimely and unusual demise ensured his remembrance. After all of his dangerous adventures, Neal's fate was left to a fishing trip in early September 1946. Three newspaper articles covered the story.

"A fishing trip today had cost the life of Master Sergeant Vernon H. Neal, former Randolph high school football star, who had been in the United States Marines for 10 years.

Sergeant Neal, 28, died in a naval hospital near Memphis, Tenn., Monday night, from gangrene, which set in after a fish hook had lodged in one of his legs. He was 80 miles from a doctor when the accident occurred and the infection developed before he could be moved to a hospital.

The former Randolph athlete, accompanied by his wife, Sue, and son [Vernie's step-son] Jimmy, had visited at the home of his parents, Mr. and Mrs. Roy S. Neal, in Randolph, only two weeks ago. They went on the fishing trip with friends in Tennessee while on their way back to the sergeant's base at Santa Ana, Calif.

The wife was at Sergeant Neal's bedside when he died. The body will be shipped to Randolph for burial…

Sergeant Neal left an outstanding war record. He was at Pearl Harbor when the Japanese staged their sneak attack. He was one of the first marines to land on Guadalcanal and took part in the bitter fighting which led to America's capture of the strategic island. He also was on Midway Island during the war.

The sergeant only recently had reenlisted for a three-year period…" [70]

In the early summer of 2004 the old brick high school was demolished, a somewhat thoughtless act that greatly disturbed the "old school" alumni. Gone was the place of many pleasant childhood memories, cherished acquaintances, and what now seem to be trivial anxieties. Also gone are most of the Class of '36 - only two remain at this time. The greatest generation is quickly succumbing to Father Time.

Author's note: The other day my 10 year old granddaughter, Izabella, noticed my pecking on the keyboard and curiously asked, "What are you writing about Papa?" I told her that I was writing about a soldier who was killed in World War II. She then asked how old he was when he died. I told her that Barney Wise was 27 years old. Then with a perception beyond her 10 years, she solemnly remarked, "Gee, he sure missed out on a lot."

CHAPTER NOTES
HENRY BERNARD WISE, CLASS of '36

1. Pierre A. Rinfret, "Infantry Training In WWII, as I experienced it.", www.parida.com/training, p 1.
2. *Ibid.*, p 2-3.
3. 70th Infantry Association, Infantry Structure, at trailblazersww2.org/history...
4. *Speedometer*, Portage County Schools yearbook. p 54.
5. Joseph E. Persico, *Eleventh Month, Eleventh Day, Eleventh Hour.* (New York: Random House, 2004), p 385; Francis A. March, *History of the World War.* (Chicago: The United Publishers of the United States and Canada, 1919), *p 32.*
6. *Akron Beacon Journal*, "Slay Mexicans For Murder Of Akron Rancher," January 24, 1916, p 1.
7. *Ibid.*, p 2.
8. *Ravenna Republican,* "Randolph," January 27, 1916.
9. John and Alice Durant, *Pictorial History of American Presidents.* (New York: A. S. Barnes and Company, 1955), p 238-241.
10. *Ravenna Republican,* "Liquor Arrests Bring Big Fines For Two Parties," January 23, 1922, p 1.
11. *Akron Beacon Journal,* January 23, 1922, entertainment section.
12. *Akron beacon Journal,* "Profound Grief Grips Eighteen Million Catholic Subjects in United States When Death Calls Pontiff to Final Rest" and "Pope Sought To Stop Warfare Spreading To Other Nations," January 23, 1922, p 12.
13. Durant, *American Presidents,* p 241.
14. *Evening Record,* "Hoover Goes In Seclusion," January 23, 1929.
15. *Evening Record,* "Four measures Await Action" and "Says Boys Enjoy Going to School," January 23, 1929, p 1.
16. *The Evening Record and Daily Courier-Tribune,* "Ravenna, Randolph, Aurora Win Opening County High Battles," September 21, 1935.
17. *Evening Record Courier -Tribune,* "Randolph Tigers After Revenge Saturday," September 24, 1935.
18. *Evening Record Courier-Tribune*, "Suffield Whips Randolph, 19-0." (The actual score was 13-0.) September 30, 1935.

19. *Evening Record Courier Tribune*, October 5, 1935.
20. *Evening Record Courier-Tribune*, "Randolph Tops Aurora In Year's Biggest Upset, 6-0," October 12, 1935.
21. *Evening Record Courier-Tribune*, October 19, 1935.
22. *Evening Record Courier-Tribune*, October 25, 1935.
23. *Evening Record Courier-Tribune*, November 2, 1935.
24. *Evening record Courier -Tribune*, "Randolph Pins 20-0 Loss On Hilltop Outfit," November 9, 1935.
25. *Evening Record Courier-Tribune*, November 16, 1935.
25. *Evening Record Courier-Tribune*, "Roudebush Leads Powerful Red Devils In Slaughter Of G-men," November 23, 1935.
26. *Evening Record Courier-Tribune*, "Quell Strikers After 24 Hours Of Rioting," November 21, 1935, p 1.
27. *Evening Record Courier-Tribune*, "Football Claims 46 Men, Boys In '35; Equals Peak," December 3, 1935.
28. *The Speedometer*, Portage County 1936 yearbook.
29. *Evening Record Courier-Tribune*, December 7, 1935.
30. *Evening Record Courier-Tribune*, "Mantua Village Tops Center...", December 14, 1935.
31. *Evening Record Courier-Tribune*, "Coach Moyer's Randolph Tigers Make habit Of Upsetting Unwary Opponents," December 16, 1935.
32. *Evening Record Courier-Tribune*, "Suffield Snuffs Randolph Hopes..." December 21, 1935.
33. *Evening Record Courier-Tribune*, January 23, 1936, p 1.
34. *Evening Record Courier-Tribune*, "New Sidewalks At Randolph Are Completed," January 24, 1936.
35. *Evening Record Courier-Tribune*, "Rev. Bertram To Deliver Address At Randolph P-T." February 20, 1936.
36. *Evening Record Courier-Tribune*, "Oh, Susan!" It's Comedy At Randolph" February 17, 1936.
37. *Evening Record Courier-Tribune*, February 20, 1936.
38. *Evening Record Courier-Tribune*, February 24, 1936.
39. *Evening Record-Courier Tribune*, February 27, 1936.
40. *Evening Record Courier-Tribune*, "Tigers Hang Up 32-22 Surprise Win; Freedom Is 24-12 Victim," February 28, 1936.
41. *Evening Record Courier-Tribune*, "Randolph, Darkhorse Team, Slated To Play, 'David Role' " February 29, 1936.
42. *Evening Record Courier-Tribune*, "Randolph Tops Suffield;

Wins 1st Cage Title," March 2, 1936.
43. *Evening Record Courier-Tribune,* "Suffield, Randolph Land Three Places Each On Tourney Team," March 3, 1936.
44. *Evening Record Courier-Tribune,* March 6, 1936.
45. *Evening Record Courier-Tribune,* "Canton Bulldogs Outspeed Ravens In 31-18 Rout; Randolph Loses To Canton Twp., 23-11" March 7, 1936.
46. *Evening Record Courier-Tribune,* "Observe Class Night Tuesday" May 14, 1936, p 2; "Carl Lang Is Valedictorian At Graduation," May 23, 1936, p 4.
47. Personal information for Scott Brockett was derived from an interview with Mary Jane Brockett, Scott's wife, in interviews dating from 2006-2007. Personal information for Vernon Neal was derived from interviews with his nephews, Fred Neal and David Neal in 2007.
48. *Evening Record,* "Leathernecks' Blasting Japs On Guadalcanal, Marine Says," December 11, 1941, p 1.
49. The newspaper article taken from Nellie Stanford's scrapbook is undated. Paul Knapp was interviewed in April 2007. The 98 year old veteran could not remember the details of his or his brother's service, but he proudly stated that there was " nothing that my brother couldn't do ... he was one swell guy and a good brother of ours."
50. Nellie Stanford's scrapbook. The dates of the articles were omitted. Whenever Paul Nau was home on furlough, someone reported it to the newspaper.
51. Marie Bettes Kropp. Marie's father, William Bettes, Sr., assisted the Portage County draft board. He kept a record of Portage County inductees and particularly information on the Randolph soldiers.
52. "26th Infantry Division," Division History, yd-info.net, p 4.
53. Pierre A. Winfret, Yankee Division Web Site, Winfret.com, p 3.
54. James Haare, BOOKS1924@cs.com. E-mail to the author on August 2, 2005.
55. Hugh M. Cole, "United States Army in World War II European Theater of Operations, The Lorraine Campaign," (Center of Military History United States Army, 1997), "The XII Corps Resumes the Offensive," iblio.org/hyperwar/Usa... p 8.
56. *Ibid.,* p 6.
57. "26th Infantry Division, 101st Regiment," yd-info.net, p 4.
58. Cole, "The XII Corps Resumes the Offensive,"

59. *Ibid.*
60. "Medal of Honor: Alfred Wilson," history.amedd.army.mil...
61. James Haahr, *The Command is Forward,* Commandant's War Diary, p 74.
62. Haahr, From the Forward by Anthony Kemp. Jameshaahr.com.
63. Judy Wakefield, "At Long Last," Oct. 18, 2001, andovertownsman.com/news...
64. Haahr, p 74.
65. Cole, "The XII Corps Resumes the Offensive," p 12-13. Also the U.S. Army Human Resources Command, "Individual Deceased Personal File" for Henry B. Wise.
66. "Individual Deceased Personal File" for Henry B. Wise.
67. *Evening Record*, "Randolph Soldier, 27, Dies Of Wounds In France Nov. 11," Nov. 27, 1944, p 1, 6.
68. "Individual Deceased Personal File" for Henry B. Wise.
69. Ibid.
70. The newspaper articles are from Nellie Stanford's collection. One article is from the *Evening Record*. "Military Rites Set Saturday For Sgt. Neal, 28, Randolph," the September 12, 1946 edition. Two other articles were undated and could not be found on microfilm: "Fishing Injury Claims Life Of Ex-Randolph Grid Star," and "Fish Hook Wound Kills Marine Vet." Contrary to the newspaper reports, Fred Neal, Vernon's nephew, heard that Vernon died from a household accident. While visiting an old marine buddy, Vernon and Sue had to sleep on a metal-framed folding cot. During the night, Vernon got up to get his wife a glass of water and stepped on the hook that held the metal frame together when folded. He cut his foot, and the infection set in.

CHAPTER FOUR
P.F.C. WILLIAM H. BETTES

Part I
"Somebody's darling, Somebody's pride..."

So begins the chorus of a southern Civil War song which would later be heard in the 1939 movie classic, "Gone With the Wind." [1]

The Randolph, Ohio local news for March 19, 1919 proudly proclaimed the birth of "Somebody's darling, Somebody's pride," William H. Bettes. "A baby boy arrived Thursday of last week [March 13, 1919] at the home of Mr. and Mrs. Edgar Bettes." [2]

On Billy's date of birth and ensuing days, other darlings and prides were arriving home from the Great War - The War to make the World Safe for Democracy - The War to End All Wars - WWI. More than 8,000 Yanks were to arrive in New York City on that date. [3]

The *Ravenna Republican* announced that the Portage County men in Co. C, 136th Machine Gun Battalion left France on March 12th. Originally, the local boys volunteered for Co. M of the 10th Regiment Ohio National Guards. With all the feverish patriotic meetings and speeches reminiscent of the Civil War's onset, Co. M was quickly filled by eager young men. Now, the Soldier's Homecoming Celebration Committee was hoping that Co. C could stop in Ravenna, the county seat, to make a parade or other demonstration. [4]

Pvt. C. H. Marrott, a Cuyahoga Falls resident, was one of the lucky ones to arrive back home in January. After being hounded by reporters, "He reluctantly and briefly stated that he participated in the second battle of the Marne, at Cantigny where he was gassed and slightly wounded by shrapnel, and also put out of the fighting for a time by shell shock, and he participated in the skirmishes on the Somme.

Asked if he had shot or killed any Germans, he smiled. 'If one wants to brag he can say he did,' replied Private Marrott. 'Undoubtedly some of the shots I fired hit Huns, but I have no proof that the fellows who fell were killed by my shots or by the shots of others. It is enough to know that they were killed.' He also admitted taking part in raids into enemy trenches and dug-outs and bringing back prisoners and of assisting in cleaning out machine gun nests, but not once did he claim any personal glory, always giving credit to 'the boys' or to 'we.' Asked for the greatest impressions he obtained from his trip to France, he said: 'The thing that impressed me the most was the fact that the French people are so far behind the Americans in everything." [5] [In 25 years, Billy Bettes was also destined to go to France and to experience some of Pvt. Marrott's travails - and then some more.]

The blood of an earlier American warrior flowed through the veins of the infant Bettes boy. His great-great-great grandfather, Nathaniel Bettes, was one of the Minutemen who answered the rebel cause after Lexington and then participated in the siege of Boston. Nathaniel's extensive service took him to Quebec, Canada, where Gen. Benedict Arnold attempted to take the fortress. He was at Saratoga when Gen. Burgoyne surrendered to the colonial army. Bettes also endured the harsh winter at Valley Forge and participated in the Battle of Monmouth in 1778. Having enlisted as a private, in 1779 Nathaniel achieved the rank of Captain in the Massachusetts Militia and the Continental Army.

Thirty years after his discharge from the army on April 15, 1780, Capt. Nathaniel Bettes decided to take advantage of the Massachusetts land grants given to Revolutionary War veterans. Twenty household members - three children by his first wife, ten by his second wife, and other relatives - in their oxen-drawn covered wagons bravely headed to the Ohio country. The arduous trek over mountains, through dense forests, and across rivers took six weeks. At last, they settled at what became known as Bettes Corners in Tallmadge Township. The rugged Revolutionary soldier resided in the area until his death in 1840 at the age of 93. [6]

Many stories could also be told about Billy's great-great uncle, William Henry West Bettes, who served as a recruiter and Lieutenant in the 6th Ohio Cavalry during the Civil War. Toward the end of the war, Bettes was a captain in the 184th Ohio Volunteer Infantry. Prior to the Civil War, Bettes moved to Randolph, and in 1857 he married Lodema Brockett. As a young man, Bettes was a teacher, and consequently his Civil War letters to the Ravenna *Democrat* were quite informative, as if the readers were his students. His discourses ranged from the mundane affairs of camp life to the actual pursuit of the enemy. Bettes loved his community and neighbors as long as they were not pro-slavery sympathizers or "Copperheads." Following the war, he served as a Justice of the Peace for Randolph Township. For over fifty years he contributed Randolph news to the local newspapers in his educational and sometimes witty style. [7]

Billy's grandfather and great grandfather were doctors in Randolph. As for Billy's dad, Edgar, life centered around his Randolph farm with his wife Alice (Jobes), oldest daughter Betsey (Born April 14, 1917), Billy, and youngest daughter Marie (Born September 13, 1924). Edgar took his profession seriously, and he served as chairman of the Portage County Farm Bureau and chairman on the board of the Federal Land Bank. [8]

For a six year old lad such as Billy Bettes, the mid-1920's offered a host of heroes. In sports, Tris Speaker batted .389 for the 1925 Cleveland Indians, but his valiant effort could not keep the Tribe from falling 27 ½ games behind the Washington Senators. The New York Yankees even fared worse and were a game behind the Indians in the final standings. However, the salad days of Ruth, Gehrig, and the Bronx Bombers were just around the corner.

In 1925, Red Grange, the All-American runner from the University of Illinois, went on a barnstorming tour with George Halas' Chicago Bears. The "Galloping Ghost" was credited with making professional football a respectable entity. On October 5, Grange appeared on the cover of *Time*.

In the boxing world, Jack Dempsey, the "Manassas Mauler," was the adored and popular heavyweight champ until he battled the ex-Marine and World War I veteran, Gene Tunney. The gutsy and skilled challenger out-boxed the aging slugger in both of their two bouts. The rematch generated an unheard of 2 million dollar gate.

Bobby Jones had conquered his famous temper and was now dominating the golf world.

The Big Ten track and field championships usually went to the University of Michigan.

The fledgling professional American Basketball League was dominated by teams such as the Cleveland Rosenblooms, New York Celtics, Boston Whirlwinds, and Philadelphia Sphas.

The demise of one sports hero saddened the 1925 sports world. Christy Mathewson, the New York Giants pitcher who had 373 wins in his career, passed away at the age of 45. Mathewson enlisted for World War I even though he was 37. Commissioned a captain, he was gassed during a training exercise in France. The damage to his lungs plus the contraction of tuberculosis was one battle that Christy could not win. [9]

Locally, young Bettes could rub elbows with old and young military heroes and be regaled by their deeds. On Memorial Day 1925 there were still 19 men left from the once 3000 strong G.A.R. post in Ravenna. The oldest man was over 93. On the same day, the National Commander of the American Legion spoke to the American youth:

"To you from failing hand we throw
the torch, be yours to hold it high!" [10]

In December, Randolph's own G.A.R. post, Vactor B. Stanford # 647, "served their annual oyster dinner the day being perfect. A goodly number being present to enjoy the bountiful repast. The afternoon was spent in visiting and reminiscence. Guests were present from Akron, Canton, and Atwater. A most delightful time was spent by all." [11]

In other news, the local newspaper was running a serial of Edna Ferber's *So Big*, a recent big seller. In July the Scopes "Monkey Trial" in Tennessee made front page headlines everywhere. In March the League of Nations continued to flounder as the British and all of her dominions rejected the disarmament protocol. Columbia records advertised such records as "Whoopee," "Sittin' on Top of the World," and "Ain't You Comin' Out Tonight." [12]

With the stock market crash and the onset of the Great Depression, America's tune changed and a different attitude prevailed. Now there were songs like "Brother, Can You Spare a Dime?"

When Franklin Roosevelt defeated Herbert Hoover by a landslide in the 1932 election, the headlines blared "Roosevelt Sweeps Country." The Democrats took all of the major posts. However, there were no expressions of "Now we are saved." The American majority simply felt that Hoover and the Republicans had not done the job and blamed them for the fix that they were in. As for the new fellow and his party, they would wait and see - and hope. [13]

Marie Kropp Bettes (Bill's younger sister): "Our folks had a dairy and the people across the street, the Honeywells, had a big apple and peaches orchard. He raised a lot of potatoes and melons, and they had a woods where they made maple syrup. My mom and dad would help cut the potatoes [for planting], and my dad would help for a dollar a day. Mom would used to go pick strawberries for a farmer, and we all worked. We managed to keep our heads above water. We canned over 500 jars. One thing about living on a farm, we had our chickens for our meat and eggs, your milk and stuff; we canned over a hundred jars of peaches. We canned anything you could get your hands on. We didn't have a freezer, so a lots of times we had these crocks; we would fry the pork chops and pour the grease over them [and they would keep like in a freezer]. We didn't butcher till cold weather... We used to have to shock wheat and oats.

[The Bettes' did all of their farm work with work horses in the 1930's. When they eventually bought a tractor, her father said, "That thing won't stop when you say whoa to it."]

She [Marie's mom] sent cream to the creamery. When I first milked the cows by hand, I thought my arms would kill me. And we had a thousand 3-day old chicks and 250-300 layers.

Of course, we had the fair... They used to have a football game on Saturday afternoons. That was the highlight of the fair.

When we went to school, everybody was in the same position. No one had more money than this one. We were all farmers." [14]

Bill's senior year of high school began on September 8, 1936, when a record 403 students entered the "Haven of Education." Twenty-seven of them were to graduate in the spring of 1937.

The chronicler for the yearbook wrote: "A sea of innocent, guileless faces greeted us from the freshmen's homeroom. They smiled shyly on upper classmen hoping no one would taunt them with that epithet that wilts even the most enthusiastic of freshmen,

"Greenie." The sophomores strutted in their new found dignity and the juniors resented the seniors' freezing stares and otherwise superior attitude which met their friendly advancements." Even with this perceived caste system, there was hardly any "trouble in River City."

Edgar B. Groom, the new principal, welcomed six new teachers to his staff. The entire staff and student body would experience Mr. Groom's innovative and progressive ideas. "A number of additions and improvements have been made since school opened. Two new subjects, public speaking and debating, have been added to our educational curriculum. Dramatics have played an important part in school entertainments and assembly programs have been comprised of student talent... The senior class chose a blood-curdling mystery, "The Whispering Room." [This was presented on March 4. The senior high operetta, "Ask the Professor," followed on March 20.]... The honor roll system has been introduced, creating an atmosphere of friendly scholastic rivalry. A Booster Club and Athletic Association have done much to enliven school spirit and clear our athletic association from debt. An enthusiastic response has greeted "Pep" meetings under direction of the Athletic Association. New basketball equipment has been purchased from the funds; a dramatic production paid for the refinishing of the gymnasium floor. A radio was purchased so that students may enjoy music with their dinner. This feature is as good as you can get at the Waldorf Astoria Hotel."

The football team was considered to be quite successful. "Our coach has enforced strict training rules and the results have been sufficient evidence of its worth." Among the team was Bill Bettes who sported #1 on his jersey. At a time when the lineups were printed in each newspaper game account, Bill's name never appeared. Thus he apparently loved the game and being part of the team. Said his sister Marie, "He wasn't an outstanding player, he was average. He had a bunch of friends to play football and baseball in the front yard, and they liked to play cards. [As for girls' sports], it was a no-no to play basketball in school; so I took home ec to spend some time, because that would take up two periods a day." [15]

The well-behaved Bill must have had some music appreciation because he also participated in the mixed chorus.

A month and a half before graduation, Bill turned eighteen.

On his birthday there was "earth-shaking" news in Portage County. The newspaper editor weighed in on the recent earthquake in the area. "The recent jiggling of this part of Ohio by a slight tremor caused geologists to study the question of earthquakes in this region with renewed interest. [There had been recent severe quakes in Japan and the far east, so could that happen here?] Ohio's quake came at the end of a mild winter, which had brought floods of unprecedented volume. There was no connection between the causes of the quakes and the floods. The earth quivers are attributable to maladjustments of the earth's crust back in the ice age more than 25,000 years ago." [16]

A distant, seemingly innocuous situation also concerned the editor - the price of paper. Most likely, his average readers and especially the young could have cared less about the rising price of pulp. For that matter, neither did the rising costs of brass, copper, and zinc alloys really affect the average citizen. However, American business was dealing with the devil in Europe, and in two years this small rumbling of war would eventually have a huge impact on all of them. The editor stated that the price of pulp in America had risen two to three times in the past three months because of the large quantities being shipped to European nations at a higher profit. Thus, there was a pulp shortage in the United States. "... The pulp is being used for the purpose of making explosives, in preparation for an impending war, or for the purpose of rearmament on a scale never before witnessed in Europe, or any other section of the world...They are preparing for war, they need the pulp, and they are willing to pay the price for it." [17]

Even if a young man did notice such forebodings, there wasn't anything he could do about it. Besides he had to make his own way in these tough financial times. Betsey Bettes: "He went to Actual Business College. He worked at the swamps [muck farms] for a couple of summers. Then he worked at a little shop in Ravenna. He wanted to farm. He did no good at the business college; he didn't want to be inside." [18]

Bill missed the peace time drafts and the early calls after the attack on Pearl Harbor. The 24-year old Bettes worked on his father's farm. If he were drafted, he could probably avoid serving. He was an only son and he worked in a vital industry that depended upon him - farming. His father handled some of the hardship cases for the draft board - those which involved farming - and although he was not part of the draft board, he may have had some influence in the matter. Nevertheless, when Bill's draft notice arrived, he did not pursue a hardship status. He was inducted into the army on July 5, 1943. Prior to leaving home, Bill helped with the haying. The Bettes didn't bail their hay, it was pitch forked onto the farm wagon on which eighteen year old Marie was working. Marie remembered, "He came home on leave in November. Then he left for Ft. Meade. The next time we heard from him, he was over in England." [19]

Part II
NORMANDY

P.F.C. Bill Bettes' lot was cast with the 9th Division's 60th Infantry Regiment.. While Bettes was stateside, the 60th had landed in North Africa in November 1942 and experienced combat until late May 1943. Then came a month of rest and training before being shipped near Palermo, Sicily in early August for the final push against the German and Italian troops on the island. On the night of November 8, 1943 the combat experienced 9th Division headed for England and the D-Day build-up. [20]

In the past year's operations the 60th Infantry had been somewhat reduced in strength by combat deaths, wounds, accidents, dysentery, and other factors. Thus, Bill Bettes and other incoming G.I.'s were the early replacements. P.F.C. Donald Cross, a replacement rifleman of Co. F in Bill's battalion, remarked, "I felt lost amongst all strangers [and] felt like a misfit. After one established himself, things changed." Eventually, Cross thought the veterans were "happy to receive us to fill out our squad. In fact one Sargt. told us, 'I've gone through Africa all the way, but this doesn't make me bulletproof.' "After being part of another unit stateside, P.F.C. Guy Wetherell wasn't too pleased either when he joined the 60th Infantry in May 1944. Said Wetherell, "I certainly hate to see the boys all split up. That's the only thing the boys don't like." In another few months, replacements of these replacements would not be received as kindly because a combat veteran often refused to make friends with some inexperienced dogface who would soon be killed or maimed. [21]

The 9th Division settled into the Winchester area to reorganize, "rest," and train. One of the first priorities was to educate the Yanks to British customs, idioms, currency, and the proper behavior. After all, some of the British already held three things against the Americans: they were over-paid; they were over-sexed; and they were over here. Hopefully, the Yanks would be on their best behavior when they received their passes to see the sights in Winchester and London. The curious ones could see historic Winchester Cathedral, Buckingham Palace, Piccadilly Circus, the bombed out areas, the underground, equally curious girls, and much more. For Bill Bettes, this life was nothing like the rural quietude in old Portage County.

By April 2, 1944 all leaves and furloughs were canceled, and the training schedule was stepped up. The Division was put on a 6-hour alert status on May 27. The men now knew that the big day was close at hand. The anxiety heightened when they were moved to the marshaling areas on June 3. Activity and sounds of preparation appeared everywhere - thousands upon thousands of troops and sailors crowding the seaports, a huge armada of ships gathering along the coast, and the roar of aircraft overhead. [22]

Pvt. Wetherell of the 3rd Battalion arrived at the Southhampton docks on the evening of June 9. Three days ago the allies landed in Normandy and established a beachhead on Fortress Europe. Now the 9th Division and others were assigned to come ashore and expand that beachhead by cutting off the Germans in the Cotentin Peninsula and to take the harbor facilities in the port of Cherbourg. So, Wetherell and the rest of the 60th Infantry departed England and slipped into the darkness before midnight. [23]

Maj. Gen. Manton S. Eddy's 9th Division debarked on Utah beach on June 10. Originally, the division's intentions were to move inland and turn to the right toward the Douve River line in the Columby-Orglandes area. However, German resistance denied this area to the 9th, and the Americans had to improvise. On June 12 Gen. Collins, VII Corps commander, ordered the 82nd Airborne Division to advance across the Douve River line and the 9th Division to cross the Mederet River, a branch of the Douve. Meanwhile, Wetherell in the 3rd Battalion assembled in the St. Marie du Mont vicinity.[24]

While the 9th Division moved to its jump-off point on the 13th, the 101st Airborne was holding off a German counter-attack at

First Squad - Top Row - Sgt. Paul Alexander, PFC Henderson, PFC Paick, Pvt. Minnick, PFC Flynn. Bottom Row - Sgt. McGrath, PFC Raick, PFC Bettes, PFC Hannah. [as written on the photo back]

Carantan.

The 60th Infantry launched its June 14 attack in columns of battalions with the 3rd Battalion in the lead. Their initial objective was to take Renouf, and then to swing to the high ground west of Orglandes. The men were under constant rifle, mortar, and artillery fire, so the movement was slow. Next to the professional German Army, the biggest problem was the excellent defensive ground that they occupied -- the hedgerows. "Each hedgerow became a separate objective, each enclosed field a battlefield, and the line of advance was often determined more by the configuration of the hedgerows than by the contour of the terrain. Observation was limited to a few hundred yards or less. Antitank guns had poor fields of fire. Control was difficult to maintain, and the maneuver of units hard to coordinate. Tanks could only move across country only if preceded by dozers punching holes in the banks; and because of the tightness of these defenses, attacking infantry often had to advance to the very hedgerow behind which the enemy had established his defense in order to get at him. The battle was thus often joined at ranges of a few yards, and grenades had to be used to rout the enemy." [25]

However, the two lead companies reached Renouf by mid-afternoon and finally occupied the town by 6 o'clock. The 2nd Battalion (Bettes' unit) moved up on the right; and advancing abreast with the 3rd Battalion, they reached the Valognes-Pont l'Abbe highway by dark. [26] All of this is easier said than done and omits the heroism and sacrifice of the individual American soldier.

Captain Matt Urban led Company F in the 2nd Battalion. "On 14 June, Captain Urban's company, attacking at Renouf, France, encountered heavy enemy small arms and tank fire. The enemy tanks were unmercifully raking his unit's positions and inflicting heavy casualties. Captain Urban, realizing that his company was in imminent danger of being decimated, armed himself with a bazooka. He worked his way with an ammo carrier through hedgerows, under a continuing barrage of fire, to a point near the tanks. He brazenly exposed himself to the enemy fire and, firing the bazooka, destroyed both tanks. Responding to Captain Urban's action, his company moved forward and routed the enemy. Later that same day, still in the attack near Orglandes, Captain Urban was wounded in the leg by direct fire from a 37mm tank-gun. He refused evacuation and continued to lead his company until they moved into defensive positions for the night." [27]

SSG Paul E. Alexander led his squad of Company G, which included Bill Bettes, into the murderous enemy fire on the 14th. "When his company had been held up over an hour by extremely heavy machine gun fire from an enemy strongpoint, Staff Sergeant Alexander led his squad forward to attack the enemy position. As he moved ahead of his men across the fire-swept terrain, Staff Sergeant Alexander was seriously wounded, but nevertheless continued to lead his squad and direct their attack. He personally threw hand grenades into four enemy machine gun positions completely silencing the guns and inflicting numerous casualties on the enemy. Staff Sergeant Alexander lost his life as a result of this action, but the extraordinary heroism and undaunted courage he displayed were an inspiring example to his men, in keeping with the highest traditions of the Armed Forces." Alexander received the Distinguished Service Cross and he was buried in the American Cemetery overlooking Omaha Beach. [28]

To compensate for their numerical inferiority, the Germans fought in small groups and took advantage of good defensive ground. The Americans intended to keep them from being reinforced and better organized by quickly pushing to the Douve River line. In this kill-or-be-killed maelstrom there would be no time for mourning Paul Alexander.

The 60th Infantry moved out at the first rays of light on 15 June. The G.I.'s immediately ran into a determined German resistance. "The 60th Infantry lost two anti-tank guns. By 0900 the regiment had advanced… beyond the Orglandes-Bonneville road, where the 1st Battalion on the right was strongly counter-attacked by four tanks and an estimated battalion of infantry. It was thrown back 500 yards to the road. The commanders of both Companies A and B were lost in this action and the battalion suffered other casualties. The 2nd Battalion [including Bill Bettes], immediately to the rear, countered the enemy thrust, however, and regained half the ground." [29]

Capt. Matt Urban also jumped off with the 2nd Battalion at 0500. "…still in the attack near Orglandes, Captain Urban, although badly wounded, directed his company in another attack. One hour later he was again wounded. Suffering from two wounds, one serious, he was evacuated to England." [30]

On 16 June the 2nd Battalion (60th Inf.) pushed off to take Ste. Colombe and to affect a bridgehead over the Douve River. The Douve in itself was not a formidable obstacle. It split into three small streams spanned by three bridges, one hardly more than a culvert that connected Ste. Colombe on the east bank with Nehou on the west. (The area south of Nehou was reportedly heavily mined.) The ground in the area was relatively firm. Other advantages for the offensive were that neither town occupied a commanding position, the river banks rose gradually, and the hedgerows made for poor observations. Nevertheless, it would be another grueling, murderous day.

"While the 1st Battalion took over the clearing of Reigneville, the 2nd Battalion, under Lt. Col. Michael B. Kauffman, swung cross country, south of Reigneville, and headed for the main crossroads in a column of companies. Company E led, followed by Company F, each with a platoon of heavy machine guns, which had to be hand-carried. Machine-gun fire from houses down the road was encountered at the crossroads, but a Company platoon crossed the road, worked its way up to the houses, killed several Germans, and took sixteen or seventeen prisoners. A wide arc was made to the north to avoid tanks which had been observed on the road, and Ste. Colombe was entered without opposition." [31]

There would be no rest. "Company E led the movement from Ste. Colombe, some men riding on tanks of Company B, 746th Tank Battalion. Without supporting fire, the 2nd Battalion pushed into the river bed and seized the first and second bridges intact. As the third bridge was out, the tanks turned back. When all three rifle companies were on the causeway, enemy shells began to land and some small-arms fire was received from Nehou. Despite the lack of tank support, Company E established itself on the west bank and held there in the face of artillery fire from enemy self-propelled guns somewhere in the vicinity of Nehou. The company's ammunition ran low and its situation became precarious. Parts of Company F and Company G started across, but finding themselves under enemy fire, some dug in between the bridges and others were pulled back to Ste. Colombe. Colonel Kauffman asked for relief, but he was told by General Collins to hold on, that the 3rd battalion would move to his aid. The ammunition shortage was eased when the battalion commander returned from Regiment with a loaded 2 ½ ton truck. Company G [with Bill Bettes] then managed to join Company E on the west bank.

But the attack on Nehou was postponed until the next day. The battalion was badly shaken; there still was no tank support; and darkness was approaching. That night the 3rd Battalion joined the exhausted 2nd battalion to strengthen the position on the west bank." [32]

The Douve River line finally had been attained but at a cost. Now, the 9th Division would try to cross the rest of the Cotentin Peninsula to the ocean and thereby force the Germans into evacuating the peninsula and Cherbourg or to be cut off and trapped.

June 17 would be a long, long day for the tired, sleep-deprived G.I.'s of the 60th Infantry. At 0600 they advanced from the bridgehead at Ste. Colombe. The Germans had evacuated Nehou, so the American columns moved down the road against small but deadly delaying enemy units. The 2nd Battalion (with Bill Bettes) pushed westward through St. Pierre-d'Artheglise to the high ground. "The progress had been so good all day that General Collins ordered the 9th Division to go as far as possible that night and to complete the sealing off of the peninsula. At 2210 General Eddy, passing the 60th Infantry [command post] group on the road, said, 'We're going all the way tonight.' "[33]

That night the actual cutting of the peninsula was achieved by the 82nd Airborne Division south of St. Sauveur-le Vicomte. The 47th Infantry (sister regiment to the 60th) cut the highway at Gde. Huanville. "Barneville-Sur-Mer, on the west coast of the Cotentin, was reached early on 18 June by the 3rd Battalion, 60th Infantry. This completed the blocking of the western corridor." [34]

The 60th Infantry's northern flank was stretched and exposed to a German counter-attack.. Into this brink was pushed the 1st battalion of the 39th Infantry, which was assigned earlier in the day as a reserve to the 60th. In the pre-dawn hours of June 18, heavy machine-pistol and machinegun fire shattered the darkness. "It seemed to cover the entire battalion front. Riflemen in Companies A and B began to return the enemy fire and were able to fight largely from their bivouac positions. Machine guns and mortars were quickly unloaded from vehicles and started to fire without observation. In the darkness, which made it difficult to find targets, a hot fire developed, the enemy advancing at times to within grenade-throwing distance. But the riflemen gave no ground, and 900 rounds were fired by the mortars, sometimes at ranges of 20 yards. Fighting at close quarters, one machine gunner found his fire masked by a herd of cows. A sergeant in Company A attempted to clear the cows from the line of fire by throwing stones and shell cases. Finally, he gave up. 'Mow em' down, Mike,' he told his gunner." [35]

With no artillery or anti-tank support, the companies disengaged the enemy and moved back to a stronger position.

Now, the American divisions turned toward the tip of the peninsula for the assault on Cherbourg. It would not be easy since Der Fuhrer had ordered his commander to defend the port city to the death.

From left to right across the Cotentin were the 9th Div., the fresh 79th Div., and the veteran 4th Div. The 4th Cavalry Squadron filled the gap between the 9th and 79th Divisions. At 0550 June 19, the 60th Infantry Regiment moved out on the extreme left flank of the battle line. The terrain became hillier with more pronounced ridges, deeper valleys, and frequent wooded areas.

That morning the weather began to worsen. A fierce storm - some said the worst in decades - began to whip up the English Channel. In the 25-32 knot winds, large tree branches were in motion, telegraph wires whistled, and occasionally there was difficulty walking against the wind. If there were a mademoiselle with an umbrella in the area, she might have it blown inside out.. Back at Omaha Beach - approximately 25 miles from the 60th Infantry - the landing facilities were taking a pounding. On June 21, the artificial "mulberry" harbors were destroyed. The wind moderated on the night of the 21st, but it wasn't until 23 June that the DUKW's were able to unload supplies. [36]

Nevertheless, the 60th Infantry easily advanced 10 miles on the 19th until around noon they were slowed by increasing artillery fire. On the following day, the 1st and 2nd Battalions were assigned objectives at Flottemanville. Again, initial progress was easy but the two battalions were stopped cold in front of Gourbesville. On the 21st, the 9th Division spent the day in reorganizing and the deadly business of patrolling.

From 4-6 miles from Cherbourg the German defenses commanded a collar of steep hills, and a belt of concrete and field fortifications girded the semicircular line. Although outnumbered, the German Army had ample supplies and ammunition, a good defensive position, the will to fight, and Hitler's order not to surrender. Thus on

22 June the Germans declined to answer the American offer of surrender.[37]

The weather finally cleared enough for air support, so at 1240 June 22 medium and fighter bombers zoomed overhead to soften the enemy for a ground attack. In short, the air attack was not a success, and mistakes were made. By 1300 the 60th, 47th, and 22nd Infantry Regiments were all calling headquarters to report that they were being strafed and bombed by their own planes. Cursing the air corps and the brass commanding this operation, the G.I.'s hunkered down. Finally, in the late afternoon all of the American divisions assaulted the fortified German line. It would prove to be a meat grinder for two days.[38]

In this methodical reduction of German strong points was 2nd Lt. John E. Butts, 60th Infantry, Company E (in Bill Bettes' 2nd Battalion). John Butts "Heroically led his platoon against the enemy in Normandy, France, on 14, 16, and 23 June 1944. Although painfully wounded on the 14th near Orglandes and again on the 16th while spearheading an attack to establish a bridgehead across the Douve River, he refused medical aid and remained with his platoon. A week later near Flottemanville Hague, he led an assault on a tactically important and stubbornly defended hill studded with tanks, pillboxes, and machinegun emplacements, and protected by concentrated artillery and mortar fire. As the attack was launched, 2nd Lt. Butts, at the head of his platoon, was critically wounded by German machinegun fire. Although weakened by his injuries, he rallied his men and directed 1 squad to make a flanking movement while he alone made a frontal assault to draw the hostile fire upon himself. Once more he was struck, but by grim determination and sheer courage continued to crawl ahead. When within ten yards of his objective, he was killed by direct fire." His platoon took the strong point and contributed to his battalion's success. 2nd Lt. John E. Butts received the Medal of Honor.[39]

The German line cracked on June 24; however, pockets of stiff resistance remained. The 9th Division attacked on June 29 with the 60th Infantry in the center and astride the main cape highway. After reaching the main road junction southeast of Beaumont-Hague, the regiment was checked. "There the enemy had taken a stand behind an antitank ditch defended by antitank guns and emplaced machine guns which in a singularly barren terrain had clear fields of fire. The 1st Battalion was stopped, but the 3rd Battalion with tank destroyer and tank support smashed through the north end of the line just south of Fleury. It came within about 1,000 yards of Beaumont-Hague but did not attempt to go farther as the Germans still held at the road junction. The road junction was overrun the next day (30 June) by the 2nd Battalion.) Just beyond it Capt. Stephen W. Sprindis led his Company E in a classic infantry charge over open ground with all three platoons advancing in a line of skirmishers firing as they charged. Despite the lack of artillery support the men kept going against enemy machine gun and mortar fire. At the same time Company F on the right advanced with tanks up the main road. Both attacks gathered momentum against an enemy whose zeal for fighting was easily dampened in these last days, and the two companies drove into Beaumont-Hague." [40]

The last harbor forts in Cherbourg surrendered on June 29; however, after German demolitions and the allied shelling and bombing, the port facilities were in shambles. It was not a clear-cut surrender where the enemy held up the white flag in unison and quit fighting. Pockets of resistance remained and the deadly mop-up continued.

On July 1, all organized German resistance on the Cotentin Peninsula ended when the 9th Division captured Cap de la Hague in the extreme northern sector. [41]

Part III
The Breakout

The allies needed mobility to defeat the German armies; and their commanding generals dreaded the prospects of being pinned down in the hedgerows and marshes in what would be similar to the trench warfare of WWI. Thus, even before Cherbourg fell to the Americans, the VII Corps' General Collins received his turn-around orders from Gen. Omar Bradley. Collins was to turn south and occupy part of the line in front of the Carantan marshes. Bradley gave him one day for rest, two to move, another for reconnaissance, and a fifth to issue attack orders. Said Bradley: It was a tall order for "Lightning Joe" Collins, a taller one yet for his troops. But I dared not give the enemy more time to dig in on that front." [42]

In the first week of July, the 9th Division was held at Les Pieux, where the men received hot food and showers. Letters were written home. (Back home, Bill Bettes' family was probably bringing in the new-mown hay.) It was a brief respite when the G.I. could reflect on what he had witnessed, how lucky he was to be alive, and about his friends who didn't make it. One private admitted to *Stars and Stripes*: "At first I was shy. I didn't know the ropes and I hated to make any noise. When I heard something, I hesitated and didn't do anything. But now I know the score. I'm out to kill every German I can get. The American soldier has to learn how to hate and he has to learn to kill right away. Don't ask any questions, shoot and keep shooting..." [43]

By July 5 the VII Corps was slowly advancing to the south toward Periers on the road leading from St. Lo to Lessay on the west coast of the Cotentin Peninsula. On July 6 German resistance became fierce as two fanatical SS divisions, the 2nd and 17th Armored, blocked the VII Corps front. By July 9, the rest of the 9th Division caught up with the VII Corps and moved into the sector east of the Taute River. On July 11, the Panzerlehr Division counter-attacked and broke the 9th Division line. A combined action of infantry, artillery, and air power drove the Germans back [44]

To make matters worse, if possible, the 60th Infantry was back in that damned hedgerow country. Said Sgt. Maj. Charles Wilsher of the 3rd Battalion: "Hedgerow country. Small fields with thick dirt embankments, trees and brush growing out of them. The Germans had dug deep trenches behind the hedgerows and covered them with timbers, so it was almost impossible for artillery to get at them. They had machine guns emplaced so they could fire through the hedgerows and had placed tanks, covering them with bushes. You had to practically dig them out...[They] would withdraw a few hedgerows, leaving a small force to fight. It was slow going but we kept driving them out. Their snipers would kill off a few of us and then want to surrender. We didn't take many prisoners." [45]

Around this time, 2nd Lt. Orville Stangl joined the 60th Infantry. He recalled: "The closer we got to BN the more casualties we were seeing, wrecked equipment, dead farm animals, dead German soldiers, and occasional American dead... the stench of war was everywhere, a smell hard to get used to at first, but in time was accepted as being normal on the front. It is a stench that can't be described, and one that will remain in my memory forever." [46]

From July 13-24, it was a war of attrition along the American front in a slow, casualty-ridden advance toward St. Lo. Meanwhile, General Bradley was devising a plan to break the deadly stalemate, namely, Operation Cobra which began on the 24th.

Bradley chose a corridor that lay between the villages of La Chapelle-Enjuger and Hebecrevon, a few kilometers north of the main road between St. Lo and Coutances. Following a saturated bombing attack, key units for the breakthrough were the VII Corps' 4th, 9th, and 30th Divisions. Then the 1st Division, 2nd and 3rd Armored Divisions were to pour through the opening. [47]

The initial air attack began on the 24th as bombers and fighter planes swept over the corridor dropping bombs that created huge craters and threw hot metal and flying debris in greater arcs. Bradley expected the air corps to attack parallel to the American lines; however, many of the bombers flew perpendicular over the G.I.s down below. Consequently, short drops struck friendly troops, killing or wounding 150 men. The attack was a disaster. This experience had to angrily remind the 60th Infantry of the botched bombing near Cherbourg nearly a month ago. [48]

A second attempt was made on the 25th. "For three hours, 1,500 B-17 and B-24 bombers pummeled the target, supported by medium bombers and fighter bombers attacking with napalm… 45-tonne [sic] Panther tanks were lifted off the ground by the force of the explosions and torn apart like children's toys. Infantrymen were buried alive in their shelters." That included more bomb "shorts" on the U. S. Infantry, which brought the two-day total to 558 casualties. In addition, the initial break-through would be a tough fight. [49]

Capt. Matt Urban, who had been wounded on June 15 near Orglandes and evacuated to England, learned about the desperate fighting in Normandy from another wounded man. Still wearing his bandages, Urban deserted the hospital and hitched his way back to his Company F, 60th Infantry Regiment. "Urban joined his demoralized company the morning of July 25th. As a sergeant remembered, "The sight of him limping up the road, all smiles, raring to lead the attack, once more brought the morale of the battle-weary men to the highest peak." Urban remembered the day well, "I was full of anger, remorse, and despair. I'd seen my men mutilated, chopped up. I was seeking revenge. I was like a tiger. It was all bubbling up inside of me, and it exploded." [50]

"Arriving at the 2nd Battalion Command Post at 1130 hours, 25 July, he [Urban] found that his unit had jumped-off at 1100 hours in the first attack of Operation Cobra. Still limping from his leg wound, Captain Urban made his way forward to take command of his company. He found his company held up by strong enemy opposition. Two supporting tanks had been destroyed and another, intact but with no tank commander or gunner, was not moving. He located a lieutenant in charge of the support tanks and directed a plan of attack to eliminate the enemy strong-point. The lieutenant and a sergeant were immediately killed by the heavy enemy fire when they tried to mount the tank. Captain Urban, though physically hampered by his leg wound and knowing quick action had to be taken, dashed through the scathing fire and mounted the tank. With enemy bullets ricocheting from the tank, Captain Urban ordered the tank forward and, completely exposed to the enemy fire, manned the machine gun and placed devastating fire on the enemy. His action, in the face of enemy fire, galvanized the battalion into action and they attacked and destroyed the enemy position. Captain Urban was wounded in the chest by shell fragments and, disregarding the recommendation of the Battalion Surgeon, again refused evacuation. On 6 August, Captain Urban became the commander of the 2nd Battalion." [51]

Fierce fighting, such as Capt. Urban's actions, occurred throughout the corridor on the 25th; but on the 26th Collin's VII Corps advanced 10 kilometers at the cost of 1,060 more casualties.

The German front finally cracked on the 28th. At 5 P.M. the American 4th Armored Division entered Coustances to the east of St. Lo, and Operation Cobra was a success. Now the American Army would resemble a giant swinging door, heading south and sweeping around to the east in an effort to entrap the German Army.

The VII Corps continued to press southward and by the 31st was moving toward Brecey. Meanwhile, on the VII's left, the XIX Corps was catching hell from a fierce German counter-attack. On August 1, both Corps continued the advance toward the Vire area northeast of Avranches, which was already under American control.

On August 3, the VII Corps took Mortain and reinforced that position on the 4th. Some units of the VII Corps headed toward Mayenne. On the 5th the VII Corps was moving to the southeast of

Mortain. The circle was tightening on the German Army. However, instead of retreating and regrouping, Der Fuhrer ordered his army to attack. So, in the early morning hours of August 7, the Germans struck between the VII and XIX Corps and managed to retake Mortain. The superior American air power greatly helped to stem the Nazi tide.[52]

Amidst the inferno, one of the deafening explosions hit near P.F.C. Bill Bettes, creating a concussion, cordite odor, and lethal flying debris. After all the narrow escapes from Utah Beach to Cherbourg and through the breakout, his luck ran out as slivers of hot shrapnel penetrated his body. Shouts of "Medic!" somehow penetrated the pandemonium. For him the war was over, and another battle was beginning.

Part IV
"Who'll Tell His Mother…"[53]

With painful shrapnel wounds to his head, chest, and abdomen, Bill Bettes was carried back to the nearest aid station. A Medic administered morphine to the alleviate the pain, and then he pinned the used syrette to Bill's collar to prevent overdosing of unconscious patients. Usually, the ½ grain injection from the toothpaste-shaped tube, combined with physical exhaustion, was sufficient to knock the patient out, with the casualty often waking up in the hospital.[54]

The badly wounded G.I. was evacuated to the 7th General Hospital, North Mimms, Herts, England. The bed-ridden, convalescent days dragged into September, October, November, and December.

Bill's sister Marie: "He was flown back to England. They tried to ship him home, but there was something with his liver. They gave him 73 transfusions. He kept hemorrhaging."

Bill's sister Betsey: Everything was censored, you know. He wrote and said that his head had healed up. Every so often, we received a letter from the War Department saying he was improving and satisfactory. [Then] we began getting letters saying that he wasn't improving satisfactory. Then in the next day or so, we would get a letter from Bill saying that he was not allowed to write anything in these letters."

Marie: "Things got so bad that he couldn't write, so the nurse, Lois Blakeley, a Red Cross nurse, wrote. He would tell her what he wanted to say and she would send the letters."

Bill's last letter was dated December 14, 1944. The next day, he died. An acute abscess of the liver was given as the official cause of death. At 1500 hours December 19, Billy Bettes was laid to rest in the Cambridge American Military Cemetery with a temporary wooden cross on his grave.[55]

A "man from Atwater" notified the family of Bill's death. Betsey: "There was sort of a mix-up. The Red Cross called. We hadn't heard from the War Department. The Red Cross notified the War Department, and then we did get a telegram." [The Battle of the Bulge was in progress at this time.]

Marie: It was a rough time... It was just the way things were at the time... It was so intense and everything."

Betsy: "It wasn't till January 2nd that they finally got it straightened around. The telegram might be in Bill's suitcase."[56]

It must have been a somber assignment for the Armed Services personnel to deal with the thousands upon thousands of grieving families like the Bettes family, but the task was respectfully handled. Yet, each correspondence was a painful reminder of the tragedy. In late June 1945 the Quartermaster Depot in Kansas City forwarded a $21.55 check to Bill's dad, "representing funds of your son, Private First Class William H. Bettes." Another letter was mailed on August 7 notifying the family that a carton of Bill's personal effects was being shipped. Bill's last worldly possessions were: A leather wallet with miscellaneous papers, a box of soap, a pack of personal letters, two French coins, a deck of cards, a blue cigarette lighter, scissors, an Expert Rifleman medal, eight 3-cent postage stamps, envelopes, a double edge razor, a Purple heart ribbon, and one piece of shrapnel. An asterisk noted that Bill's wallet, photos, and Rifle Medal were damaged by shrapnel.[57]

Then came the agonizing decision of whether to bring the decomposed body home or to let the remains lie in a military cemetery on foreign soil. Like the notification of Bill's death, the disposition of his remains was also a confusing matter. His father's deep anxiety can be seen in the letter he wrote to the Quartermaster General on April 19, 1947.

"We were very glad to receive your letter of April 4th and the information which you gave us.

We would like to know whether or not the Military Cemetery at Cambridge, England is going to be a National Cemetery or if the bodies will be moved from there to the National Cemetery. We would also like to have any literature or pictures of the Cemetery and how it is maintained etc. We have wanted to know these things for a long time, but didn't know who the right one was to get this information from.

This is a rather difficult decision to make, therefore we would appreciate as much information as possible before making a final decision." [58]

Marie Bettes Kropp: "After Bill died, Mom got a pen friend. Their names were Gotobed. They were old maids. We would send them money and they would go up to the cemetery and put flowers on [Bill's grave]. After they passed away, their niece laid them. Then they formed this organization where you send money over two months before - they call it Remembrance day - they don't call it Memorial Day. They sent us a program. We were lucky to have contact with people who would visit the grave and take flowers." [59]

After many tears and probably some sleepless nights, Bill's mother made the final decision to have her son's remains lie in the United States Military Cemetery at Cambridge, England. Her husband then wrote to the Chief Memorial Division.

"In reply to your letter of June 19, 1947 in regards to the burial of PFC William H. Bettes, it is our wish that the final burial of the deceased to be in US Military Cemetery, Cambridge, England.

We will appreciate any information that may be of interest to us regarding the Cemetery if you care to send to us.

We would also like to know if there any histories or records being printed about the Ninth Division of the First Army in which my son served. We would appreciate it if you would tell us if there is anything available and in what manner it can be obtained." [60]

On January 18, 1949 - five years and one month after Bill Bettes' death - the QM General notified Mr. Bettes that his son's remains were permanently interred and that the cemetery was under the supervision of the American Battle Monuments Commission. Still, there was some confusion, and in an exchange of telephone calls in late April 1950, Mr. Bettes and the QM Department cleared up the misunderstandings.

There never was a funeral or memorial service for Bill Bettes, but his army buddies never forgot him or his family. There was "just a little gathering at the Methodist church. Nice letters came from the chaplain and the commanding officer... Charlie Minnick [of Bill's squad] from Virginia came to visit. Sgt. McGrath, an officer from Connecticut - he and his wife came to visit. They always sent Christmas cards until he passed away. He called Mom on her 80th birthday. We were lucky to hear from those people."

It had been over sixty-one years since Bill's death; and sitting across the kitchen table from Betsey and Marie, the sorrow on their faces and in their voices remained as they told the story of their brother's life and death. Betsey said, "If he was living, he'd be 86 years old."

Marie summed it up: "If Bill would have come back, I think we would have owned the Viola Bettes' place... He had a lot of friends. He was popular. He was very well liked. And I'm not saying that because he was my brother... We never had any closure."

CHAPTER NOTES
P.F.C. WILLIAM H. BETTES

1. "Songs of the Civil War," Sony Music Entertainment, 1991. Track twelve of this CD is "Somebody's Darling." Marie Revenal de la Coste was moved to write a poem about the suffering and deaths that she witnessed in the hospital wards. She submitted her poem to a Savannah music publisher, who then forwarded it to John Hill Hewitt, a noted southern composer. Hewitt fashioned the music for the verse and created the chorus.
2. *The Ravenna Republican* (Ravenna, Ohio), "Randolph," March 24, 1919.
3. *Akron Beacon Journal* (Akron, Ohio), "8,000 Yanks Due To Arrive Today," March 13, 1919.
4. *Ravenna Republican*, "Company C On Way Home With Entire 37th Division," March 17, 1919, p 1. Company C's complete history is told in Edythe G. Dean's *Over the Top and Back* (New York: Vantage Press, 2005).
5. *Beacon Journal*, "Soldier Modest About War Record," March 13, 1919.
6. "Bettes Family History," given to the author by Marie Kropp Bettes in 2005.
7. Richard J. Staats *A Grassroots History of the American Civil War, Volume IV, The Life and Times of Colonel William Stedman of the 6th Ohio Cavalry* and *The History of the 6th Ohio Volunteer Cavalry 1861-1865* (Westminster, Md.: Heritage Books, Inc.). For additional information on William Henry West Bettes.
8. "Bettes Family History" and interviews with Marie Bettes Kropp.
9. For the sports heroes, see Wikipedia on-line.
10. *Ravenna Republican*, May 29, 1925, p 1.
11. *Ravenna Republican*, "Randolph," December 23, 1925.
12. *Ravenna Republican*, March 13, 1925.
13. *The Evening Record* (Ravenna, Ohio), November 9, 1932.
14. Interview with Betsey Bettes and Marie Bettes Kropp on July 5, 2005.
15. Ibid.
16. *The Evening Record and the Daily Courier-Tribune* (Ravenna-Kent, Ohio), March 13, 1937, p 2.
17. Ibid.

18. Interview of July 5, 2005.
19. Interview of July 5, 2005.
20. Lonesentry.com. "Hitler's Nemesis: The 9th Infantry Division - WWII G.I. Stories Booklet," p 5-10.
21. Militaryhistoryonline.com "G.I. Wetherell: The Story of a 'Go Devil' " p 3.
22. "Hitler's Nemesis," p 10-11.
23. Wetherell, "Story of a Go Devil," p 4.
24. Army.mil "Securing the Douve Line: Utah Beach to Cherbourg," p 10-11.
25. Ibid. p 10.
26. Ibid. p 12.
27. Oldreliable.org "9th Infantry Division Medal Of Honor Recipients," p 15.
28. Legionofvalor.com "Distinguished Service Cross Recipients," SSG Paul E. Alexander, p 1.
29. "Securing the Douve Line," p 13.
30. Oldreliable.org, Medal of Honor Recipients, p 15.
31. "Securing the Douve Line," p 15-16.
32. Ibid. p 16.
33. Ibiblio.org/hyperwar, "Utah Beach to Cherbourg, Sealing Off the Peninsula," p 2.
34. Ibid. p 3.
35. Ibid. p 4.
36. Hyperwar: "Cross Channel Invasion," p 29-30. For the weather effects, see disaster center.com, "Conversion table for knots to miles per hour. "30 knots equal 34.6 MPH.
37. "Cross Channel Invasion," p 26.
38. "Utah Beach to Cherbourg," p 2-3.
39. Army.mil, "The Normandy Invasion: Medal of Honor Recipients," p 1.
40. Hyperwar: "Cross Cannel Invasion," p 41.
41. Hal Buell, *World War II, A Complete Photographic History* (New York: Black Dog and Leventhal Publishers, Inc., 2002), p 507.
42. Omar Bradley, *A Soldier's Story* (New York: Henry Holt and Company, 1951), p 319.
43. Wetherell, "Story of a Go Devil," p 8.
44. Buell, *World War II*, p 511-514.
45. Wetherell, "Story of a Go Devil," p 6.

46. Ibid.
47. Normandiememoire.com: "Operation Cobra: the break-out," p 1.
48. Ibid.
49. Col. Vincent J. Esposito, Chief Editor, *The West Point Atlas Of American Wars, Vol.* II (New York: Frederick A. Praeger, Inc., 1959), Map 53; also "Operation Cobra," p 2.
50. Freerepublic.com, "The Freeper Foxhole Remembers Lt. Col. Matt Louis Urban," Feb. 11, 2004.
51. Oldreliable.org, "9th Infantry Division Medal Of Honor Recipients," p 15.
52. Buell, *World War II*, p 525-531.
53. "Songs of the Civil War." See footnote 1. "Somebody's darling, Somebody's pride; Who'll tell his mother where her boy died?"
54. Home.att.net, "History of WWII Medicine," p 8.
55. Department of the Army, U.S. Army Human Resources Command. Individual Deceased Personal File for William H. Bettes.
56. Quotes from Betsey Bettes and Marie Bettes Kropp are in the interview of July 5, 2005.
57. U.S. Army Human Resources Command, Individual Deceased Personal File for William H. Bettes.
58. William E. bettes letter to the Quartermaster General, Thomas B. Larkin. Individual Deceased Personal File for William H. Bettes.
59. Interview of July 5, 2005.
60. Individual Deceased Personal File.

CHAPTER FIVE

P.F.C. GEORGE M. BUZEK

Part I
A Happy Life

When young George Buzek was running late for school or in a hurry to greet the new day, he had a knack for putting on his sox and pants while hopping and walking. To Ann Buzek, her little brother was an energetic, happy, joking comic who enjoyed playing tricks on his sister. The lad also immensely enjoyed belting out the seemingly endless stanzas and chorus of his favorite tune, "She'll Be Comin' Round the Mountain." For a young boy, life was good on the farm near Greensburg, Ohio.

George loved to play baseball, and Ann said that he was "real good" at pitching horseshoes. The petite Ann, who had thrown more than a few ringers in her time, was also proud of her own horseshoe prowess. In time, the diminutive Ann considered her brother as a lean, "real tall" young man - George was 5' 10".

The Buzeks were new Americans. Andrew and Maria Buzek were married on Valentine's Day, 1899 at Glozan, Yugoslavia. In 1905, the 26 year old Andrew, full of heartache and promises, left his young wife and journeyed to America. Although he wanted to be a farmer, Andrew worked in a machine shop so that he could afford to bring his wife to America. After three long years of waiting, Maria joined her husband in the United States. The Buzeks produced six more Americans, George being the fifth child.

In 1908, Andrew was one of the organizers and charter members of St. John Slovac Lutheran Church in Akron. The church became a part of the Buzek family life.

Andrew and Maria were destined to celebrate 69 years of marriage. "Their advice to newlyweds: Love, trust and have faith in God and in each other. Try to live according to God's law and the

Golden Rule." [1] Andrew added, "You must have faith in your spouse, be religious and be a conscientious worker." [2]

Andrew Buzek achieved his dream of becoming an American farmer when he operated a farm on Massilon Road in the Greensburg school district. However, the Great Depression made life difficult for everyone. When asked how things were for her in the 1930's, Ann Buzek remarked with an emphatic, "Rough." Then for good measure, she repeated the word. (Ann chose not to complete high school because she did not have good shoes.) The family lost their farm in 1934 and moved to a potato farm in Randolph Township in Portage County.

George wanted to finish his senior year with his friends at Greensburg High School; so he was permitted to reside with second cousin Sam Buzek's family, who also operated a farm along Massilon Road.

George's school persona was quite different from that shared with his immediate family and close friends. Those who remembered George in later years recalled that he was quiet and polite. Cousin Sam remembered George as a quiet, pleasant man, a real gentleman. Sam laughingly said that George's only sin was getting caught smoking in school, which was rather common in those days. Next to George's picture in the 1935 yearbook was the following statement: "There is always safety in silence." His only listed extra-curricular activity was interclass baseball in his junior year. He gave his nickname as "Mike." But in spite of his reserved character, George was not a loner. [3]

He and other Greensburg teenagers liked to hang out at Bolin's "fillin' station" on the narrow two-lane Massilon Road. Russell Bolin, a junior, was the son of the proprietor; and if there were any two opposite characters, it was George and Russell. Thus, the witty last will and testament in the 1935 yearbook read: "To Russell Bolin, George Buzek leaves his love (?) for studying. No danger of them ever getting hit by a bookworm." (Russell went on to become senior class president, outstanding athlete, and active in nearly every school function.) In the graduating class' prophecy for ten years in the future, "Governor Rueschman is giving a commemoration speech. Clark Witsaman, George Buzek, and Sam Stevenou are Arvine's body guards."

In spite of hard economic times, life went on. As in all generations, the youth intended to enjoy their youth to the fullest. There was some room for optimism. After all, President Roosevelt's alphabet agencies promised a better tomorrow; and in Europe the German dictator was cooing about peace. On May 21, 1935 (graduation time in those days) Adolf Hitler declared to the Reichstag: "Germany has no intention of arming to the skies. We believe that if the people of the world would unite jointly in destroying all of their fire, gas, and explosive bombs this would be a cheaper affair than destroying each other. I cannot close my address better than by repeating our confession of faith in peace. If these professions were put to the proof by a sincere effort on all sides to adopt measures that will really preserve the peace, there would be more tranquility in Europe. Such an accord should be preferred to the anxieties that now prevail, which are converting every major power in Europe into an armed camp prepared at a moment's notice to resort to war." [4]

No teenager in the 1935 graduating class at Greensburg High School, or any high school across the land, could imagine or prophesy how much pain, anxiety, suffering, and even death that lay in store for some of them within the next ten years.

After graduation George joined the family on the potato farm in Randolph Township. In May 1935 consumers paid 25 cents for nine pounds of potatoes, which left the farmer little profit for his extensive labor. If you wanted steak to go with your potatoes, the cost was 18 cents per pound. A sample of other advertised prices in the Akron area were: *Akron Beacon Journal* 3 cents; 8 piece twin bed outfit $39; push reel lawn mower $4.98; electric ringer washer $39; 10 lbs. sugar 56 cents; 2 cans of soup 19 cents; 2 lbs. butter 57 cents; and 1 lb. of wieners 19 cents. [5]

Prices were certainly low, but generally the incomes were even lower. Unemployment was at 20.1 per cent. In May 1935 Babe Ruth was one of the relatively few who had no financial worries. The 41 year old Yankee slugger was talking retirement. Nevertheless, Ann Buzek recalled that her brother had a "happy, fun-loving life" at this time.

The fun-loving George attended a Polish dance in Ravenna some time in the early 1940's, and there he met Helen Dalaski. The couple were married on August 29, 1942 at the Buzek family's

"Mike" Buzek

Greensburg High School graduation picture, Class of 1935. Later in the year, George moved to Randolph Township in Portage County.

P.F.C. GEORGE BUZEK
This photograph was taken at Camp Shelby, Miss.

church, St. John Lutheran in Akron. Things were looking up for the newlyweds as George's draft number failed to come up, and he was now employed at Ferry Machine Co. in Kent. All of that changed the following spring when George became a part of Uncle Sam's payroll on May 8, 1943.

Part II
Life Becomes Expendable

Following a furlough home in October 1943, George's lot was cast as a replacement in the 36th Infantry Division, 142nd Regiment, Company K. At this time, the 36th Division was already engaged with the Nazis in Italy.

The division was initially comprised of the Texas National Guard; but in time it would lose some of its Texas character. On September 13, 1941 Maj. Gen. Fred L. Walker, an Ohioan, took command of the division. Walker, a graduate engineer of Ohio State University, had been commissioned a lieutenant in the regular army in 1911. When Gen. Pershing went chasing after Pancho Villa in Mexico from 1916-1917, Walker was a member of the expedition. During World War I, Walker was a battalion commander in the 3rd Division, in which he earned a Distinguished Service Medal for repelling a major German attack along the Marne River. During his WWI stint, Walker was wounded. Under Gen. Walker, PFC Buzek would be in good hands. The general knew what combat was about; and although he knew that men died in war, he would not needlessly expend them for trivial gains or personal glory. However, that could not be said for some of Walker's superiors. [6]

The 36th Infantry Division participated in three large scale maneuvers before being entrained to New York City. The 142nd regiment sailed from New York harbor on April 1, 1943. Twelve days later, the 142nd landed at Oran in North Africa. The 36th Division continued to train, and some of the exercises were amphibious landings to prepare them for the invasion of Italy. Prime Minister Winston Churchill referred to this theater as the "soft underbelly" of Europe. The 36th would soon learn differently; in fact, Italy could just as well be named the "meat grinder" of Europe, which seemed to be never-ending.

At 0330 on September 9, 1943, Gen. Mark Clark launched the assault on Salerno, Italy. On the right flank the inexperienced 36th Division landed at Paestum along a six-mile front. In the vain hope of surprising the Germans, the division went in without naval or air support. However, the Germans were not fooled, and they took a heavy toll of the Americans wading ashore. While exploding shells wreaked havoc on the water craft behind them, the GI's had to crawl through barbed wire, face machine guns, and work past enemy tanks.

"As Sergeant Manuel S. Gonzales of Company F, 142nd Infantry Regiment, crept toward a German emplacement, with machine-gun fire whistling just over his head, a tracer bullet hit the pack on his back and set it afire. He slipped out of the pack and kept crawling. A grenade fragment wounded him, but still he kept going until he was close enough to wipe out the gun crew with his own grenade." [7] In the next few days, the 36th slugged its way inland to Hill 424 near Altavilla, about twelve miles from the beach.

The Germans expertly regrouped. Their troops in Southern Italy eluded the British Eighth Army, which was coming up "the boot." Reinforcements flowed to the Salerno landing site, and by September 12, Gen. Albert Kesselring ordered the German counter-attack. At daybreak the Germans assaulted Hill 424, and by noon the position was in their possession. At 1530 on September 15, a strong German attack forced the Sele River and pierced the American lines. A battalion of the 36th Division was completely overrun. In the confusion and panic, the Americans were in danger of being pushed into the Gulf of Salerno. The artillery massed and fired their guns point-blank at the near-victorious Germans. In the night, the Americans struggle to reestablish their lines; and two battalions of the 82nd Airborne dropped in to reinforce the beachhead. The Germans continued probing attacks on the 14th, but allied naval and air support broke up the attacks. Allied reinforcements continued to pour in, and by the 15th the beachhead was safe. [8]

Throughout the Salerno battle, bravery was not lacking in the inexperienced 36th Division. For their conspicuous actions, four men received the Medal of Honor. "T/Sgt. Charles E. "Commando" Kelly, Pittsburgh, held off the Germans alone by throwing mortar shells when there were no more grenades. On Hill 424, Pvt. William Crawford, Pueblo, Colo., grenaded several machine gun nests, captured another machine gun position and fought the enemy until he was captured. Lt. Arnold Bjorklund, Wash., grabbed an enemy rifle and destroyed two German machine guns with it. T/Sgt. James Logan, Luling, Tex., single-handedly wiped out machine gun nests which held up an entire battalion, advanced alone to rout snipers which covered his unit's position." [9]

On September 18, the Germans pulled back from the beachhead. Although it was a concession to the allied landing, the Germans withdrew to nearly impregnable defensive positions and intended to make the allies pay for any advance with staggering casualties. As it was, the nine-day battle for Salerno cost the Americans 500 killed, 1,200 wounded, and 1,200 missing. The British suffered 5,000 casualties. [10]

In the aftermath of finger-pointing and casting blame for the near total disaster, Gen. Mark Clark thought the 36 Division's performance in the Salerno landing was poor. However, Gen. Fred Walker thought the criticism was unjust and that in the end his troops were victorious. [11]

The 36th Division pulled back to defensive positions on the right of the line, while the allies slowly pressed forward on the left toward Naples. The severely battered city fell to the British on October 1. On October 4, Generals Eisenhower and Alexander issued a rosy forecast that the allies would be in Rome by the end of the month.

The British Eighth Army plodding up the boot finally linked up with the Salerno pocket, and the allied front now extended across the Italian peninsula, a distance of approximately 90 miles. On the western side of the front the British 48th Div., 7th Armored Div., and 58th Div. fought with the American 3rd, 34th, and 45th Divisions. Progress was slow and bloody. The American Fifth Army crossed the Volturno River on October 13.. By the end of the month, Rome wasn't very much closer, thus making Eisenhower and Alexander not very good prognosticators.

On November 5, the Fifth Army launched a series of attacks to break through the German's Reinhard line. Amidst horrible weather conditions, the attacks went on for ten long grueling days. On November 15, Alexander finally called a halt to the sputtering offensive to allow his battle-fatigued troops a respite and to regroup his forces. [12]

Having been replenished with replacement GI's, the 36th Division (141st, 142nd, and 143rd Infantry Regiments) moved into the front lines as part of Gen. Alexander's regrouping on November 15. The 36th Division faced the enemy in the lower Liri Valley just north of Venafro.

This was not "Sunny Italy" as seen in the travel brochures. There were no scenic Italian seaside villas or pastoral peasant scenes. Here the steep-sided volcanic remains jutted upwards of 3,000 feet like gigantic canine teeth. There were only two main roads leading to Rome, and from their commanding perches the Germans certainly would not allow anything to pass. In some sectors the roads amounted to twisting mountain lanes; in others barely a path wended up and around the rocky escarpments.

Rushing swiftly through the mountains and to the sea were a multitude of ice cold rivers which were easily defended by the Germans. A casual backpacker on vacation would find it extremely difficult to cross this terrain, much less an armed, equipment-laden GI. It was the kind of terrain where a few brave, skilled units could hold off attacking armies; and that is exactly what the Germans did.

The German infantry, panzer units, and paratroopers were an implacable foe. Gen. Alexander recalled entering a ward of wounded German soldiers. The German sergeant called the men to attention, "Achtung, Herr General!" The wounded men lay to rigid attention with their arms stiffly at their sides. Alexander ordered them to carry on, or they would have remained in that position. Said the British general, "Whatever we may feel about the German, we must admit that German soldiers were extremely tough and brave." [13]

The tough and brave Germans were well-entrenched upon the heights. They had blasted deep bunkers into the volcanic rock and constructed others from reinforced concrete. After the severest shelling, they would emerge from their shelters and resume the lethal defense. From the heights the Germans could see everything, but down below the GI's had little to hide behind. Digging foxholes in the volcanic rock was nigh impossible.

The Germans possessed the best artillery piece of the war in the 88. Their panzer tanks were second to none. Thousands upon thousands of deadly mines had been planted in the areas that the GI's were most likely to tread. When stepped on by the unlucky and unwary GI, the "Bouncing Betty" sprung from the ground and exploded at waist height, sending flying steel shrapnel in all directions. Just a tiny sliver in a critical area meant instant death. The wooded Shuh mines blew off a foot, or a hand if the GI was crawling. Machine gun nests spit bullets in a crossfire from their slotted bunkers. Expert snipers picked off unwary GI's, especially the officers. Although outnumbered in the air, the Luftwaffe still had fangs and could roar down on unsuspecting targets.

In the mountains the GI's depended on mules to carry in rations, ammunition, and water. Where the mules could not or would not go, the GI's had to lug the supplies the rest of the way. It took hours - usually at night - to carry the wounded down the mountains.

Another enemy was the weather. At night the temperature plunged below freezing. One could get a mixture of torrential rain, snow, sleet, and pea-soup fog. There was trench foot, colds, pneumonia, and constant shivering to worry about. Perhaps there were occasional thoughts about leaving one's miserable shelter and going on patrol, which would at least allow some movement and a chance to generate some heat. However, being assigned to a patrol was akin to receiving a death sentence.

Into this maelstrom came PFC George Buzek and other replacement troops. Odors of cordite and rotting flesh greeted them. Eardrum-shattering explosions rocked the earth sending deadly steel fragments, hurtling rocks, and granite slivers whizzing through the air. The night was even worse - flashes of light and wondering if the next shell had your number. What were the damned German patrols doing out there in the blackness? Vehement swearing mixed with ardent prayers. As the dawn ushered in another day of rain and wet snow, the survivors could see the guts of their buddies strewn on the ground; and they soon suspected that the same fate awaited them. Was there any sanity at the top of the command? [14]

The rosy forecast for the end of October had long passed; and the allies certainly would not be in Rome for Thanksgiving. On November 25, the Allied Supreme Command approved Operation Shingle, an end-run amphibious assault at Anzio. However, the current allied line had to get closer to Anzio to affect a link-up with the beachhead. Thus on November 30, the allies prepared for the aptly named Operation Raincoat.

On December 3, the 142nd Infantry Regiment executed their part by advancing on Mount Maggiore, the northwest tip of the Mount Camino hill mass. After a massive artillery bombardment the attack started in the wet darkness at 0300, and by 1700 the 142nd was at the top. The outnumbered Germans made several fanatical attacks trying to drive the Americans off the mountain top, but the 142nd held on. "Resupply was a major problem, the terrain here being so steep that even mules could not clamber up some of the slopes. Almost constant rain added to the general difficulty. Frequently, it was impossible for Allied air force units to get into the air, let alone support the ground attack." [15]

"Behind every mountain in Italy there is another. Now the Allied soldiers faced Monte Lungo - a prominence right in the middle of the Mignano corridor, between the railway to Rome and Highway 6. To the right of the highway was Monte Sammucro, towering to almost 4,000 feet, with the village of San Pietro on its lower slope." [16]

After a night-long approach march through heavy fog, the 142nd's sister regiment, the 143rd, sent two battalions to attack San Pietro. They got within 400 yards of the town and were pinned down for two days. At dawn of the 8th, the other battalion crept to within hand grenade range and successfully rushed the peak of Monte Sammucro.

The 36th Division continued the effort to take San Pietro, but to no avail. Over on Mount Lungo, the 142nd Regiment made their assault at 1730 on December 15. By 1000 the next morning, they were at the top. Now, San Pietro was a trap for the Germans, so they abandoned the ruins and fell back to the western end of Mount Sammucro. There they repulsed the American II Corps till near the end of the month.

The Allies would not be in Rome by Christmas; and on New Year's Eve a raging blizzard swept the mountains making life even more miserable for the combatants. [17]

In the first two weeks of January, the Germans begrudgingly fell back to the Gustav Line. Their strong defensive position ran from the Tyrrhenian Sea, up the Garigliano and Rapido Rivers, through the Monte Cassino bastion, and to the Adriatic Sea.

Beginning on January 20, Allied attacks on the Gustav Line

were intended to distract the Germans from the Anzio landing area. In addition, there were hopes of puncturing the dominant position. The 36th Division was assigned to pierce the Gustav Line at the Rapido River west of Cassino.

"The river itself was an obstacle. Unfordable, eight to twelve feet deep, 40 to 50 feet wide, with steep banks, a swift current, ice-cold water and no bridges... Overlooking the river on the German side were series of strong points sheltering riflemen, machine gunners, mortars, antitank guns. Dug-in tanks and concrete bunkers were so arranged as to give mutual protection by interlocking fire. The Germans had cut down trees and brush to permit clear fields of fire. They had strung barbed wire to snag and hold attacking forces. They had planted mines along likely approach routes. Supported by considerable artillery, the 15th Panzer Grenadiers who defended the Rapido River were confident they could turn back any attempt to cross.... The low ground on the American side of the Rapido was flat and bare for a mile or so back from the river. Much of it was covered with deep mud. There were no good highways, only farm roads, dirt tracks not strong enough to hold up under the beating of the heavy vehicles of an infantry division. Getting to the river bank itself would be tough. Getting across the river would be worse." [18]

Gen. Walker had thoughts of asking to be relieved from command; however upon reflection, he felt a loyalty to his men and that he could do a better job than a newcomer. Walker wrote: "I knew that the men, who trusted me, were about to undergo unnecessary losses and hardship that I could not prevent. I had been in command of the division for two and a half years. I knew a great many soldiers by name. I had met their families when we had been stationed in Texas. Although everyone knows that war is merciless, I made it my business to keep down losses and hardship by careful planning. It is bad enough to expend men for legitimate military objectives. It is criminal to waste them as a result of unrealistic and careless planning." [19]

Walker decided to make the difficult crossing in the darkness. Three hours after sunset at 2000 hours, the 141st and 143rd Infantry Regiments moved out in a cold heavy fog. (P.F.C. George Buzek and the rest of the 142nd were fortunate to be in the corps reserve and unavailable for the attack..) The alert Panzer Grenadiers zeroed in their artillery on the crossing. In the dark and bedlam, most of the GI's failed to make the crossing. The few that did manage to get across paid dearly for their success. Walker was ordered to make another attack. Across the river the sounds of exploding shells, staccato firing, and the screams of their badly wounded comrades echoed onto the American side of the river. Many more GI's joined the ranks of the dead, the mangled, and the POW's. The commander of the 15th Panzer Grenadier Division counted 430 American dead and 770 captured on his side of the Rapido. Another 900 casualties were on the American side. German losses were minimal - less than 250. [20]

With the 141st and 143rd Regiments shot up, the 142nd was assigned to the 34th Infantry Division. The 34th was another division that had valiantly tried to do the impossible many times; and now it was being asked to do it again. Another battle for Cassino began on January 24, 1944.

Five miles to the east of Cassino the French Expeditionary Force was ordered to assault Monte Belvedere and Colle Abate. (For their part in the battle, the two French divisions would sustain 2,500 casualties.) Between the French forces and Cassino, the 34th Division was ordered to push across the Rapido River, swing west behind Cassino, and push to the crucial Route 6. The 142nd went in between the 34th Division and the French. "It was very tough going; the mountains were rocky, strewn with boulders and cut by ravines and gullies. Digging foxholes on the rocky ground was out of the question, and each feature was exposed to fire from surrounding points. The ravines were no better since the gorse growing there, far from giving cover, had been sown with mines, booby-traps and hidden barbed wire by the defenders. The Germans had three months to prepare their defensive positions using dynamite and to stockpile ammunition and stores." [21]

Val Przgocki, a combat medic with the 111th Medical Battalion, recalled the attack with a touch of gallows humor and irony. "Our litter squad was attached to the first aid station of the First battalion of the 142nd Regiment. We had orders to get behind the Monte Cassino Abbey at the base of Mt. Cairo. I don't know why we tried to infiltrate in broad daylight as the Germans always held the high ground and were always looking down our throats. As we moved out single file, the German snipers opened up on us and held up the whole battalion. We took cover behind a stone wall so as not to be a target. One of the infantry G.I.'s said to me that he will get that sniper as soon as he fires another round and exposes his hiding place. He poked his head over the stone wall to get a bead on the sniper when a bullet hit his helmet and glanced off. Another inch or two and he would have had it between the eyes. We all laughed as he grabbed his helmet and sat down next to me. He stated that let somebody else get him. As we ran to avoid the sniper shots, I forgot to pick up my ditty bag, and when we reached a dry river bed I had to return to retrieve my ditty bag. It maybe was an omen as when I was sliding down to the riverbed, a big artillery shell landed nearby. The second one landed right smack into the riverbed and exploded amongst the medics. It raised me up in the air about two feet and the smoke and dust clouded the area. Medics were hollering for medics as three were killed and one had his leg blown off. Another had shrapnel in his back. Two had some shrapnel but were able to walk.

As soon as the third shell landed, the infantry battalion took off towards their objective and left us. Those of us who were not injured put a tourniquet on the one that lost his leg and we patched up the others... We later heard the 210 pound patient that had a small shrapnel wound in his back died. The one that lost his leg lived." [22]

The Americans scrambled and clawed to the high ground northeast of the Monastery. "How they even managed to establish themselves there, in such bleak weather and supplied by mules that took seven hours to reach them, is almost impossible to imagine. The icy, wind swept ridge known as Snakeshead, fifteen hundred yards from their goal, was the main feature they held, but it was also essential to capture Albaneta Farm and Point 593, which the Germans and Italians aptly called Calvary." [23]

The Americans came within a mile of taking Route 6 - in fact, they could see the elusive goal. At Cassino one regiment established a foothold in the edge of town. "The stone walls of the old Italian houses were so thick that it took as many as nine bazooka rockets to blow a hole three feet in diameter; among the houses, the Germans had built steel-reinforced concrete bunkers so strong that 105mm shells were ineffective against them. A maze of tunnels and trenches linked these strong points, enabling the defenders to dart back and forth at will." [24] This American attack ultimately failed.

The last attack was made on 11 February, when violent rain and snow reduced visibility to a few yards. The Germans had thrown them back from the features Point 593 and Albaneta again and again." [25]

On February 11, after a final three day assault on Monastery Hill and Cassino town, the Americans were withdrawn. "The U.S. II Corps, after two and a half weeks of torrid battle, was fought out. The performance of the 34th Division [and the 142nd Regiment] in the mountains is considered to rank as one of the finest feats of arms carried out by any soldiers during the war. In return, they sustained losses of about 80% in the Infantry battalions, some 2,200 casualties." [26]

P.F.C. George M. Buzek was among the casualties. It was not a "million dollar" wound that could send a fellow stateside, but it was serious enough to get a GI out of the grim front line and bitter weather. George surely wrote many letters and v-mails while in the service, but only a scant sample remain. Through v-mail George kept the folks at home apprised of his condition. On February 17 he penciled an unsteady note to his sister Ann.

Dear family,

This is no second grader writing but me. My right hand is bandaged so I'm writing with my left hand, with quite some difficulties. I didn't write for a long time, so I thought I'd say hello to all. I got wounded in my right hand and am in a hospital, but am feeling fine. I can't write for a while, so say hello to the folks and all.

Love, George

In an undated v-mail, George wrote to his older brother Dan. Although he is still writing with his opposite hand, the practice has made his writing more legible.

Dear family,

Just a few lines to let you know I'm all right and not to worry. It's really hard to write with my left hand. Don't write much until my bandage gets off my finger.

Hope Mom is well now and at home with all of you. Anxious to know your farm plan for this year.

I'm listening to radio and just taking it easy. Love to all.

George

On February 23, George wrote to Dan at Route 1, Atwater,

Ohio.
Dear Danny & Virginia,

Well, I'm still writing in my crude penmanship, but I guess I'll have to for several weeks. I have to laugh [at] the way I hold this pen between my fingers; it <u>ain't</u> like the teachers taught me but it will be in about a week. I finally got a chance to answer Mrs. [unreadable last name] letter today. She will probably come over to say she received a letter from me. She is a kind, considerate person and I think she gets along with Helen & Virginia... I've been here a relatively short time compared with most of the boys, but it seems like a long time to me. Things are really tough, and I thought basic training was hard. I think when I get home I'll be well-satisfied to be a farmer. George

On March 8, George again wrote to his older brother.

Dear family,

I received a letter from Virginia and am glad everything [is] O.K. at home. I'm sorry to hear that Danny might have to leave for the service. It's going to be hard for the folks & Virginia and the children. I hope he won't have to go.

I thought I would go to town to try to find Ronny something, but didn't go. So, I'll have to go some other time if I get a chance.

I'm feeling fine and expect to leave here in a few days. The weather is fine and everything is green. The gardens are well-started and there are plenty of flowers around. Not in cities though.

Love to you all, George

On March 18, George wrote to his mother. His letter shows that he likes the 1940's farm life; however, Helen seems to prefer the city life. He also has thoughts of what Mother's Day will be like in 1944.

Dear family,

Well, just think how lucky I am being out on a nice spring day while you people have snow at home. It is starting to be spring here and the days are warm, the nights still get slightly chilly.

I wrote Helen a letter today also. Myself, I feel good and I hope all of you got rid of your colds. Say hello to Helen. Tell her we'll move out to a farm after the war and to get used to the outhouse & to pumping water while she is out there. Well, I could think about it anyhow.

Don't have much to write, but do wish you, Mom, a happy

Mother's Day. We'll all be home for next year's Mother's Day and have lovely flowers. Tell Ronny I said hello.   George

While George was convalescing, the Allies futilely continued to hammer the Gustav Line and Cassino; and the Germans still had them pinned down at Anzio. Failed German counter-attacks merely added to both sides' casualty lists.

However, in May the Allies were prepared for another concerted effort to break the German strangle hold. Replacement troops and returned wounded again filled the ranks of the divisions.

After eight days of bloody fighting, the monastery atop Monte Cassino finally fell to the Polish II Corps on May 18. The keystone to the German line had been removed and the Gustav Line began to unravel. On May 25 the Allies coming up the coast finally linked up with the Anzio beachhead.

Meanwhile, the 36th Division made an amphibious landing at the Anzio beachhead on the 22nd. It pushed to Valletri on the perimeter.

In his years as a West Point cadet, Mark Clark surely studied American campaigns and learned that the great generals concentrated on destroying the enemy's armies, not capturing territories or cities. Clark now had the opportunity to trap the German army or a large segment of it; however, he was obsessed with breaking the German lines barring the path to Rome. After all of the bitter failures in the Italian Campaign, Clark could be a modern-day Caesar conquering Rome. First, he would have to edge out the equally ambitious British.

The Germans moved back to the unfinished Caesar Line at the base of the Alban Hills. A reconnaissance patrol of the 36th Division discovered Monte Artemisio behind Valletri to be lightly defended. To exploit this lucky break, no chances were to be taken. Ruthless measures, stealth, and murderous hand-to-hand combat would prevail. The 141st and 142nd Regiments would make the assault. The 142nd's role would be to loop around and establish roadblocks to close the northern escape routes from Valletri. This required a communication line of eight miles that ran over a ridge from two to three thousand feet high.[27]

In the evening of May 30, two GI's brought a captured sniper to Regimental H.Q. The German sniper had killed their Lieutenant. What if the sniper should escape and blab what he had seen? Besides, he was in the way. In effect, the two men were ordered to take the despicable sniper down the road and not tell the officers what happened. Moments later, a rifle shot was heard in the forest. [28]

Among 8,000 men the word was passed along by whispers or hand signals. Passing through the lines, they would be surrounded, and one stupid shot could wreck the entire operation and get them all slaughtered. There was to be no rifle fire - if necessary, kill with a knife, garrote, or bayonet. Use a grenade only if absolutely necessary. No more smoking or talking, keep five yard intervals. [29]

"We marched all night," recalled one soldier. "We had all been cautioned to maintain absolute silence, and when the troops learned what we were doing, this became the quietest bunch of guys I have ever seen. All night long I never heard so much as a small clink from a piece of equipment." [30]

In the darkness, the two regiments silently ascended through the vineyards on the lower slopes. Next came the steeper slope with its sharp rocks and thorny bushes.

Among the ranks were former college boys, farm lads, factory workers, and big city kids - all now being ordered to perform the work of hardened gangsters. But many of them had been steeled by Salerno, San Pietro, the Rapido slaughter, and Albaneta Farm. Now it was payback time. German sentries were jumped from behind and had their throats slit or garroted.

On the left the silence was broken by the 141st, firing for all they were worth as a diversion for their sister regiment. Harvey Reves, a medic with Company B, 11th Medical Battalion, was with the 2nd Battalion, 142nd Regiment. "At dawn we took a break in a small canyon. I went to sleep immediately but was soon awakened by bursting mortar shells and Val PryzgockI [see footnote 22] yelling at me to help him with a wounded Sgt. When I got there the Sgt. was dead and his Lt. was crying. We quickly moved to another wounded nearby, patched him up and put him on a litter, and then Val took a chunk of shrapnel in his leg. After I patched him, the column started moving out and Val was evacuated by Jeep along with others. There were many wounded there and some dead…" [31]

By 0635 the 142nd regiment had arrived at the summit. They captured three artillery observers, and turned southwest along the ridge to 2,500' Maschio dell' Artemisio. In spite of harassing German artillery fire, by darkness, the entire ridge was in the hands of the 141st and 142nd. When he heard the news, Gen. Clark reportedly said it "caused all of us to turn handsprings." The road to Rome was now open. [32]

On June 1, Gen. Walker led his troops into Valletri from the rear. His elation was shattered when his close friend, Col. Harold Reese, was killed from a blast from a retreating German 88mm. [33]

At the dawn of June 2, the 142nd and 143rd advanced 4 ½ miles over rolling farm land to Monte Cavo and Rocca di Papa. The 142nd positioned itself directly east of 3,136' Monte Cavo. [34]

American units won the race for Rome on June 4. George Buzek and the 36th Division also got their march through Rome, but it was an unspectacular hike just before midnight of June 4. As Walker's division trudged through the blacked-out Roman streets to the Tiber bridges, the soldiers could hear their own tramping boots, the drone of truck motors, and the liberated Italian people clapping in the darkened windows.

Gen. Mark Clark made his grand entrance into the Italian capital on June 5 for his photo-ops with his corps commanders, resistance leaders, and politicians.

Part III
A Life Ends In Italy

On the home front in Akron, George's wife, parents, and other relatives nervously followed the progress of the allies in Italy. In late May the *Beacon Journal's* front pages featured the Italian Campaign. On the 26th, the newspaper carried news from Allied headquarters in Naples: "Allied forces rolled back the Germans today in swift new advances toward Rome at both ends of the Italian battle line." [35]

On the 29th, the story line read: "Foe Viciously Battles Yankees 16 Miles From Rome." Anxiety levels increased for the Buzek family when they read that three Akron men were killed in the fighting near Rome. [36]

On June 2, the newspaper printed: "Allies Smash Main Highway Near Valmonte, Cracking Anchor In Nazi Line," and that the U.S. infantry had entered Valletri yesterday.

June 5 brought the glorious news that the allies had entered

Rome. However, the large photograph on page five illustrated the price exacted for the Eternal City's liberation. A Fifth Army firing squad was sending a volley over row upon row of white crosses at the American Cemetery at Nettuno. The exercises, which included an address by Lt. Gen. Mark Clark, had been conducted on Memorial Day. [37]

D-Day news dwarfed any other topic on June 6. On the following day, a front page article read: Akron Mothers Pray For Safety Of Their Sons." Solemn prayer services were conducted at St. Vincent's catholic church, the Goodyear Tire Company's theater, the Akron Jewish Center, the YMCA, and other places. [38] In many cases it was past time to pray for the sons and time to pray for the mothers whose sons were already dead. Such was the case for Maria Buzek.

While Gen. Clark was schmoozing and getting photographed in Rome, the 142nd Regiment was in pursuit of the retreating German Army, which was putting up a stiff rear guard fight. Some time on June 5 just north of Rome, a shell fragment ripped into George's back, and the 27 year old private died.

On the fallen soldier's body were his last worldly possessions: pictures, two prayer books, three knives, mirror, comb, ring, S.S. card, identification card, driver's license, induction notice, money order receipt, wallet, purple heart ribbon, and $8.61.

On the evening of June 7, the shrouded body of George Buzek was laid to rest beside a fellow Company K man at the American Military Cemetery at Nettuno, Italy. George's Protestant white cross joined the multitude of others in the countless rows. [39]

Helen Buzek was eight months pregnant when the bad news arrived at her Akron doorstep in June 1944. Her brother, John Dalaski, was recently announced as killed in action after being missing for a year. John was a gunner whose plane disappeared on a raid over Germany. Now, the father of her unborn child was dead. [40]

For the next three and a half years, correspondence from the Buzek family to the U.S. Army evidenced frustration, anger, anguish, and misunderstandings. On the Army's part, the Quartermaster Department dutifully followed the prescribed red tape trail as tactfully as possible. The two main concerns of both parties were George's personal effects and where he would be permanently buried.

On September 16, 1944 the Quartermaster Depot in Kansas

City sent Helen an $8.61 check. At this time no other personal effects had been forwarded to them. The "Administrative Assistant" added: It is probable that additional effects of Private Buzek will reach this Bureau at a later date. As it is my intention to forward any such property to you immediately upon arrival here, I ask that you please notify us, without fail, in the event there is any change in your address within the next six months. I wish to express my sympathy in the loss of your husband." For this matter in the future, Helen was told to refer to case #96772D.

On September 21, Helen signed and dated the letter (acknowledging the receipt of the check) and returned it in the SASE. She then wrote a note to the QM Dept. It was dated August 21, but the month evidently was a mistake.

Dear Sir:

Writing a few lines in reply to #96772D. My address is 45 Sommers Ct. If possible please try and locate his other personal belongings because I would like to have them as a keepsake.

Sincerely Yours,
Mrs. Helen Buzek.

On November 2, 1944, Helen wrote another note to the Army in which there seems to be a justified impatient tone.

Dear Sir:

I am writing to in reference to AG 201, Buzek, George M. PC-N NAT 139. I have never received any word whether he was buried or not and would like to know. Other families receive word where their boys or husbands are buried and their number of the grave. I have never received any further word beside the telegram in June saying that my husband was killed in action on June 5, 1944 in Italy. I will appreciate a reply as soon as possible. Thank You.

Sincerely Yours,
Mrs. Helen Buzek

Helen's letter apparently bounced around from office to office, because the Army's reply took 71 days. Helen was informed that : The official report of interment received in this office shows that the remains of your husband were interred in the American Cemetery, Nettuno, Italy, Grave 4851, Row 69, Plot 2-J, with a Pro-Protestant ceremony conducted at the grave by an Army Chaplain. A temporary marker with a fitting inscription thereon has been erected and the grave properly recorded. The cemetery is under immediate supervision of our military authorities." A copy of her letter was forwarded to Kansas City regarding the personal effects.

On April 11, 1945 the Army informed Helen that they had received some additional property belonging to George. The items were nail clippers, a flashlight, and a wrist watch band.

Helen immediately responded.

Dear Sir:

Writing in regards to 96772. Received a letter from you that was written January 24, 1945 saying that the personal effects of my husband would be released and sent to me in the near future.

A few days ago I received a letter from P. L. Koob 2nd Lt. Q.M.C. Officer in charge saying that they have received additional property of my husband and are sending it to me. I have received the package and was very much disappointed of its contents. I received a batterie [sic], pen, nail clippers and a watch strap but no watch.

I have been hoping to receive my husband's wrist watch so that the baby will have a keepsake of its father. Also my husband had a bible with his name on it and a few other articles, but mainly I would like to have his watch if possible. I can't understand why I haven't received any of his clothes or other belongings, also why I received the additional property before the other. I hope to have more information about that.

Sincerely Yours,
Helen Buzek

On May 11, 1945 the QM Dept. informed Helen that the clothing was government issue, and by regulations was retained by the government. Furthermore, "I regret to advise that we have no information regarding the watch about which you inquire. All the property of Private Buzek received at this Bureau to date, has been forwarded to you."

Five months later, October 24, 1945, George's personal effects were finally examined in Kansas City. An examiner noted that there was a "very bad odor" and "knives rusty." Thus, on November 1, the Army sent a warning to Helen.

"Not infrequently, due to exposure to the weather and other conditions, certain articles received here have a peculiar or sometimes even disagreeable odor. Such an odor may develop from the length of time the articles have been packaged in transit from overseas. All of your husband's effects received here are in this condition. Since it is our desire to spare the recipient any avoidable unpleasant reaction, I wish to acquaint you with this condition and ask that you tell me whether you, nevertheless, desire these articles sent you... If your reply in this regard is not received here within fifteen days from the date of this letter, it necessarily will be assumed that the articles are unacceptable." The "Individual Deceased Personal File" showed no record of Helen's decision, and the remaining family members were unaware of such personal effects.

Almost two years later, March 7, 1947, Helen had to decide whether her husband's remains, which were now in a skeletal condition, should be permanently interred at Nettuno or shipped home. She read the "Request For Disposition Of Remains" form and put an X in the box next to "Be interred in a permanent American military cemetery overseas." The notarized form was then mailed to the Quartermaster Department; but this was not the end of the matter.

George's parents wanted their son's remains to be sent home. They could then at least visit the gravesite, thus they were upset over their daughter-in-law's decision. Consequently, they sent their own letter to the Quartermaster General on October 22, 1947.
"Dear Sir:

We, the undersigned, the parents of George M. Buzek wish to make a request for the disposition of the remains of our son. We would very much appreciate your sending us the necessary form to make this request.

The official report shows that he is interred in the American Military Cemetery, at Nettuno, Italy..." Andrew and Maria signed the typed letter.

In a relatively fast time, the Army responded to the Buzeks on November 7, 1947. The essential paragraph must have been disheartening. "The 'Request for Disposition of Remains' questionnaire was mailed to Mrs. Helen Buzek who, according to the present records of the Department of the Army, is the only next of kin legally authorized to direct the final disposition of the remains of your son."

Not to be deterred, George's parents apparently went to work on Helen. The harried widow relented, and wrote to the Army.
"Dear Sir:

Writing in regards to the burial of my late husband P.F.C. George Buzek. I have already filed a Request for Disposition of Remains but now I have changed my mind and would like to have him brought back home because of my little daughter. Please send me the forms to fill out again..."

Four months later, March 17, 1948, the Army responded to Helen's letter. All she had to do was to send them the name and address of the funeral director to receive the remains. This information would then be added to her Disposition Form, and "action will be taken to comply with your request."

Whether Helen sent the information is unknown. What is known is that the Army notified Helen (December 2, 1948) that George was permanently interred at Nettuno, Italy.

On Memorial Day 1945, Gen. Lucian Truscott still commanded the U.S. Fifth Army, and he was scheduled to speak at the ceremonies at the Anzio-Nettuno American Cemetery. Behind the podium were over 20,000 temporary white wooden crosses marking the American graves. In the next few years, some of the remains would be disinterred and shipped to sites in the United States. The remainder, including George Buzek and one other man from Randolph Township, would rest forever beneath Italian soil.

According to Bill Mauldin, when it was Truscott's turn to speak to the audience and assembled VIP's, he turned his back to them and addressed the corpses that he had commanded at that place. "He apologized to the dead men for their presence here. He said that everybody tells leaders it is not their fault that men get killed in war, but that every leader knows in his heart this is not altogether true. He said he hoped that anybody here through any mistake of his would forgive him, but he realized that was asking a hell of a lot under the circumstances... Truscott said he would not speak about the glorious dead because he didn't see much glory in getting killed in your late teens or early twenties. He promised that in the future if he ran into anybody, especially old men, who thought that death in battle was glorious, he would straighten them out. He said he thought that was the least he could do." [41]

CHAPTER NOTES
P.F.C. George M. Buzek

1. This quote was found on a yellowed newspaper article in Ann Buzek's mementoes. There was no date or newspaper title for the article. The previous comments regarding George Buzek's youth were acquired in an interview with Ann at her Akron home in the summer of 2005. Ann Buzek passed away on Dec. 19, 2006.
2. *Akron Beacon Journal*, obituary for Andrew Buzek, August 29, 1968.
3. Interview with Marguerite Kleckner, class of 1935 at Greensburg High School. Mrs. Kleckner generously loaned the author her 1935 yearbook to make copies. Incidentally, she and her sister were the star players on the girl's basketball team which won the county champion-ship. From our conversation, a telephone interview with Sam Buzek ensued.
4. *Beacon Journal*, "Dictator Hitler's Speech," p 4, May 22, 1935.
5. *Beacon Journal*, May 22, 1935.
6. "36th Division in World War II, Division Commanders," Texas Military Forces Museum, texasmilitaryforcesmuseum.org/36thdivision. Also "History Of The 36th Infantry Division In World War II," ghg.net/burtond/36th/36infhist.html.
7. Robert Wallace, *The Italian Campaign*, (Alexandria, Va.: Time-Life Books, 1981), p 55.
8. Col. Vincent J. Esposito, Chief Editor, *The West Point Atlas of American Wars, Vol. II* (New York: Frederick A. Praeger, Publishers, 1959), Maps 94, 95, 96.
9. "The Story of the 36th Division," Lone Sentry.com, p 3.
10. Wallace, *The Italian Campaign*, p 63.
11. Dan Kurzman, *The Race for Rome* (Garden City, New York: Doubleday & Company, Inc., 1975), p 305.
12. Hal Buell, *World War II, A Complete Photographic History* (New York: Black Dog & Levinthal Publishers, Inc., 2002), pp 386-395.
13. Wallace, *The Italian Campaign*, pp 102-103.
14. Raleigh Trevelyan, *Rome '44, The Battle for the Eternal City* (New York: The Viking Press, 1981), p 129.
15. Esposito, *West Point Atlas, Vol. II*, map 100.
16. Wallace, *The Italian Campaign*, p 109.
17. Esposito, *West Point Atlas*, map 100.
18. 36th Infantry Division Association, "General Walker's Story of

the Rapido Crossing," www.kwanah.com/36division... p 2-3.
19. *Ibid.* p 4.
20. *Ibid.* p 9.
21. "Battle of Monte Cassino - Wikipedia, the free encyclopedia," en.wikipedia.org...p 5.
22. "Personal Accounts of WWII Medics," home.att.net/~steinert... p 8, Nov. 26, 2007.
23. Trevelyan, *Rome 44*, p 132.
24. Wallace, *The Italian Campaign,* p 137.
25. Trevelyan, *Rome 44,* p 133.
26. "Battle of Monte Cassino, wikipedia... p 6.
27. Ernest F. Fisher, Jr., *Cassino to the Alps* (Washington, D.C.: U.S. Government Printing Office, 1977)), p 186.
28. Dan Kurzman, *The Race for Rome*, (Garden City, New York: Doubleday & Company, Inc., 1975), p 310.
29. *Ibid.*, p 311.
30. Wallace, *The Italian Campaign,* p 151.
31. "Personal Accounts of WWII Medics," home.att.net/~steinert... p 13-14, Nov. 26, 2007.
32. Fisher, *Cassino to the Alps,* p 188.
33. Kurzman, *Race for Rome,* p 311.
34. Fisher, *Cassino to the Alps,* p 201.
35. *Akron* Beacon *Journal,* May 26, 1944, p 1.
36. *Beacon Journal,* May 29, 1944, p 1.
37. *Beacon Journal,* June 5, 1944, p 1 and 5.
38. *Beacon Journal,* June 7, 1944, p 1.
39. U.S. Army Human Resources Command, "Individual Deceased Personal File." George Buzek's burial information is taken from this source.
40. A yellowed newspaper article with George's picture and death notice was given to the author by George's sister. Some of the information in the article was incorrect.
41. Bill Mauldin, *The Brass Ring* (New York: W. W. Norton & Company, Inc., 1971), p 272.

DONALD DIBBLE
"Thinks much and speaks little."

Donald Dibble - 2nd Row, far right in the white jersey.

CHAPTER SIX

PVT. DONALD DIBBLE, A PEACEFUL MAN

Part I
Good Times Among The Bad Times

Springtime 1931- You would have thought that the Great Depression had completely by-passed the small community of Randolph, Ohio. Judging by the extensive local newspaper coverage, there was not a sign of whining complaints, of pocketbooks being pinched, or of flagging confidence in the government. Many former residents still came into town to visit friends and relatives. Some of the town folks jumped into the old flivver and jostled over the rugged roads to be guests elsewhere. Besides, as one old-timer saw it, "What the hell, we were all in the same boat."

In that merry month of May civic responsibilities and appreciation of the past were still maintained. Memorial Day services were to be held at the Town Hall yard: "All G.A.R., Spanish American and World War veterans are given a special invitation to be in the parade. Let us all be present to honor those who have given the supreme sacrifice for us. The soldiers' graves will be decorated by the American Legion Saturday forenoon." [1]

In spite of the dire economic circumstances, there were signs of genuine progress: "The regular meeting of the Farm Bureau will be held in the school house Monday evening June 1. Mr. Kranz of the Ohio Edison Co. of Akron will give an illustrated lecture on Rural Electrification. The public is invited. Come and bring your electric problems and have them solved."

High school graduation took place on Friday night May 22 in the high school auditorium. The gym and gallery were filled to capacity, and the folks listened attentively to the program for the eleven graduates. Their class motto was: "We Launch Tonight. Where will we Anchor." The class flower (pink tea rose) and the class colors (Green and Pink) must have been chosen by the girls in the senior class.

Among the excited graduates was Donald Dibble, sharply

dressed in his suit and tie, sandy-red hair combed straight back, the naturally wavy hair piling up on top. Next to Donald's senior picture in the yearbook was the phrase: "Thinks much and speaks little." Although he may have been a little shy, Donald had played left guard on the football team. (Next to him on the line at center was Bobby Hilliard, a junior.[2])

Donald also played trombone in the school orchestra, and musical talent seemed to run in the family. Donald's brother, Chester, was noted for being a pianist. His mother, Gertie, mentioned that the Dibbles played in the speakeasies during Prohibition. In later years, her husband, Harvey, would be remembered by local dance fans as the bass violinist in old-time orchestras.

Harvey Dibble was a "stationary engineer" and a sawmill operator in his younger years. Being a licensed boiler man, he was the custodian at the Randolph school for seven years before his retirement. Harvey also served as secretary of the Randolph Fair Board. However, there was a dark side to Harvey Dibble. He was an alcoholic who would come home drunk and take it out on his wife and whip the kids. Donald and his brother Roger would move in with some neighbors when things got bad. [3]

On Saturday evening May 23, the alumni took over the high school gym. This proud and friendly gathering was an institution in the community. "Approximately 80 people partook of a delicious chicken dinner served by the Randolph Junior Citizens Club... Everyone seemed to be in exceptionally good spirits and spent a very enjoyable evening... All but one of the class of 1931 was present."

On the program was Donald's brother, Chester, who performed "a brilliantly executed piano solo." Chester also "gave a few timely words of advice and a hearty welcome to the class of 1931."

Five years later - For the rural folks in the county the weather is always an easy conversation starter; and in 1936 it was even easier. From January to March the subnormal temperatures made the winter one of the coldest in the 1930's. The wind whistled over the bleak stubbled fields, and the wind chill was horrible. Folks in their multi-layered clothes were unrecognizable as they waddled hunched over through the drifting snow. Then, with a sudden early spring thaw, floods and mud dominated the landscape.

The weather bounced the other way as the summer of '36 became one of the hottest on record. Starting in June, week after week people sweltered in their un-air conditioned homes and apartments. Deaths from heat stroke escalated across the Midwest. As the summer wore on, crops withered in the fields, and grain prices began to soar. Folks wondered how could the Great Depression get any worse. Oddly enough, Billie Holliday was crooning George Gershwin's latest popular tune, "Summertime." "Summertime and the livin' is easy. Fish are jumpin' and the cotton is high..."

Across America the Great Depression inexorably wore on. Although there were signs of better times to come, the unemployment rate was still at 16.9 percent. Some tried the so-called easy path of crime. Bank robbers, gangsters, and hucksters of all kinds roved the countryside. It proved to be a very unstable profession as newspaper front pages announced that some were gunned down and others received a state execution.

Labor unrest brought many strikes in '36. One of the bitterest was the sit-down strike at the Goodyear Tire and Rubber Company in Akron from February to March. Outside the shops tensions led to occasional bloody scuffles between the union men, company "enforcers," and police.

Internationally, the world seemed to be going to hell in a hand basket as Germany, Italy, and Japan escalated their aggressive aims.

Apparently, Hollywood and Broadway figured that the theater-going public saw enough depressing dramas in their own everyday lives; thus a plethora of inane, light-hearted stories flooded the silver screen and stage. Fred Astaire pranced around magnificent sets, the good guy always came out best, and love conquered all. The Sons of the Pioneers were introducing "Cool Water," and the citified Bing Crosby was crooning "I'm An Old Cow Hand." The amazing thing about the singing cowboys is that they could mosey down the dusty trail, bouncing and rocking in the saddle, strumming a guitar, and not miss a vocal note or a chord.

However, for young lovers this, as in all ages, was the best of times. "The Way You Look Tonight" was a special love song of 1936. It expressed the lovers' feelings so well that the tune echoed down to young lovers of succeeding generations.

"Some day, when I'm awfully low,

When the world is cold,
I will feel a glow just thinking of you...
And the way you look tonight..."

Thus, love and marriage came to the Dibble family in early 1936. Helen Dibble, a "Popular Randolph Girl," was a 1928 Randolph High School graduate and a 1931 graduate from the Alliance City Hospital nurses training school. The young nurse desired a special date for her wedding, and in 1936 there was a date better than Valentines Day. She chose leap year's day, and on that cold February 29th she walked down the short aisle of the Randolph Christian Church. The single ring ceremony certainly was a Dibble family affair. In fact, Helen's bridegroom, Ken Clayton, seemed to be an inconsequential participant according to the newspaper account.

"The bride wore a beautiful purple crushed velvet gown with silver accessories and carried white rose buds. She was attended by Miss Dorothy Hill of Ravenna, who wore green crepe and a corsage of white rose buds.

The bridegroom was attended by Donald Dibble, brother of the bride. [Donald surely had his eyes on the lovely Miss Hill.] Mrs. Maxine Belding sang two selections: "I Love You Truly" and "Sweethearts Forever." She was accompanied on the piano by Chester Dibble, another brother of the bride. The ushers were Howard Coler and Roger Dibble.

The church was decorated with pink and white crepe paper, palms, and candelabras..." [4]

During his sister's wedding ceremony, Donald cast adoring glances at the radiant maid of honor, and he felt that he was the luckiest man on the earth. Dorothy Hill had miraculously accepted his proposal, and they were to be married on May 2.

Dorothy's and Donald's wedding was the prominent story in the Women's Features of the Evening Record for May 7. "...Miss Doris Hill, sister of the bride, was maid of honor and Roger Dibble, brother of the groom, was the best man. The bride wore a gown of pink wool with silver and white accessories and wore a corsage of white roses and lilies of the valley. Her attendant wore a frock of lavender crepe with accessories. Following the ceremony [in Akron] the members of the immediate families were served a dinner at

Donald and Dorothy (Hill) Dibble

DONALD DIBBLE & wife

Pvt. Donald A. Dibble

the home of the bride..." [5]

A month later the Women's Features reported: "Mrs. Dibble, Recent Bride, Honor Guest at Miscellaneous Shower." "...A delicious 6 o'clock dinner was served to ten guests. A bowl of deep red and yellow roses centered the table. Following the dinner the bride was presented with many lovely gifts and the remainder of the evening was spent in playing cards and music..." [6]

These were surely good times in a trying era as Donald and Dorothy settled into their apartment on South Chestnut Street in Ravenna. Donald could walk down the hill to his place of employment, the Cleveland Worsted Mills. Here, as in many places across the nation, job security was a fragile thing. The average guy was caught between a rock and a hard spot as unionizes, strikers, and tight-fisted management dueled in the work place. However, on the weekends the young couple could take some of their meager earnings and walk hand in hand two blocks up the street to the town's Main Street. There, they could window shop, buy a soda at the drugstore counter, and take in a movie.

Spencer Tracy and Clark Gable were two of the dominant male stars in the '30's. Tracy won the Oscar in 1937 for his role in "Captains Courageous, and Gable hit his peak in '39 as Rhett Butler in GWTW. Walt Disney's new and wonderful animated films dazzled the movie-goers. "Snow White and the Seven Dwarfs" debuted in 1937, and one its songs, "Whistle While You Work," was one of the top hits. Whatever was on the bill, you got your money's worth by seeing the main feature and a "B" movie. A cartoon was always good for some laughs, and this year Daffy Duck was introduced to the public. Sometimes a movie was serialized, whereby the viewer was treated to perhaps a 5-10 minute segment of it. To see the next episode, one had to come back the following weekend.

Then came the news reel, in which there were amazing items like the opening of the Golden Gate Bridge in 1937 and the operation of Hoover Dam. After four years of planning, the New York City World's Fair opened in 1939. This oasis of progress in the Great Depression eventually attracted 44 million visitors. On the negative and disturbing side, German planes joined Francisco Franco's army in the Spanish Civil War. By November,1937 approximately 35,000 Spaniards had been executed. In December of the same year, the

Japanese Army began a three-month slaughter of over 250,000 Chinese civilians. The isolationists in America were quite thankful for the Atlantic and Pacific Oceans.

If one was into reading mysteries, Agatha Christie's *Death on the Nile* was now in print; and John Steinbeck's *Of Mice and Men* was a thought-provoker.

Having been a high school football player, Donald may have been interested in the NFL championship game of 1937, which was a 28-21 victory for the Redskins over the Bears. These two teams were the dominant professional teams of the era; however their success was broken in 1939 when the Packers beat the Giants 20-0.

In the meantime, Donald and Dorothy went about their daily lives, worshipped side by side in their church, and enjoyed their family ties, especially at Thanksgiving and Christmas.

With the peace time draft in 1941, Donald and Dorothy closely followed the national news, world events, and the local draft board notices. By 1943, Donald was a married man and over thirty years old, but he and Dorothy had no children.

Part II
The Quiet Man Becomes a Soldier

Uncle Sam needed more men, and thus Donald Dibble was inducted into the service on October 26, 1943, just three days after his 31st birthday. He kissed his tearful wife good-bye at the Ravenna bus terminal, and with the other somber-faced draftees gazed out the windows at the passing autumn scenery on the route to Cleveland. Nothing much registered except thoughts of the past and what lay in store for him.

After the customary, and often cursory, physical examination, Donald boarded the train for Camp Blanding, Florida. His lot was cast with the medical detachment trainees who were undergoing basic training in this all-male city of soldiers. One medic recalled Camp Blanding as a "strenuous period of training. The ability to endure forced marches under a burning sun inures the men to physical hardship."[7] Day after day, the army plied its routine of long marches, calisthenics, inspections, enforced-discipline, punishment, and specialized instructions in order to transform the freedom-loving citizen into a dutiful, order-taking, and responsive soldier.

At last, Donald's furlough arrived in the early spring of 1944. The time with his wife, family, and friends seemed to fly by; and soon it was time to say more tearful good-byes at the train station. The train chugged toward Camp Meade, Maryland. His next destination was a crowded, smelly troop ship bound for the Mediterranean theater of war and the 6th Infantry Regiment. The 6th IR had been bloodied by Rommel's Afrika Corps in the blinding heat and wind-blown sand in the North African campaign. It was now taking fearful losses in the steep mountains and deadly valleys of the Italian peninsula. Due to attrition, replacements were desperately needed. Donald would serve in the 3rd battalion of the regiment's medical detachment.

Being a private, Donald was in the lower echelon of the detachment. In each battalion "the enlisted personnel included a section Sergeant, (a Staff Sergeant), a Corporal and a complement of 22 additional highly skilled technicians in the area of first aid, litter bearers, drivers, etc.... Each Company in the regiment was assigned two (2) aid men. These men lived with the company and moved with them on every move. They were exposed to enemy fire just the same as riflemen. And, on many occasions, were exposed to a higher degree than the rifleman. His responsibility was to locate wounded men, quickly assess the severity of the wound and immediately start the action necessary to relieve the wounded man of pain and suffering. In many instances the Aid Man had to comfort those soldiers who were more mentally wounded than physical. The Aid Man and the other soldiers in the company had to work very closely together in retrieving wounded men from precarious situations and the subsequent evacuations" [8]

In spite of his training, there was plenty the 31-year old private could not comprehend until he actually came under fire. One Aid man recalled: "We were not strangers with the platoon we served with, everyone was a comrade. And unlike the other members of the platoon who can't stop to aid a wounded buddy, have no idea how it tears the aid man apart to witness one of his buddies wounded and helpless. We eat, sleep, laugh, and yes even cry with these comrades, we become a family, and like any family, death affects us all... I can never describe the feeling you get when you see your closest friend dead from his wounds, and knowing that you were unable to save his life..." It is no wonder that historian Stephen Ambrose wrote, "It was the universal opinion of the frontline infantry that the medics were the bravest of all." [9] All of this lay in store for Private Dibble.

While Donald was on his way to Camp Blanding in sunny Florida, the 6th IR was landing on the beaches north of Naples on October 28, 1943. Any advancement was bought dearly in flesh and blood as the Germans commanded the advantageous high ground and were adept at every aspect of combat. By December, the regiment received casualties from anti-personnel mines and artillery fire; and the cold, wet weather led to many cases of trench foot. In the January heavy snow and bone-chilling temperatures, the regiment engaged the enemy at the mine-infested Mt. Lungo and Mt. Porchia. The battle for the crests seesawed back and forth as the Germans counter-attacked. The 6th IR dug in, and after January 8 the men were relieved by the 141st Infantry. The battle had cost the regiment 7 officers and 106 men killed in action, 328 evacuated wounded, and 71 lost in action. Obviously, there was plenty of work for the medical detachments.[10]

The regiment received little respite as it was included in the Anzio inferno. Throughout March, April, and into May it was pinned down in the cold rain and mud while air bursts, artillery and mortar fire kept everyone's head down in the slop. More casualties came from patrol activity. This is the world that awaited Private Dibble if he and the transport ships could get past the Luftwaffe's new radio-guided bombs.

In the wreckage-strewn harbor, barrage balloons hovered over the transport ships. Not very far away, artillery fire sounded like continuous thunder. The fresh troops and materiel began to stream off the ships. A different kind of cargo was going in the opposite direction.

Boarding the nearby hospital ships are the walking wounded wearing an assortment of head, arm, hand, and shoulder bandages. Some quietly tell of the fighting as they saw it, and a few smile wanly and joke about going back - sardonic American humor at its best. On the upper deck those with minor wounds are walking about drinking hot coffee from huge mugs. Some of the men going onboard are not talking. They are carried on the ships on stretchers, bits of their clothing lying pathetically across their blanketed figures. A few look at the sky with unseeing eyes. A few are smoking.

"The stretcher bearers are Negroes and everybody watching is impressed by their care of the wounded. They walk gently down slippery planks, carefully balancing their burdens so that no jolt will increase the pain. They smooth blankets that are ruffled by the wind." Then they slowly walk back to shore for another wounded man.

Every once in a while there is a stretcher tagged with a POW sign. And with just as great care a wounded German is lifted onto the ship. There aren't many of these today.

Some who are coming back will never talk again. Their stories are finished. They are completely covered with a blanket.

As the ambulances roll up to the unloading areas, they meet a convoy of men, tanks, and trucks. "The men who move into war are as silent as those who are coming out." [11]

When Pvt. Dibble came ashore at Anzio, the 3rd battalion was a small part of the stalemate. Yet, casualties mounted from patrol activity and artillery bombardments, and the medical detachment men had to be out where the action was the hottest.

On May 23, 1944 the battalion joined in the massive and horrific Anzio breakout. By June 3, the unit was moving up Highway 7 and entered Rome at dusk. There was not much time to bask in the excited welcome of the liberated Romans, as the battalion assembled near Grosetto on June 18-20. It went on the attack for 18 days through the hills and over secondary roads. At first the advance was relatively easy against the retreating German Army; but supply problems, the terrain, and the regrouped German units brought the movement to a crawl.

On July 20, the 6th I.R.'s three battalions were reorganized. Dibble's 3rd battalion became the 14th Armored Infantry Battalion, which continued the attack toward the north side of the Arno River. [12]

On September 1, elements of the 1st Armored Division crossed the Arno River between Pisa and Florence. Facing the Americans were the 16th SS Panzer; a more hardened, experienced, ruthless, and fanatical foe could not be found.

The 14th Armored battalion shifted to the II Corps on its right, which was thrusting up the center of the "boot." For three weeks, the outfit tried to push the Germans back in the central Apennine Mountains, some of which abruptly rise to over 3,300 feet. However, by the end of October the Germans were firmly entrenched in the Gothic Line which ran across Italy from Lake Comacchio near the east coast to 9 miles south of Bologna in the center and to about 12 miles north of Pisa on the west coast. A period of attacks and counterattacks by both sides ensued, but a long, cold winter stalemate faced the combatants.

There was no special battle name to commemorate the names of the fallen, and November 5, 1944 held no special significance for anyone except for the families of the fallen soldiers. On that date the bodies of Pvt. Donald Dibble and some of his fellow soldiers were discovered near Vado, Italy.

Most soldiers carried a wristwatch, a wallet, photographs, the latest letters from home, and perhaps some special mementos that meant something only to the owner. None of these things were found on Donald's body. Perhaps like their American counterparts, the German troops in the vicinity were souvenir hunters or just curious to see what the enemy possessed. Perhaps there was something more sinister since Donald was found with "penetrating wounds to the head and back." [13]

Many years later, Donald's brother Roger said that Donald was executed by a German firing squad. No one knew his source for that information, although it is known that the Americans were facing the dreaded SS troops who would have shot a medic or anyone else with no qualms. At other times, Roger would begin to tell his son about Donald, but the emotions would well up and Roger could not continue talking. When the author spoke with Roger Dibble, the Randolph resident was in his upper 80's and suffering from Alzheimer's disease. Roger did not remember ever having a brother named Donald.

Eventually, Dorothy was faced with the agonizing decision of where Donald's final resting place should be. In August 1948, Pvt. Donald A. Dibble was permanently laid to rest in the U. S. Military Cemetery at Florence, Italy next to 4,401 other United States soldiers.

Dorothy remarried in July 1949 and had one daughter. The wedded bliss did not last long as Dorothy died in July 1955 at the age of 41.

All that remained of this World War II tragedy was a lot of might-have-beens.

The final resting place for Pvt. Donald A. Dibble Florence American Cemetery (photograph by Wikimedia Commons)

CHAPTER NOTES
Private Donald Dibble

1. *The Evening Record* (Ravenna, Ohio), "Randolph," May 26, 1931. The local Randolph news and alumni information comes from this newspaper article.
2. See Robert Hilliard of Chapter One. Bob also died in Italy.
3. *Evening Record*, "H. J. Dibble, 67, Randolph, Dies," January 10, 1944, p 1. Personal information comes from an interview with Gary Dibble, son of Roger Dibble.
4. *Evening Record*, "Popular Randolph Girl Becomes Bride At Pretty Church Wedding," March 2, 1936.
5. *Evening Record*, "Miss Dorothy Hill Becomes bride Of Donald Dibble Of Randolph," May 7, 1936.
6. *Evening Record*, "Mrs. Dibble, Recent Bride, Honor Guest at Miscellaneous Shower," June 10, 1936.
7. "From the National Archives, Medical Detachment 16th Infantry History," warchronical.com/16th Infantry…
8. The 30th Infantry Division Veterans of WWII/Combat Medics, 30thinfantry.org/medics…
9. World War II Combat Medic, home.att.net/~steinert First quote is by Albert Gentile, Aid-Man for Company B, 333rd Infantry, 84th Infantry Division, WWII.
10. Sixth Regiment U. States Infantry History, fortatkinsononline.org./6thInfyHistory… p 7-8.
11. Marjorie Avery, "Wounded Handled Carefully," *Akron Beacon Journal*, June 15, 1944. Marjorie Avery witnessed the evacuation of the wounded following D-Day at Normandy. What she saw could have been witnessed at other ports in the European theater and on the Pacific Islands. Parts of Avery's report have been paraphrased for this section.
12. "Sixth Regiment U. States Infantry History." fortatkinsononline.Org/6[th]InfyHistory… The Italian Campaign itinerary for the 6th I. R. is taken from this source.
13. Department of the Army, U. S. Army Human Resources Command. "Individual Deceased Personal File" for Donald A. Dibble.

CHAPTER SEVEN

GEORGE REISINGER, JR.
SEAMAN FIRST CLASS USN

Part I
The North Atlantic, 1942

From Eric the Red and the marauding Vikings to the modern day sailors who bravely dare to go down to the sea in ships, the North Atlantic has been a trial to one's very soul. World War II sailors, who experienced nature's perils on the high seas, retained vivid memories of their ordeals.

"At times the sea was smooth like a mirror, but in contrast, it would almost lie flat when the gale made it lie down, and dragged out white foam from what should have been the tops of waves. This was always followed by masses of water being scooped up, making long deep valleys through which ships would thunder, squealing and groaning like a human in pain. We could see for miles from the top of a wave and then next, a gleaming green sheet of water towering over us which thundered away into a dark valley. In the Pentland Skerries, even without a storm, foaming currents run in all directions." [1]

The sea is an ever-changing entity, which can be awe-inspiring or terrifying. A British officer recalled: "...it was late afternoon and the weather had turned a little rough. The scudding cloud and hazy yellow sun in the southwest, and the sea which was being whipped into spray seemed a dirty brown." [2]

In other seasons, the ships blindly plowed through the billowing seas. "Thick fog and heavy snow, which could last from two to eight days, would disperse the convoy. A normal thing. No zig-zagging, just course altering at principal route-turning points." [3]

Then, there was the physical effect upon the crews. "A ship's roll from the bridge is unbelievable, screws raising out of the water, and the ship falling on seas like thunder." Furthermore, "Newfoundland is a violent place with comparative calm changing to roaring winds, with people struggling against horizontal rain and sleet in the half light of the underworld." [4]

"…The constant motion of the ship which became very tiring due to the continuous tensing of the muscles the whole time, the misery of keeping watch in severe weather and danger of moving along the upper deck even when secured to the lines rigged for this purpose, the clamping down of potholes which resulted in all spaces below quickly becoming fuggy and smelly and the condensation on the cold steel sides of the ship resulting in the whole of the ship's interior being continually wet. Above all, was the fact that our whole mode of life was one of expectation of Action Stations at any time." [5]

A sailor on a corvette remarked: "It was sheer unmitigated hell… The mess decks were usually a shambles and the wear and tear on bodies and tempers was something I shall never forget. But we were young and tough and, in a sense, we gloried in our misery and made light of it." [6]

Whether inside the vessel or scrambling on the windblown decks, the sailor's faith and fate rested in the hands of his own ability, his shipmates, the Captain, and his God.

In 1942, the German u-boats added to the menace. By the end of the year, their torpedoes would send 1,160 allied ships to the bottom of the Atlantic Ocean. Death could be instant, or it could come slowly as the victim floundered in the frigid waters hoping against hope for a miraculous deliverance, only to succumb to the cold numbness and silently sink beneath the waves. The aftermath was not a pristine seascape, but a horrible scene of oil slicks, shattered debris, and mangled human bodies. One British eyewitness related a haunting memory. "…A new ship called H.M.S. Pintail came out to join us, I think from Harwich. We plodded along over a mirror-like sea, the sun glittered and flashed from the water as she glided past us. We were so envious of her power and grace. Suddenly she speeded up, and carving white wings of water, she cut across our bows. There was a huge explosion and she heeled onto her side, still cutting through water, with a white wave curling over her decks, ripping off depth charges, and men like cotton reels and dolls, like a dying animal, and then NOTHING! Everything vanished! There ahead of us was the mirror-like sunlit sea, but nothing else. We were stunned. Then suddenly the scene changed, becoming macabre. Bodies came to the surface. Not exactly complete men, but parts missing, and entrails floating after some bodies. It was pitiful. It still flashes into my mind and it hurts. Time does not heal." [7]

In spite of nature's wrath and the stealthy German u-boats, war supplies, foodstuffs, and United States troops were desperately needed in Great Britain and North Africa. One link in the supply line - convoy AT-20 - gathered off the coast of Halifax, Nova Scotia in August 1942. The USS Ingraham and other screening destroyers herded the convoy ships like good shepherds. Since the convoy was transporting troops, the ships intended to sail at a "fast" 15 knot speed. It would not be easy. One day out of Halifax: "The fog was nasty, cotton-thick in patches, but thinning here and there into open spaces ("fog-dogs" in the vernacular) which appeared unrepentantly, like clearings in a misty forest. One minute a ship was plowing blindly through an opalescent cloud, [the] next minute she was in the clear, exposed." [8] In the darkness of night on a rolling sea, conditions were worse.

The USS Ingraham and her crew of 229 men and officers were in harm's way. On board the Ingraham was Seaman 1/c George Reisinger, Jr.

Part II
Young George

In their silver-haired years, George's school mates just could not remember him. Ponder as hard as they could, the name George Reisinger drew a blank. Even so, one can deduce what young George was not. He was not the class' Mr. Personality, most friendly, most athletic, the funniest, the mouthiest, the class bully, the brightest nor the most stupid student, the best dressed, or the best anything. Everyone remembers them. He apparently was just a quiet, very average kid.

George's family spoke German in their household, so perhaps George had difficulty understanding the words of his teachers and fellow students when he first attended Randolph Elementary School. Maybe he was self-conscious of an accent.

1st Grade Class, Randolph School, Mrs. Burky, teacher

6th Grade Class, Randolph School

Freshman Class, Randolph School

George Reisinger, Jr. - 1941

The Weitzel Photo Studio
801 SO. MAIN ST.

HyperWar: USS Ingraham (DD-444)

In George's first grade class picture (circa 1929), he is the sixth student from the left in the second row. Obviously, no one told the 6-year olds to smile or say "cheese" because most of them are pretty glum. Fourth from the left in the front row is Dorothy ("Squirt") Francisco whose brother Robert would be killed in Europe in WWII. In the same row and second from the right is Marjorie Leech. Her brother Elmer would be killed off the North African coast in WWII.

In George's sixth grade class picture (circa 1934), some of the students look more chipper. George is again the sixth student from the left in row two (chin partially hidden). Dorothy Francisco is fifth from the left in the front row. Marie Bettes is in row three, fifth from the left. Her brother Bill would be killed in France in 1944. Also in row three, third from the left, is Bob Foster, who was a great source of information for this project and a WWII Navy man. In 1944, Bob's brother-in-law, Robert Hillard, would be killed in Italy. Of the twenty boys in the class, twelve would serve in the armed forces during WWII.

In the freshman group picture, George is again the sixth student from the left in the second row. If the taller kids were put in the back rows as usual, then George was one of the smaller boys in the class. George may have dropped out of school before his senior year. He did not graduate from Randolph High School.

While George's former schoolmates were completing their junior year in high school, he reported to the USN Recruiting Station in Cleveland on March 18, 1941. The next day, his Navy life began at the USN Training Station at Great Lakes, Illinois. From that time until May 29, the Navy worked on turning George and his fellow landlubbers into seamen. Following boot camp, Reisinger was assigned a two-week stint on board the USS Melville. The Melville was an old destroyer tender which was launched in 1913 and saw service in World War I.

From June 12 to July 19, 1941 George was stationed at the Charleston Navy Yard. On the 19th he began service aboard the USS Ingraham (444), a new destroyer that was launched just the previous February. The Ingraham began escorting convoys in December 1941; and during 1942 she escorted convoys through the perilous North Atlantic between the United States, Iceland, and the United Kingdom. If George had joined the Navy to see the world, he certainly was seeing a good portion of the dangerous parts.

Prior to rendezvousing with Convoy AT-20, the young seaman sent letters from New York City to his sister Eva. He was looking forward to visiting her on his next leave.

Part III
In Peril On The Sea

The midshipmen at the United States Naval Academy frequently raise their voices in what has been known as *The Navy Hymn*. The actual title is *Eternal Father, Strong To Save* with the words written by William Whiting in 1860 and the music by John B. Dykes in 1861. This fervent musical prayer was the favorite hymn of President Franklin D. Roosevelt.

> Eternal Father, strong to save,
> Whose arm hath bound the restless wave,
> Who bid'st the mighty ocean deep
> Its own appointed limits keep;
> Oh, hear us when we cry to Thee,
> For those in peril on the sea. [9]

Convoy AT-20, the USS Ingraham, and Seaman First Class George Reisinger, Jr. were in peril on the sea and certainly needed the Eternal Father's saving grace.

August 22, 1942 - In the 4 AM darkness, the ships glided out of Halifax, Nova Scotia and into the vast North Atlantic. Compared to previous convoys, it was a small assembly of ten escorted ships. However, there was an unprecedented protective array of a battleship, a light cruiser, and a full squadron of nine of the newest U. S. destroyers. By 6 AM, the ships were aligned in columns for the relatively fast crossing to Greenoch, Scotland. The chief reasons for the speed and maximum protection were the approximately 50,000 soldiers and priority supplies on board the troop ships. [10]

Twelve hours later, a radar contact unleashed a chain of events which would irrevocably lead to disaster. At 6 PM, the troopship Letitia reported the contact, and the USS Swanson and the USS Ingraham were sent to investigate. The destroyers patrolled the area but were unable to determine the source of the radar contact. Perhaps it was due to whales or porpoises. Fortunately, there were no signs of the dreaded U-boats. The convoy then attempted to resume its original alignment.[11]

During the 20-24 watch (8 PM to midnight), the convoy sailed into a swirling horizontal fog with visibility varying from one quarter to three quarters of a mile. Vertically, the fog was not deep, as occasionally the moonlight glowed eerily through the foggy wisps.[12]

With the increased possibility of a collision or ship dispersion, the expected 15 knot speed had to be reduced, and all leading ships were ordered to close up and to launch towing spars. The conning officer on each ship strained to keep the forward ship's spar in sight.[13]

The USS Buck Incident - At 2205 (10:05 PM), a radio message directed the USS Buck (DD420) to escort the Letitia to her assigned position in the convoy. The 3-year old destroyer cautiously steamed toward the transport ship with visibility near zero. In the dense fog the Buck had to get into bullhorn range to help direct the Letitia.

At 2225 the Buck was now in a crossing position in the convoy column. Suddenly out of the fog at only 30 yards loomed the transport Awatea. The lookout's warning was too late, and the Awatea rammed the Buck's starboard quarter. "The steep bow of the Awatea nearly severed Buck. A 300 pound depth charge from one of Buck's K-guns dropped over the side and exploded, damaging Buck's port propeller. Buck broke away, badly hurt, and helpless." [14]

The Ingraham Collision - The Ingraham was ordered to investigate a reported collision in the convoy, and through the darkness she cut across the convoy's path in the blinding fog. Steaming just as blindly toward the destroyer was the USS Chemung, a repenishment oiler. On board the Ingraham was Seaman 1/c Luther Wilhelm. "On the night of 22 of August, I was in the Number 2 handling room reading the funny papers. Suddenly, I felt a big boom, the ship quivering, leaning to starboard, and jerking about. My immediate thinking was that we were hit by several torpedoes. I yelled up into the voice tube to the Number 2 gun turret above but received no answer. I then went about calling the bridge, and also received no answer. The other guys with me in Number 2 handling room just stared at me in silence. I yelled to them that 'we have to get out of here' but to no avail. I undogged the hatch and felt the ship sinking beneath me. As I was climbing the ladder to the mount on the starboard side main deck, the water was lapping at my heels. I just let go and started to swimming away from the ship..." [15]

Franklyn E. Dailey, Jr. was on board the USS Edison (DD439). "Lying nearly on her side, Ingraham blew up with an orange flash of such intensity that it cut through the fog and was visible on the Edison's bridge. Ensign R.F. (Dick) Hofer, the junior watch officer on Edison's bridge, reported the flash in Edison's log at 2235 by Edison's chronometer. Because I was so new at watch standing underway, I was up on the bridge early to relieve Dick Hofer, and was just getting night-vision when I too saw the flash." [16]

Luther Wilhelm: "The Ingraham went down by the stern, after capsizing to starboard, in less than 2 minutes. There was a major explosion as the stern went under, caused by the depth charges going off. I was in the water for two and ½ hours until the USS Bristol DD453 picked me up. I was sent to a hospital in Nova Scotia after leaving the Bristol. I never saw any of my shipmates again." [17]

There were not many shipmates left for Wilhelm to see. Of the 229 crew members, only 11 survived - one officer and 10 ratings. George Reisinger, Jr. was not one of them. [18]

The surviving officer was Ensign Melvin Brown, a Naval Academy classmate of Franklyn Dailey. Dailey: "Ensign Brown was in the Ingraham's main gun director when she rolled over. He survived drowning mainly because he was wearing a kapok life jacket with a ring that curled from its vest on the chest up around and behind the neck. This jacket could hold an unconscious man's head out of water." [19]

The telegram reached Atwater, Ohio just before noon on August 25, 1942. It was delivered to George's father. The senior Reisinger read: "The Navy Department regrets to inform you that your son George Reisinger Jr Seaman First Class USN is missing in the performance of his duty and in the service of his country. The Department appreciates your great anxiety but details not now available and delay in receipt thereof must necessarily be expected. To prevent possible aid to our enemies please do not divulge the name of the ship or station. Rear Admiral Randall Jacobs, Chief of Naval Personnel." Not until the summer of 2007 did the remaining family learn of the circumstances leading to George's death. [20]

[The USS Buck - In the collision with the Awatea, the Buck

lost seven crew members. In spite of extensive damage, she was towed back to Boston where she arrived on August 26, 1942. After repairs, the Buck returned to escort duty until June 1943, when she was assigned patrol duty off the coast of North Africa. Following another escort trip to the United States, the Buck supported the invasion of Italy. On October 9, 1943 while patroling off the coast of Salerno, the Buck was struck by at least one torpedo, possibly two. Within four minutes she sank beneath the waves with only 97 survivors. [21]

The USS Awatea - Almost three months after the collision with the USS Buck, the Awatea participated in the North African landings, Operation Torch. After unloading her troops, the ship was bombed and strafed off the coast of Algeria. At 11 P.M. November 11, 1942 the Awatea sank to the bottom of the Mediterranean Sea.

The USS Chemung - The oiler that sank the Ingraham limped back to Boston. After repairs, the Chemung also participated in the North African invasion. In late autumn 1945, the Chemung sailed into the Pacific Theater. She survived the war. [22]]

The East Coast Memorial to the Missing at Sea honors the 4,601 Americans who lost their lives in the Atlantic Ocean during World War II. At its dedication on May 23, 1963 the keynote speaker was President John F. Kennedy, a sailor who personally knew the perils of the sea and war from the destruction of his PT 109. The President's remarks were applicable to Americans in the past, at the present, and in the future.

"We commemorate them particularly appropriately here in the shadow of the Statue of Liberty. I am sure that their families who will come here and read their names may wonder on the occasion whether this rather extraordinary act on their behalf was worthwhile. It is, after all, against the law of nature for parents to bury their children. Children should bury their fathers, and when it is necessary for a father or mother to bury a son who may range from 18 to 28 with all of his life before him, it represents a special wrench. And I am sure they wonder, with all of the bright promises particularly of World War I and then World War II, what it all meant that we should be in such hazard today.I suppose it means that every generation of Americans must be expected in their time to do their part to maintain freedom for their country and freedom for those associated with it;

that there is no final victory but rather all Americans must be always prepared to play their proper part in a difficult and dangerous world. These 4500 Americans did - dying in the Western Atlantic - and nearly 20 years later it is appropriate for us to remember them and also remember those who in 1963 are doing the same thing not in the Western Atlantic but much further from our shores, who also on sea and land are bearing the burden of our defense." [23]

The name of George Reisinger, Jr., Seaman First Class, is inscribed on a plaque at the East Coast Memorial to the Missing at Sea.

CHAPTER NOTES
George Reisinger, Jr.
Seaman First Class USN

1. "The Life of a Seasick Sailor," WW2 People's War, www.bbc.uk/Ww2peopleswar/stories....
2. Martin Middlebrook, *Convoy* (New York: William Morrow and Company, Inc., 1977), p 103-104.
3. *Ibid.,* p 108.
4. Griffith Bailey Coale, Commander, USNR, "World War II Navy Art: A Vision of History," Department of the Navy - Naval History Center, Washington, D.C. history.navy.mil/ac/wwii/history...
5. Middlebrook, *Convoy*, p 130.
6. Middlebrook, p 105.
7. "The Life of a Seasick Sailor," BBC - WW2 People's War...
8. "WW II Troop Convoy Loses two Destroyers Off Halifax," www.daileyint.com/seawar/seawar4...
9. "Eternal Father, Strong To Save," www.cyberhymnal.org...
10. Franklyn E. Dailey Jr., "No 'Abandon Ship' for Ingraham," www.Daileyint.com/seawar/apejtwas... p 1.
11. See footnote 8. p 7.
12. Dailey, "No 'Abandon Ship' for Ingraham," p 5.
13. See footnote 8, p 5.
14. Dailey, Convoy loses two destroyers off Halifax, p 7.
15. Luther Wilhelm, "A Survivor's Tale," www. geocities.com/Pentagon/barracks... p 1.
16. Dailey, loses two destroyers, p 7.
17. Luther, Survivor's Tale. p 1.
18. Allied Warships, USS Ingraham (I) (DD 444), ww.uboat.net/allies/warships/ship...
19. Dailey, loses two destroyers, p 7-8.
20. Interview with Betty Tanaska, a niece of George Reisinger. Betty graciously donated George's service pictures and furnished a copy of the telegram.
21. "USS Buck," Dome Island Press, www.domeisland.com/gold later/ussbuck...
22. Information on the Awatea and Chemung can be located online at Wikipedia.
23. The American Presidency Project. John F. Kennedy. "Remarks in New York City at the Dedication of the East Coast Memorial to the Missing at Sea." May 23rd, 1963. www.presidency.ucsb.edu/ws...

CHAPTER EIGHT

PRIVATE ELMER L. LEECH
AVIATION ENGINEER

Part I
Out of Poverty

It was a cold bleak Christmas in the Great Depression. Like the freezing winter weather, gloom and hopelessness hovered over many a household; and the words "Peace on Earth and good will toward men" had a hollow ring to them. Francis Knapp's mother decided to do something about that, at least in her neighborhood. So, with little Francis in tow, she delivered food and gifts to the Leech family who lived in a drafty, former one-room schoolhouse. The residence was a step up from the log cabin in which they had previously resided. At any rate, Francis always remembered that the Leech family were the poorest people that he had ever seen.

Steve Feciuch was a lifetime friend of Bill Leech and of course knew Bill's brother Elmer. Steve remembered that although the family was poor, they were all hard workers. Elmer G. Leech, the dad, worked for various farmers for lodging. He and the boys would milk from 20-30 cows twice each day in addition to the other farm chores. The boys also worked on the muck farms in the Hartville area where the wages were a pittance but at least it was something.

Steve met Bill when they were about eight years old. The boys loved to fish and hunt, both for the sport and camaraderie, as well as putting something on the dinner table. [In their older years, the two close friends would make hunting and fishing trips to the Pennsylvania mountains.] Playing ball in the pastures was also great fun. As teenagers, the boys worked at Congress Lake Country Club where on Monday evenings they were allowed to golf and do the watering at the same time. Steve always remembered Bill as a "good

guy, well-liked, and a good businessman who treated people well."
Bill's climb out of poverty was interrupted by the war, in which he was a machine-gunner and fought in the hell of Anzio. After the war, Bill gradually built a successful limestone, sand, gravel, and hauling business. Bill Leech became a wealthy man, but Steve said that his lifetime friend "never let it go to his head."
Whether Elmer Leech would have been a partner with his brother or have enjoyed the same success is a matter of conjecture. Fate had other things in store for him. Elmer preferred to be called Bud. Bud Leech was a small fellow - 5'7 ½ ", 127 pounds. He had blue eyes and reddish-brown hair. The last time that Steve saw Bud was when the young man, who was going off to war, dropped by the Feciuch home to say goodbye. They wished Bud good luck and never saw him again. [1]

Bud Leech's 1942 Christmas present was a greetings letter from Uncle Sam. He was inducted into the service on January 2, 1943; and after reporting to Cleveland, Bud did his boot camp at Camp Perry, Ohio. In February, he boarded the train for Dyersburg, Mississippi, where he became a private in the 853rd Engineer Battalion, Aviation. [2]

An engineer battalion's training could cover a wide range of experiences: building docks, bombing targets, bridges, roads, air strips, buildings, and camouflaged works. Some men received specialized training in communication lines, camouflage, chemical warfare, vehicle operation, heavy equipment operation, administration, and pipe line work. "In addition, special emphasis was placed on tactical training on hikes and overnight problems to prepare the men for combat conditions. Subjects of vital importance were fire control, scouting, cover and concealment." [3]

Part II
The Rohna

It seemed as if destiny was reaching out to several U. S. units and drawing them to Oran, Algeria. Sgt. Carl Schoenacher, who had enlisted in the Army Air Corps in 1940, was stationed in Iceland as a radio support technician. Aboard ship to Oran, he and his close friend, Sgt. Bill Reid, studied Reid's book on the new Goren contract bridge system. A couple on-lookers challenged the two sergeants with the taunt, "You play the book, we'll play the cards." Schoenacher recalled, "I do not recall the stakes. They were small. The difference was in the partial score hands. We would bid and make them. They would either pass or overbid to game. Slowly we accepted their credit. By the time we docked at Oran (Algeria) they owed us several bucks." Carl and Bill never collected the debt. They were destined to be passengers on the British troop ship, HMTS Rohna. [4]

Bennie J. McRae, Jr. left Hampton Roads on October 5, 1943. His outfit, the 858th Engineer Aviation Battalion, sailed on two Liberty Ships bound for Oran. (The 858th was destined to work on the Ledo Road and the Burma Road, where the men had to combat steep grades and sharp curves, 9,000 foot mountains, monsoon rains, dense jungle undergrowth, and racial prejudice in America's segregated army. The 858th was the only black unit to serve in all of the China theater.) At Oran, McRae's battalion had to cross over the decks of the Rohna to board her sister ship, the HMTS Rajula.[5]

Jim Lamson was in a company (not part of the much larger 853rd) on board the Rohna. Jim's outfit eventually sailed to Bombay, India where they boarded a very slow train to Calcutta. The unit started pole line construction out of Calcutta and into China, a task that took two years to cover 2,100 miles of communication lines. [6]

Crammed on board the Rohna were 2,193 passengers, including 1,988 U.S. troops, 7 Red Cross personnel, a crew of 198, and Bud Leech. The ship's crew consisted of British officers, Indian seamen, and an Australian captain. Leaving Oran and bound for Bombay, Rohna joined convoy KMF 26, consisting of 24 ships. [7]

Sgt. Schoenbacher: "We left Oran on Thanksgiving morning (1943). We had a Thanksgiving dinner aboard ship. It was calm but we were near the shore where there were swells that 'rocked the boat' and spoiled some meals. Once out of the harbor it was rougher, perhaps five foot waves... I remember the goat, midship starboard, not knowing why it was there, and I recall noticing that the two huge rafts on the forward well deck at a 45 degree angle were painted securely to the frame from which they were supposed to slide. We had been assured that the Mediterranean had been swept clear of Nazi U-boats. We stayed in sight of the African coast until the next afternoon, Friday November 26." [8]

As dusk was approaching on that fateful Friday, a flight of thirty German bombers roared toward the convoy. Blaring ship horns warned the troops to go below, and a steady anti-aircraft fire added more tension to a desperate situation. Several smaller planes zoomed beneath the German bombers, and at first the men thought they were allied fighters sent to protect them. When the fighters strafed the ship in front of the Rohna, they knew that they were enemy aircraft instead. [9]

Sgt. Schoenbacher: We were to stay in our bunking area and were warned not to crowd to the portholes. We were forward near the stairs, down one deck. Some fellows went to the latrine to look out. During the attack, Reid said he was going to take a look, uncharacteristic of him. I played solitaire." [10]

Jim Lamson: "So when we got out there and got under attack there, they'd blow the horn and everything for everyone to go down into the hold - different deck. I looked at the ship when I got on it and I said, I'm not going down nowhere. I'm staying on top, so I got back to the kitchen gallery. There were square portholes where they used to throw the garbage at night time. I took a look. The first bomb missed." [11]

Overhead, Maj. Hans Dochtermann pilots his Heinkel 177 long range bomber toward the Rohna. He is carrying the latest German killing innovation - two Hs293 remote-controlled glider bombs, one under each wing. The 1100 pound Hs293 looked like an unmanned airplane with stubby wings. In effect, it was the first air-launched cruise missile that glided to its target by remote radio control. Heading toward the target at 4,000 feet, Maj. Dochtermann releases the glider bombs, and Georg Zuther, his bombardier, steers them toward the troop-filled Rohna. Streaking at nearly 500 MPH, one of the bombs slams into the Rohna's port side just above the waterline, the first successful war-strike by such a weapon. It explodes in the engine room, blowing a huge hole at the waterline on the other side. [12]

Jim Lamson saw the bomb coming toward the Rohna and thought the object was a British fighter plane on fire. There was a huge WHAM! and Jim was knocked out. When he came to, he tried to help others on the ship, but he was hurting from shrapnel wounds in his legs, back, arm, and wrist. The wrist was bleeding badly, so he wrapped a handkerchief around it. Amidst the pandemonium, he crawled to the front of the boat. Unlike some who panicked and jumped in with full gear, Jim stripped off his shoes and clothes before he made the plunge. The salt water was very cold, but it helped to stem the flow of blood. Being an excellent swimmer, Jim was able to help others in difficulty. Lamson thought he was in the sea for eight or nine hours, which meant that he was bobbing in the darkness, before being picked up by the USS Pioneer, a mine sweeper. [13]

Pvt. Wayne Coy was a 20 year old private with about three months' service. When the attack commenced, Coy and others went below decks. "We just waited to be hit," he said. "Everything went dead... The water was rough [and] a bunch of us got together." Making use of their gas-filled vests, they bobbed in the waves until the USS Pioneer picked them from the sea. There were little more than 600 survivors aboard the 125 foot mine sweeper, and "They were afraid of that ship capsizing because so many people were on board." [14]

Sgt. Schoenacher: "Suddenly there was a thud. The lights went out. A strong draft scattered my [solitaire] cards. I cannot call it wind, because wind has direction. One of life's mysteries is what happened to [Sgt.] Reid. I never saw him again. Where he went I'll never know. I looked, he was not in sight... I have no idea how long I looked for him, but recall seeing Sgt. Ekiss at the top of the stairs waving for us to come up. The ship's communication system was dead. We were dead in the water. Topside there was chaos... Down the ropes I climbed. I hung near the water, then tried to time my jump to hit the crest of a wave and be carried away from the ship. When behind the ship, I was pulled under twice... To my right in the distance was a ship that seemed to stay. While on the crest of a wave, I saw three men with what appeared to be an airplane wing tank... I slid down that wave as fast as I knew how and grabbed the tank. We would tread water until we were on the crest of a wave, then kick like mad to slide down it toward the ship. We reached the ship quickly, while they were still firing anti-aircraft guns... Two sailors would drop a rope, then pull whoever grabbed it... When the fellow ahead of me grabbed for a rope, the tank flipped over onto my head because he was on the leading edge and I on the trailing edge. The stars were bright for an instance. My head and shoulders hurt, and I was slow to grab the rope. Sailors were working rapidly. After being sworn at, I grabbed the rope on the next swing. As soon as my head was above deck, an arm went under each shoulder and I was sent sliding across the wet deck, surprised, smarting, but safe." [15]

Lt. Charles Beard was an 853rd Battalion man on board the Rohna. "The first thing I did was pick up all the life vests that I could that were floating near me. I had one around my waist and one under each arm. I had that much sense about me." Most of his comrades were not so fortunate. "Some were killed by the blast. Some just gave out." For Lt. Beard, he was headed for a long night in the water - 12 hours of hell. The next day he was rescued by the British destroyer, the Holcomb. He apparently was the last survivor picked out of the water. [16]

"Between 10:30 P.M. and midnight, rescue ships, including the minesweeper USS Pioneer, the Red Cross ship Clan Campbell, and the Rohna's sister ship HMT Rajula, reported 'sailing through a sea of floating bodies.' " The sinking claimed 1,015 U. S. servicemen, three Red Cross workers, and 134 Indian crewmen and British officers, making it the worst *at-sea* disaster in U. S. history. [17] [The Rohna was second to the USS Arizona, which lost 1,177 lives at Pearl Harbor. The greatest *maritime* disaster in U. S. history occurred on April 27, 1865 when the steamboat Sultana exploded. An estimated 1,800 were killed, most of them returning Civil War soldiers and some survivors of Andersonville Prison.]

After being saved, Sgt. Schoenacher tried to find his close friend and bridge partner, Sgt. Bill Reid. "I went to the docks each time when ships carrying survivors landed. No one had seen him. I now understand how one feels to have a missing relative." [18]

Part III
The Aftermath

"For security reasons, the War Department immediately suppressed all news of the Rohna catastrophe." First, a secret weapon was involved. Then there were the propaganda and morale aspects. Details of the sinking might give the Germans a propaganda coup and let them know how well their Hs293 had worked; whereas on the U. S. home front the populace might become discouraged over such a loss and perhaps get mad as hell that so many U. S. troops were lost on a British transport ship. In the immediate aftermath of the sinking, the War Department needed time to ascertain all of the facts; and in the larger scheme of things, there were many other priorities occurring at the same time. In addition, there were American casualties taking place all over the globe, and they also had to be reported and somehow explained to the relatives stateside. In the meantime, surviving company commanders like Lt. Charles Beard were assigned to write letters to the families of their fallen buddies. Beard said that "Everything was so secret that I couldn't tell them what happened to their loved ones." The only thing he could write was that the victim was "killed in action" or "missing at sea and presumed dead." [19]

The American Graves Registration eventually reported that "A thorough and complete search of the entire coastline of the Mediterranean Sea, including all islands therein, has been accomplished by AGRS/MZ Search and Recovery Teams. Every feasible means of communication was used in an effort to notify the local population of the importance of reporting all isolated remains buried along the coasts or washed ashore. All efforts proved to be of no avail in that no identifiable remains of the subject deceased [Elmer Leech] were recovered." Thus, Bud Leech was among the 829 Rohna victims who were declared "Non-Recoverable." For their families, friends, and surviving service buddies, there was left a huge permanent void and absolutely no closure. [20]

On January 6, 1944, forty-one days after the Rohna's sinking, Bud Leech's mother, Ethel Leech, received her first telegram from the Secretary of War. It was basically a form letter with the pertinent information filled in. "The Secretary of War desires me to express his deep regret that your son, Private Elmer Leech has been reported missing in action since Twenty Six November in North Africa Area..." For Ethel there was still a ray of hope. Maybe, just maybe, Bud had somehow survived, or perhaps there was a clerical mistake somewhere. [21]

Four months later, Ethel Leech's remaining slim hopes were dashed by a second telegram received in May 1944. "The Secretary of War asks that I assure you of his deep regret in the loss of your son Private Elmer L. Leech who was previously reported missing in action. Report received in the War Department establishes the fact that your son's death occurred on twenty-seven November Nineteen Forty Three..." [22]

Like many mothers and wives, Ethel Leech wanted a remembrance of her loved one. On April 17, 1945 she wrote to the War Department.
"Dear sir

My son was killed in action on Nov. 27th 1943. they said he was on a ship that went down but I received the Purple heart and it stated that he had died from the result of wounds received in action. Could you tell me if his Personal Belongings were recovered and if they were would you please send them to me. I am his Mother and would like so much to have them. His name [is] Pvt. Elmer Leroy Leech... thank you..." [23]

During the War, the Kansas City Quartermaster Depot seemed to be in the business of conveying bad news and sincere sympathy to many families across America. On April 30, 1945 Harry Niemiec, 2nd Lt. Q.M.C., replied to Ethel Leech's inquiry. If she had any hopes when she nervously opened the envelope, they were soon dashed by Lt. Niemiec's letter.

"...The Army Effects Bureau has not received any belongings of your son, nor any other information regarding his effects.

The time that normally is required for effects to reach this Bureau from overseas, is approximately one year. Due to the lapse of time, it is reasonable to assume there were no effects of Private Leech recovered.

I appreciate your anxiety, and I am indeed sorry to convey this report. However, if this Bureau should receive information indicating the recovery of any personalty [sic] of Private Leech, I shall communicate with you promptly.

Please accept my sympathy in the loss of your son..."[24]

Perhaps, Ethel slowly and sorrowfully placed the letter upon the kitchen table, while more tears trickled down her cheeks.

On July 1, 1949 (approximately 5 years and 7 months after the sinking of the Rohna), the Army issued a "Statement of Investigation," which included the following information.

Item 1 - "...The "S.S. Rohna", was hit by an enemy glider bomb and sank in the Mediterranean Sea, fifteen miles north of Djidjelli, Algeria on 26 November 1943. The weather was cloudy and the sun was setting. The bomb struck the ship in the engine room which caught fire and flooded immediately. The vessel began listing to starboard; the flames spread quickly to practically all parts of the ship; all electrical equipment failed; and the Master decided that 'Nothing could be done' and ordered 'Abandon Ship'. The ship settled rapidly by the stern and at approximately one and one-half hours after the bomb struck, its bow disappeared below the surface of the sea."

Item two - "An investigation of the circumstances surrounding the sinking of the 'S.S. Rohna reveal the contributing factors in the extreme loss of life, and the unusual proportion of uncovered remains, to be:

A. The terrific effect of the explosion.

B. The poor condition of the ship's equipment and the conduct of its crew.

C. The difficulties encountered in the rescue operations."

Item 3 - "Original Board Proceedings, dated 30 August 1947, were not accepted due to numerous deficiencies, and a more thorough and complete investigation was required in order to insure the recovery and identification of all descendents possible..." [25]

On November 11 (Armistice Day), 1993, Charles Osgood's radio program featured the story of the Rohna. Two weeks later, he again covered the story. Osgood remarked, "It is not that we forget, it is just that we never knew." [As with the case of the Rohna, perhaps the minimal WWII history of the local men and women is not due to forgetfulness or apathy, but merely because we never knew.] [26]

On May 30, 1996, a memorial to the Rohna was unveiled at the Fort Mitchell National Cemetery in Seale, Alabama. John Fievet, a survivor of the Rohna sinking, spoke at the ceremony: "I dedicate this memorial to the memory of those who fell in the service of our country. I dedicate it in the names of those who offered their lives that justice, freedom, and democracy might survive to be the victorious ideals of the world. The lives of those who made the supreme sacrifice are glorious before us. Their deeds are an inspiration. As they served America in the time of war, yielding their last full measure of devotion, may we serve America in the time of peace. I dedicate this memorial to them, and with it, I dedicate this society to the faithful service of our country and the preservation of the memory of those who died, that liberty might live..." [27]

The House of Representatives (October 10, 2000) and the U.S. Senate (October 27, 2000) passed a resolution to honor the Rohna's victims, the survivors, and the rescuers. [28]

Elmer L. Leech's name is among the 3,724 that are inscribed

on the Tablets of the Missing at Carthage, Tunisia. At the Court of Honor is the following inscription: "SOME THERE BE WHICH HAVE NO SEPULCHRE THEIR NAME LIVETH FOR EVERMORE." On the west side of the Visitors' Building is the inscription taken from General Eisenhower's dedication of the Golden Book now enshrined in St. Paul's Cathedral in London. "HERE WE AND ALL WHO SHALL HEREAFTER LIVE IN FREEDOM WILL BE REMINDED THAT TO THESE MEN AND THEIR COMRADES WE OWE A DEBT TO BE PAID WITH GRATEFUL REMEMBRANCE OF THEIR SACRIFICE AND WITH THE HIGH RESOLVE THAT THE CAUSE FOR WHICH THEY DIED SHALL LIVE." [29]

Such are the lofty words for Bud Leech, a poverty-stricken farm lad who probably would have preferred to return home to Ohio where awaited the opportunity for success, the pursuit of happiness, and a potential family of his own.

CHAPTER NOTES
Private Elmer L. Leech, Aviation Engineer

1. Interview with Steve Feciuch, February, 2008.
2. Individual Deceased Personal File for Elmer L. Leech. U.S. Army Human Resources Command.
3. Bennie J. McRae, Jr., "858th Engineer Aviation Battalion." people.coax.net/lfw/858TH...
4. Franklyn E. Dailey, Jr. "Getting There Was Dangerous; Rohna Disaster Lay Ahead, The Triumph of Instrument Flight." daileyint.com/flying...
5. Bennie J. McRae, Jr. "858th Engineer Aviation Battalion," people.coax... p 2-3.
6. Jason A. McGarry, "Jim Lamson Full Interview," AAUP Oral History Project, Center for Oral History, University of Connecticut, march 23, 2001. Sp.uconn.edu...
7. U. S. Military Honors, "The sinking of HMT Rohna." sid-hill.com/honors/hon...
8. Franklyn E. Dailey, Jr. "Getting There Was Dangerous..."
9. "The Freeper Foxhole Remembers The Sinking of HMT Rohna." free republic.com/focus/f-vetscor...
10. Dailey, Getting There Was Dangerous..."
11. McGarry, "Jim Lamson Full Interview."

12. Michael Logue, "Sinking of the 'Rohna' - A virtually unknown WWII tragedy." hq.usace.army.mil/cepa/pubs... and The Freeper Foxhole Remembers The Sinking of HMT Rohna, p 8.
13. McGarry, "Jim Lamson Full Interview." p 3-5.
14. David Slone, Times-Union staff writer. "Rohna Survivor Tells Tale Of heroism And Patriotism." timeworks.com...
15. Dailey, "Getting There Was Dangerous," p 3.
16. Logue, "Sinking of the Rohna," p 1.
17. Logue, "Sinking of the Rohna"; U. S. Military Honors, "The sinking of HMT Rohna."
18. Dailey, "Getting There Was Dangerous," p 3.
19. Logue, "Sinking of the Rohna" p 1-2.
20. Individual Deceased Personal File for Elmer Leech. U. S. Army Human Resources Command
21. Ibid.
22. Ibid.
23. Ibid. Ethel Leech's letter to the Army.
24. Ibid. Response to Ethel leech's letter.
25. Ibid. Report of Memorial Division, Identification Branch, Final Determination Section. p 1-2.
26. "The Freeper Foxhole Remembers The Sinking of HMT Rohna."
27. Logue, "Sinking of the Rohna;" and Freeper.
28. Freeper re resolutions by Congress.
29. American Battle Monuments Commission, North Africa American Cemetery and Memorial. ABMC.gov/cemeteries. p 5, 9.

Pvt. Elmer L. (Bud) Leech (left) and his brother Bill. Bud was lost at sea on November 26, 1943, when a glider bomb struck the troop ship Rohna.

EPILOG

New Years Eve, 1945. It was a time for reflection on the monumental events of the passing year, a time for celebrating the present and just being alive, and after six years of war a time of anticipation for a new year of peace.

1945 had been a ride on an extreme emotional rollercoaster, and the *Beacon Journal* editor attempted to make sense of it all. "The days of 1945 stand out in memory as individuals, each with some world-shaking event for history to record. Each 24 hours was crammed with news - and with headaches for newspaper editors who tried vainly to find enough space on page one to properly report every happening."

In January the Allies had been eliminating Hitler's last gasp on the western front, the bloody and freezing Battle of the Bulge. In February, the Yanks entered Manila. After nearly a month of bitter fighting, Iwo Jima was captured. April saw the invasion of Okinawa, the death of President Roosevelt, the United Nations opening a conference in San Francisco, and the deaths of Mussolini and his mistress. May 7 saw Germany's official surrender. On June 21, the Americans moved closer to Tokyo when organized resistance finally ended on Okinawa. On July 28, the U.S. Senate ratified the U.N. Charter, 89-2. August ushered in the atomic age when atomic bombs were dropped on Hiroshima and Nagasaki. Japan officially surrendered aboard the U.S.S. Missouri in Tokyo Bay on September 2. Food rationing - except for sugar - ended on November 1. Three weeks later, General Motors workers went on strike for a 30 per cent raise. On December 3, President Truman proposed "fact finders" for the labor unrest. In the early winter, the Nuremburg Trials and executions began.

To the newspaper editor the extreme peak on the emotional rollercoaster ride was the pure joy of victory. "Of all the epochal events of the past 12 months, Victory is the greatest. Victory over Germany. Victory over Japan. Victory over hate, oppression, barbarism and aggression. Victory over fear and victory over killing." At the other extreme was the extreme grief that persisted throughout the land. "And in thousands of homes, deaths moved in with the arrival of terse, official messages from the war or navy department. Gold stars in service flags. He won't be coming back."

Predictions for 1946 ranged from gloom and doom to rays of

sunshine. Although higher prices and more labor strikes loomed on the horizon, farm and industrial prosperity looked good. With the war over, political partisanship was expected to obliterate statesmanship. Past scores could now be settled. "Knives are being sharpened for sitting congressmen. Many will see their last year in the capital."

On the world scene, relations with Russia were already poor and getting worse. Germany was partitioned. The United Nations was expected to begin feebly, but perhaps by the end of the year it would offer hope of permanent world peace. Would the new atomic energy be used to advance or destroy the human race?

Although great jubilation greeted Johnny's marching home again, problems of veteran readjustment and employment, housing, hospital and clothing needs were "presently apparent and will become more pressing." For some time into the future, the consumer could expect more shortages of butter, shirts, dresses, tires, new cars, and numerous related items. However, Americans had seen plenty gloom and doom from the stock market crash in '29, the Great Depression, and a devastating World War. So, as they prepared for this New Years Eve, thoughts of future troublesome possibilities temporarily faded into the background.

In the evening many church members braved the cold breeze and swirling snow flurries to attend New Years Eve services. Hymns and prayers of thanksgiving were solemnly and earnestly offered up to God.

The train station and the Greyhound Bus depot were strangely peaceful this evening. They had been jammed just before Christmas with folks coming home and others passing through to their destinations. Rail and bus traffic was expected to resume the hectic pace in the coming week.

The state liquor stores, however, were doing a booming business. Reports "indicated the community would be well doused in alcoholic beverages. Record long lines at all stores were reported throughout the day. Plentiful amounts of blended whiskies were on hand, though no bonded goods could be had."

As the darkness deepened, electric trolley cars, diesel-puffing buses, shared taxis, and scurrying pedestrians flooded the main streets. "Reservations at night clubs and bars filled all available space. Probably the happiest celebrants are the thousands of Akron area veterans, home again after years over seas. For the first time in four years uniforms did not predominate, and most of the khakis and blues that could be seen were worn by ex-soldiers and sailors who had been rushed through the discharge process to make it home for Jan. 1."

Earlier in the day, the *Beacon* admonished the revelers about excessive drinking: "If you do celebrate tonight, leave the car at home, if you can. Take a bus or a taxi. If you must drive, don't drink."

In the seconds before the clocks struck twelve, the countdowns began. Whether one was in a noisy, smoke-filled night club or sitting quietly beside the radio in the family living room and waiting for the mellow tones from Guy Lombardo's Orchestra, perhaps thoughts arose of those who would have loved to be there, but now they lay beneath the sod somewhere in Europe, on a South Pacific island, or under the ocean's waves. Many a throat filled with a painful lump and many sad tears trickled down the cheeks when the strains of "Auld Land Syne" filled the air in the first seconds of 1946:

'Should auld acquaintance be forgot
and never brought to mind?
Should auld acquaintance be forgot
and days of auld lang syne?
For auld lang syne, my dear,
for auld lang syne,
We'll take a cup of kindness yet,
for auld lang syne."

Other Heritage Books by Richard J. Staats:

*A Grassroots History of Baseball:
Days of the Rosewood Bat and the Silver Ball*

*A Grassroots History of the American Civil War, Volume I:
The Life and Times of Pvt. Ephraim Cooper,
One of Mr. Lincoln's First Volunteers*

*A Grassroots History of the American Civil War, Volume II:
The Bully Seventh Ohio Volunteer Infantry*

*A Grassroots History of the American Civil War, Volume III:
Captain Cotter's Battery*

*A Grassroots History of the American Civil War, Volume IV:
The Life and Times of Colonel William Stedman of the 6th Ohio Cavalry*

A Grassroots History of World War II: Eight Men in Granite

*The History of the 6th Ohio Volunteer Cavalry, 1861-1865:
A Journal of Patriotism, Duty and Bravery*

www.ingramcontent.com/pod-product-compliance
Lightning Source LLC
Chambersburg PA
CBHW072133220426
43664CB00013B/2226